Porches of North America

Porches

OF NORTH AMERICA

Thomas Durant Visser

UNIVERSITY PRESS OF NEW ENGLAND

Hanover and London

University Press of New England
www.upne.com
© 2012 Thomas Durant Visser
All rights reserved
Manufactured in the United States of America
Designed by Rich Hendel
Typeset in Charter and The Serif by
Passumpsic Publishing

For permission to reproduce any of the
material in this book, contact Permissions,
University Press of New England, One Court
Street, Suite 250, Lebanon NH 03766; or visit
www.upne.com

Library of Congress
Cataloging-in-Publication Data
Porches of North America /
Thomas Durant Visser. — 1st [edition].
   pages cm
Includes bibliographical references and index.
ISBN 978-1-61168-220-5 (cloth : alk. paper) —
ISBN 978-1-61168-221-2 (ebook)
1. Porches — United States.
2. Porches — Canada. I. Title.
NA7125.V57   2012
721'.84—dc23   2011046332

5 4 3 2 1

Contents

Preface

Though one may be hard-pressed to name another architectural feature that can prompt such tenacious feelings of welcome, comfort, and nostalgia, it is surprising that not more has been published on the history of porches. In response, this book examines how porches in their many forms have evolved in the United States and Canada through innovations, adaptations, and revivals.

A primary goal of this study is to provide a basic contextual and typological framework to help observers identify various common types of historic porches in North America. Many of the illustrations shown on the following pages are examples of porches drawn from historical sources and public archives, as well as from the author's field research across the United States and Canada. The hub of these research wanderings has been a home with two well-used porches and surrounding neighborhoods in Vermont, a state with one of the highest proportions of surviving heritage buildings in North America. Many of these are equipped with representative examples of porches similar in design and features to those that may be found in many other communities in North America. Examples of porch types from other regions in the continent are also discussed and shown, including some associated with important historic landmarks, those recorded by the Historic American Buildings Survey, and examples from various archival collections and published sources.

The generous assistance provided by the librarians at the University of Vermont Special Collections and at the McGill University Rare Books and Special Collections is gratefully acknowledged, as is the research support provided by the University of Vermont. Special thanks are also due to the Historic American Buildings Survey and the Library of Congress. Others who have greatly assisted with this project include my colleagues, graduate students, and alumni at the University of Vermont Historic Preservation Program and History Department; the director, editors, and staff at the University Press of New England; the professional preservationists at the Vermont Division for Historic Preservation and at other preservation offices, agencies, and organizations; the many people across the United States and Canada (and especially in Quebec) who have shared their knowledge and memories of porches; and most of all, my patient partner.

For clarity and as a starting point of reference, the word *porch* is used in this book with its broad contemporary meaning; that is, an identifiable building feature that is open on at least one side or serves as a covered entry and is large enough to shelter at least one person. In addition to traditional porches, related porchlike structures, such as stoops, porte-cocheres, and marquees are also included.

It is important to recognize, however, that the study of historic porches is made somewhat complex by the great variety of formal and informal names that have been used to describe the various types of structures and their features. As with other aspects of language, common usages of formal and vernacular names have evolved over time, as well as within regional and cultural contexts. Some linguistic usages may even reflect the geographical backgrounds of the persons using the words.

The various terms used to describe porches in this book may be divided into the following categories:

> Words that are synonymous with the broad, contemporary meaning of *porch*, but that may reflect nuances of regional parlance or historical usages, e.g., *veranda, piazza, gallery*
> Words that define specific forms of porches, e.g., *portico, loggia, colonnade*
> Words that describe identifiable styles of porches, e.g., *Gothic Revival, Italianate, Queen Anne*
> Words that describe architectural features of porches, e.g., *columns, balustrades, brackets*

To address this terminology in detail, examples and features of specific forms and features of porches are discussed and illustrated in the following chapters, and a glossary of porch terms is included at the back of the book.

The study of porches may also provide clues to understanding the cultural heritage of geographical areas. Whether or not built according standard principles of recognized architectural styles, many informal "vernacular" types of porches may provide insights into a region's cultural heritage, especially when patterns emerge across broad geographical areas. Sometimes these "folk" patterns are strongest in isolated and rural places that have been less closely connected with urban centers and learned ways. Such geographical patterns of their prevalence may thus be seen as evidence of how the development and diffusion of vernacular types of porches and other building features may reflect cultural imprints left on the land through the history of human habitation, movement, and communication.

Another goal of this study is to look beyond the formal architectural history of this building feature to examine how the various transitional spaces created by porches may imbue users with lasting impressions. Indeed, discovering evidence of the kinds of feelings that users associated with a place can be one of the most challenging tasks for architectural historians, who normally focus instead on documenting physical features of buildings and spaces. While tape measures and cameras can capture much of the tangible information that may be recorded in drawings, photographs, and written descriptions, the identification and documentation of human feelings and impressions associated with building features can be much more difficult to research, owing to the inevitable subjective nature of the inquiry. Historical and literary sources, such as diaries, journals, travelogues, novels, interviews, and oral histories, may provide some evidence of place- and space-associated feelings related to porches, however. But to decipher feelings associated with porches in more depth, it may also be important to consider how porches connect various realms as *liminal domains*, that is, as threshold spaces hosting transitional human experiences on physical, spiritual, and psychological levels.

Thus it is hoped that by combining these various lines of inquiry, this book may offer some fresh perspectives on the history of porches in North America that will help promote the understanding, appreciation, care, and preservation of this remarkable building feature in its many forms and uses.

History

The porch, the veranda, or the piazza, are highly characteristic features, and no dwelling-house can be considered complete without one or more of them.

—A. J. Downing, *Cottage Residences*, 1842

With a history that can be traced to antiquity, a wide variety of porches, including porticos, piazzas, and verandas, blossomed forth as forms of architectural plumage in North America more than two centuries ago. As places to greet the world, as shelters to celebrate arrivals and departures, and as outdoor living spaces, few architectural features evoke such rich feelings, as do porches. By their location, design, and associations, porches and porticos may provide expressions of access and engagement, of exclusion and defense, of willingness and hope, of power and authority, or of style, taste, and personality. And as transitional realms that straddle thresholds betwixt and between indoors and out, between private and public, and even perhaps between sacred and secular, porches may host many curiously memorable activities, experiences, and impressions.

The historical roots of this building feature are complex. Some observers have attempted to explain the history of porches in practical terms as structures erected to fill human needs through innovation and adaptation. Others have traced historical links that may demonstrate how such building forms as porches reflect the diffusion of knowledge conveyed through cultural contacts. Both approaches of inquiry have merit.

Evidence suggests that many indigenous peoples in North, Central, and South America were building porchlike structures long before contact with Europeans. Noteworthy surviving examples include the stone porticos, galleries, and colonnades erected by the Mayan cultures in Mexico and Belize from about 500 CE and later.[1]

Archaeological finds of post holes and post molds show that wooden posts were used by Native American peoples in the

Figure 1.1. *For these children blowing soap bubbles, the front porch provided special opportunities for enjoyment and companionship in activities best suited to the home's liminal space that straddled indoor and outdoor realms. Circa 1890s stereograph.*

American Southwest for building ramadas, the simple, open shelters supported by poles with roofs of brush or fabric.[2] Although these ramadas were often built as freestanding structures, they were also attached to dwellings to serve as porches and as open, sheltered spaces for cooking, eating, and other domestic activities. Archaeological site excavations along the Rio Grande in Texas suggest that ramadas were attached

to adobe houses as shade awnings. Radiocarbon tests have dated a collapsed roof of one of these structures—covered with grass, river reeds, sticks, poles, and mud daub—to between 1290 and 1410 CE.[3]

Examples of Native American dwellings with ramada porches constructed with local materials and traditional methods were documented for the Historic American Buildings Survey during the 1930s, and indeed, ramadas are still being built by people in the American Southwest as shade-rendering structures, using materials and techniques similar to those employed long ago.[4]

Elsewhere, other Native American peoples were constructing shelters with porch-like features before contact with Europeans. According to an early seventeenth-century account written by the French missionary Father Gabriel Sagard, indigenous bands of Huron Indians, also known as the Wendat people, who were then living in what is now central Ontario, built large bark-covered longhouses up to seventy feet in length called *ganonchia* for winter use. These were equipped at each end with an enclosed porch, called an *aque*, that was used for storing food and firewood.[5]

In the 1770s, the English botanist, William Bartram, observed dwellings with porches erected by the indigenous inhabitants of Alabama, including a council house in a Creek Indian town with what he described as a "piazza" in front with pillars formed to look like spotted serpents.[6]

Even some Inuit peoples of the Arctic regions of Canada and Alaska constructed winter shelters with enclosed porches that served as passageway entrances to provide protection from the cold and from intruders. Examples of these semi-subterranean structures built by the people who have called themselves the Siglit were documented in the Mackenzie Delta region of the Northwest Territories as early as 1865, but based on archaeological evidence, this type of dwelling feature is thought to have roots in technologies developed by people in the Bearing Strait region more than two thousand years ago.[7]

Thus as one looks across the Americas and beyond to other lands, one finds evidence that simple, open, shade-rendering

Figure 1.2. *Traditional Native American dwellings in Pinal County, Arizona, featured ramadas supported by stout mesquite uprights and roofed with arrowweed thatch and mud over cottonwood poles. The attached house has wattle-and-daub walls made from saguaro ribs and mud. Historic American Buildings Survey photograph, 1939, HABS ARIZ,11-SAC.V,5-1.*

Figure 1.3. *A simple ramada constructed of local materials revives traditions of the people of the Tohono O'odham Nation while framing a view of the Mission San Xavier del Bac, a National Historic Landmark near Tucson, Arizona.*

structures have served as transitional spaces between inside and out for millennia.[8] Whether supported by plain posts or ornate columns, open-sided, roofed appendages have been common architectural features on domestic and public buildings since antiquity and before, especially where people around the world have valued shade and protection.

In hot climates of lower latitudes where

the midday sun passes nearly overhead with little seasonal variation, porches have been recessed into buildings as loggias or have been located on south or north sides to provide shade and relief from the heat. Arcades and colonnades also have provided shade to protect exterior masonry walls from the heat of the sun, and thus have allowed interior spaces to remain more temperate. It would be a mistake to assume that porches have a history rooted only in shade-rendering benefits in hot climates, however. Indeed, in addition to the Arctic examples mentioned above, archaeologists also have found evidence of a large timber structure with a porch in Tyrone County, Ireland, that according to radiocarbon tests was constructed more than four thousand years ago.[9]

Porticos, colonnades, arcades, and various other forms of porches have long provided intermediary spaces and transitional zones intended to serve many uses as extended thresholds that straddle inside and outside realms on domestic, civic, mercantile, and religious buildings. From the simple, open sheds on primitive houses recorded in Egyptian hieroglyphics, to the grand porticos of ancient Greece, the ornamented colonnades and arcades of Rome, and the elaborate recessed porches of Renaissance cathedrals, this basic architectural concept is deeply embedded in the vocabulary and memory of human culture.

During the late Old Kingdom and early Middle Kingdom of ancient Egypt, porticos supported by pillars or columns provided shady spaces on residential buildings constructed more than 4,500 years ago.[10] The King James Version of the Bible includes more than forty references to porches, including this Old Testament description of the porch (or *ulam*) of King Solomon's Temple in Jerusalem:

And he made a porch of pillars; the length thereof was fifty cubits, and the breadth thereof thirty cubits: and the porch was before them: and the other pillars and the thick beam were before them.

Then he made a porch for the throne where he might judge, even the porch of judgment: and it was covered with cedar from one side of the floor to the other.[11]

In ancient Greece colonnades, porticos, and *stoae* (shaded passageways supported by columns) provided the public with sheltered spaces for walking, trade, and religious meetings. Indeed, the transitional function and character of these quasi-public porches, being spaces neither completely *in*, nor completely *out*, promoted a broad range of human opportunities and experiences. Symbolically, it was perhaps thus no accident that Plato's early dialogue on piety between a skeptical Socrates and Euthyphro, a staunch defender of traditional religious values, was set on the portico, or the *stoa*, of the king-archon's court, located south of the Acropolis in ancient Athens.[12]

Also, the Stoa Poikile, or "Painted Porch," built in the fifth century BCE on the north side of the Athenian agora, served as the main teaching place, circa 300 BCE, for Zeno of Citium, who is credited with founding the Stoic school of philosophy.[13] With colonnades extending longer than three hundred feet, one of the greatest examples is the Stoa of Attalos (figure 1.4), originally constructed in the Athenian agora during the rule of Attalos II between 159 BCE and 138 BCE, and reconstructed during the 1950s based on archaeological evidence.

An outstanding surviving example of a porch from ancient Greece is the Porch of the Maidens (figure 1.5) or Caryatid Porch, attached to the distinctive Erechtheum

Figure 1.4. *Doric columns on the left and Ionic columns on the right support the colonnade of the reconstructed Stoa of Attalos in Athens.*

Figure 1.5. *The Porch of the Maidens, also known as the Caryatid Porch of the Erechtheum temple, faces the Parthenon temple on the Acropolis in Athens. Circa 1900 stereograph by Underwood & Underwood.*

temple on the summit of the Acropolis in Athens. Constructed between 421 and 405 BCE, its entablature is supported on the heads of six carved-marble female figures that face east toward the Parthenon.[14]

COVERED APPROACH

The word *porch* can be traced to the Medieval English and French word *porche*. Both share a common root with the word *portico* that stems from the classical Latin, *porticus*, which was used to refer to a colonnade or an arcade. Defined in a nineteenth-century English architectural glossary as "an adjunctive erection placed over the doorway of a larger building," porches were built on many great European cathedrals, churches, and castles of the Middle Ages, as well as on dwellings and various humbler utilitarian buildings.[15] These porches could range in size from very shallow, protected entrances to grand two-story structures with second-floor spaces accessed from dwelling apartments or chapels. Before the Reformation, in keeping with their physical position as transitional liminal spaces mediating between sacred and secular realms, church porches in England and Germany were used for such functions as marriages, baptisms, and religious education, as well as for signing legal contracts. Even highly eminent persons were sometimes buried in church porches in the early Christian Church, rather than within the sacred interior sanctuaries of churches, as became customary later.[16]

When located at the entrance at the opposite end of a church or cathedral from the altar, such church porches could be part of the narthex. Some religious functions might be performed in a narthex for those people who were not allowed inside the church. Also, the term *galilee porch* has been used to describe a church or chapel porch located on the west side (which is considered less sacred) of a nave of a church or Gothic cathedral.[17]

Figure 1.6. (left) *The English architectural term,* porch, *has long described any projection intended to shelter a building entrance. A thirteenth-century example of a Gothic shallow stone porch at Uffington, Berkshire, England, is shown in this woodcut. From* A Glossary of Terms Used in Grecian, Roman, Italian, and Gothic Architecture *(1850); Rare Books and Special Collections, McGill University Library.*

Figure 1.7. (right) *This small stone porch shelters an entrance to Castle Ashby in Northampton, England, built starting in 1574. Note the small stone bench within. From* A Glossary of Terms Used in Grecian, Roman, Italian, and Gothic Architecture *(1850); Rare Books and Special Collections, McGill University Library.*

Before the mid-nineteenth century, the word *porch* was commonly used in England and in English-speaking areas of North America to describe either an open or enclosed shelter of a building entrance. English architect Richard Brown discussed it thusly in 1841: "The porch, now apended to modern residences, which is a projecting entrance with its sides enclosed, was originally to the Gothic church what the portico was to the Greek and Roman temple, and is therefore of sacred origin."[18]

To be sure, the word *porch* was also common in American parlance in the early 1800s, as is reflected in this excerpt from Clement Clarke Moore's familiar Christmas poem, "A Visit from St. Nicolas," written in 1832:

"Now, Dasher! now, Dancer! now, Prancer! Now, Vixen!

On! Comet, on! Cupid! on! Donder and Blitzen—
To the top of the porch! to the top of the wall!
Now, dash away, dash away, dash away all!"[19]

In 1841, A. J. Downing described some of the important practical and symbolic roles that porches serve for buildings: "*A Porch* strengthens or conveys expression of purpose, because, instead of leaving the entrance door bare, as in manufactories and buildings of an inferior description, it serves both as a note of preparation, and an effectual shelter and protection to the entrance. Besides this, it gives a dignity and importance to that entrance, pointing it out to the stranger as the place of approach."[20] Meanings of the words *porch* and *portico* were clarified in the 1850s with the following definitions:

> Porch, an exterior appendage to a building, forming a covered approach to a door or entrance.
>
> Portico, a covered space or projection surrounded by columns at the entrance of a building. A porch is a covered station, and a portico is a covered walk.[21]

Today, the term *porch* is used broadly across North America to describe this building feature in many forms, whereas *portico* is generally used to describe a specific type of porch with columns and other classically inspired architectural details that shelters a doorway. The identifying features of important types of porches and porticos are discussed below.

Speculations about the origins and evolution of the porch as a feature of domestic architecture in the United States and Canada have prompted some architectural historians and writers to point to Europe and elsewhere for evidence of design precedents. Even the various names given to types of this shade-rendering building feature suggest a range of exotic sources, such as *portico*, *loggia*, and *piazza* from the Mediterranean and *veranda* from the Indian subcontinent.

Some cultural geographers, anthropologists, and preservation scholars have proposed models of cultural diffusion that also include considerations of Spanish, French, English, Dutch, African, Native American, and Caribbean precedents and connections to help explain the historical spread of adoptions of some types of porches in North America. Of the latter, an example is how the *bohio*, the rectangular thatched-roofed house with an open porch or inset doorway built by the indigenous Arawaks on the island of Hispaniola and elsewhere in the

Figure 1.8. Corredores *with clay tile roofs, benches, and chairs surround a* placita *near San Diego, California, in this early-twentieth-century postcard view.*

West Indies that was documented by Spanish explorers by the sixteenth century, may have influenced vernacular coastal Creole architecture from Lousiana to the Carolinas.[22] Examples of various historic porch designs that were spread by cultural diffusion are discussed below.

LOGGIAS, *PORTALES*, AND *CORREDORES*

The Spanish colonial and Mexican architecture of the American Southwest reflects a rich history that merges Native American traditions with the region's three centuries as part of New Spain and thirty-eight years as part of Mexico before the territory from western Colorado to California was taken by the United States in 1848. In addition to recessed loggias and arcades, traditional Hispanic vernacular building features include such types of porches as *portales*, which are colonnades that face streets or market squares; and *corredores*, the covered walkways that provide access to dwelling rooms off private inner patios (or *placitas*) of Spanish colonial structures and later Spanish Colonial Revival–style residences.

Figure 1.9. *The long front* portal *contributes to the Pueblo Revival–character of the Palace of the Governors in Santa Fe, New Mexico. This landmark adobe building, which originally dates from between 1610 and 1614, was restored in 1909. Detail from Historic American Buildings Survey photograph, 1934, HABS NM,25-SANFE,2-1.*

Figure 1.10. *An elevated loggia was built into the northeast corner of the Convento, erected about 1699 at the San Esteban del Rey Mission, Acoma Pueblo, New Mexico. Historic American Buildings Survey photograph, 1934, HABS NM,31-ACOMP,2-14.*

As early as the 1500s, these various types of porches were being constructed on structures built by Spanish-speaking peoples of the American Southwest, Florida, the Caribbean, Mexico, and elsewhere in Latin America. Not only did these reflect vernacular forms of porches best suited to local climates and social contexts, but such building designs were also influenced by governmental actions. The Laws of the Indies of 1573, which governed the planning of New World Spanish colonial settlements, required that buildings facing public squares and side streets should have arcades or colonnades. Whether for military presidios or for civilian pueblos, these Spanish planning codes helped to guide the development of such communities in the present United States as Santa Fe, New Mexico, and Tucson, Arizona.[23]

One of the best-known examples of an adobe structure with a prominent *portal* is the El Palacio Real de Santa Fe, commonly known as the Palace of the Governors (figure 1.9). It was originally built about 1610 and restored to its current Pueblo Revival appearance between 1909 and 1913.[24] In addition to providing a shaded walkway along the street, this and other *portales* often are used as informal vending spaces for small merchants.

Both *portales* and *corredores* were mentioned by authors describing Spanish Colonial buildings in nineteenth-century American guide books, especially as attention turned to settling the American West after the completion of the transcontinental railroad in 1869. The following excerpt from an 1873 travelogue written by Charles Nordhoff, describes an evening's activities under the *corredor* veranda facing the open *placita* at the Santa Margarita ranch, located at what is now the Camp Pendleton Marine Corps base near Oceanside, California:

In the evening the major-domo and the older vacqueros gathered on the long verandah. While a lady was singing in the parlor, where the family and visitors gathered, I noticed three or four old men—evidently privileged characters— sitting quietly, listening, on a long bench in the hall. At meal-times, if the long dining-table was not full, two or three of these privileged characters quietly took the vacant places, far down—below the

Figure 1.11. *Two arched openings, supported by a center masonry pier and walls, create a simple arcade that forms a shaded loggia at the Gonzalez-Alvarez House in Saint Augustine, Florida. Original parts of the walls of coquina stone may date from about 1723. Historic American Buildings Survey photograph, 1965, HABS FLA,55-SAUG,11-13.*

Figure 1.12. *A* corredor *faces a* placita *at the Casa del Rancho Santa Margarita y Los Flores in Oceanside, California. Detail from Historic American Buildings Survey photograph, 1937, HABS CAL,37-OCSI.V,2-5.*

Figure 1.13. *This circa 1905 postcard view shows the* corredor *facing the patio at the reputed fictional home of Ramona, the Ygnacio del Valle Adobe at the Rancho Camulos, a National Historic Landmark in Piru, California.*

salt—ate and listened, or answered, if they were addressed. Meantime another long table was set, or had been set, under a piazza roof in the quadrangle which every Californian house incloses, and here others ate.[25]

Another richly detailed description of a *corredor* veranda on an adobe dwelling in southern California was included in the popular novel *Ramona*, written by Helen Jackson in 1884:

The house was of adobe, low, with a wide veranda on the three sides of the inner court, and a still broader one across the entire front, which looked to the south. These verandas, especially those on the inner court, were supplementary rooms to the house. The greater part of the family life went on in them. Nobody stayed inside the walls, except when it was necessary. All the kitchen work, except the actual cooking, was done here, in front of the kitchen doors and windows. Babies slept, were washed, sat in the dirt, and played, on the veranda. The women said their prayers, took their naps, and wove their lace there. Old Juanita shelled her beans there, and threw the pods down on the tile floor, till towards night they were sometimes piled high around her, like corn-husks at a husking. The herdsman and shepherds smoked there, lounged there, trained their dogs there; there the young made love, and the old dozed; the

Figure 1.14. *The circa 1834 Vallejo Adobe near Petaluma, California, features a two-story Monterey porch that is typical of the adobes constructed between the 1830s and 1850s along the California coast. Historic American Buildings Survey photograph, 1934, HABS CAL,49-PET.V,1-1.*

benches, which ran the entire length of the walls, were worn into hollows, and shone like satin; the tile floors also were broken and sunk in places, making little wells, which filled up in times of hard rains, and were then an invaluable addition to the children's resources for amusement, and also to the comfort of the dogs, cats, and fowls, who picked about among them, taking sips from each.[26]

MONTEREY PORCHES

The iconic two-story balcony porches of the Monterey-style buildings in coastal California reflect a mixture of local Hispanic traditions with Anglo designs brought by New Englanders between the 1830s and the 1850s.[27] Although some real estate agents may describe most any California house with an upstairs balcony porch as "Monterey style," an adobe house with second-story balcony built in 1853 in Monterey, California, by an immigrant from Boston, Thomas Larkin, has been regarded by some as the

first example of the Monterey style of house. Scholarly research has shown, however, that the form is actually much older.[28] The circa 1834 Vallejo Adobe (figures 1.14 and 1.15) located near Petaluma, California, is an outstanding example of this form, boasting a two-story Monterey porch more than two hundred feet long.[29]

A notable historic example of a Monterey porch that cantilevers out from the adobe walls can be found at the Pacific House, built in 1847 in Monterey, California. It is now owned by the California State Parks and operated as a museum.[30] Monterey porches continued to be constructed on adobe buildings in California throughout the Victorian era, with ornamentation reflecting influences of various popular architectural styles.[31]

FRENCH GALLERIES

The term *gallery* is used to describe various architectural features, but of particular interest are the various types of porches that may be found on buildings in the areas of North America influenced by French colonial and cultural traditions. Derived from the French word, *galerie*, for a covered promenade or porch, galleries may extend along one, several, or all sides of a building on the ground floor, or even on multiple stories. *Galerie* is also used in French to describe a *galerie basse* or *portique* on the ground floor of a building and a *galerie haute* or *loggia*, which describes a second-story balcony or *balcon* on the *premier étage* (or first upper story).[32]

The regions of North America where buildings with porches known as galleries are principally found encompass the former New France and Louisiana Territory, including Quebec, adjacent Acadian areas of the Canadian Maritime Provinces, and French-

Figure 1.15. *View from inside the Monterey porch of the circa 1834 Vallejo Adobe near Petaluma, California. Historic American Buildings Survey photograph, 1934, HABS CAL,49-PET.V,1-7.*

Figure 1.16. *A shallow, upper-story balcony Monterey porch rings the Pacific House, circa 1847, in Monterey, California. Detail from Historic American Buildings Survey photograph, 1936,* HABS CAL,27-MONT,5-1.

Figure 1.17. *Built in 1878, the Casa de Geronimo Lopez in San Fernando, California, combines the form of a traditional adobe house with a Monterey porch decorated with Eastlake motifs on the balustrade and porch post brackets. Historic American Buildings Survey photograph, 1960,* HABS CAL,19-SANF,3-4.

speaking areas of eastern Ontario, as well as the formerly French-speaking areas of Louisiana and elsewhere along the Mississippi River valley.

Both hipped roofs and gabled roofs are associated with French Colonial and Quebec galleries. These include the steeply pitched, pavilion types of hipped roofs, as well as shallow-pitched hipped roofs, double-hipped roofs, and simple gable roofs that in some examples have curved, bell-cast extended eaves. These design trends were initially inherited from northern France through the process of cultural diffusion but were refined over the centuries in the New World through incremental innovations. Examples of the characteristic Quebec form of galleries sheltered by extended bell-cast overhanging roof eaves date from the late 1600s through the present.[33]

In a design passed on from medieval French traditions, the lower curved parts of these roofs (referred to in French as *larmier incurvé* or *avant-toit courbé*) were often formed by adding extensions, known in French as *coyaux*, to the lower ends of the rafters.[34] On some traditional Quebec

houses the *coyaux* only extended a foot or two beyond the walls, and the overhanging canted eaves are unsupported by posts; on others, however, the *coyaux* project further to form shallow *galeries* supported by posts.[35]

Houses with such extended curved eaves and galleries located along the south shore of the Saint Lawrence River in Quebec were described by a traveler from the United States in the 1850s:

> The habitations are almost exclusively built of wood, and, though generally alike, I did not see any two that precisely resembled each other. They seem to have been built by men who had a decided taste for the picturesque in form, if not superior ideas in regard to comfort and utility. They are usually one story high, with steep, curved, and overhanging roofs, dormer windows in abundance, porches and piazzas of manifold varieties, and are painted after every imaginable fashion.[36]

A few well-preserved French colonial buildings with galleries survive in the United States in former Louisiana Territory

Figure 1.18. *Facing the Saint Lawrence River, a shallow gallery fronts the Marsil House, circa 1759, one of the oldest surviving buildings in Saint Lambert, Quebec.*

Figure 1.19. *The very shallow galleries along the front and rear of this nineteenth-century brick house in Napierville, Quebec, are formed with extended roof eaves supported by boxed columns, each trimmed with simple moldings forming capitals.*

Figure 1.20. *This photograph, taken sometime before 1906, of a much older log home in Tadoussac, Quebec, shows the curved roof eaves extended to provide a sheltered gallery space serving practical needs without supporting posts. Note that the heavy wooden deck that projects beyond house wall is being used for a wide variety of domestic purposes by this* habitant *family. McCord Museum, Montreal, MP-0000.1262.3.*

Figure 1.21. *Summer guests are shown posing along the shallow front gallery of a house in Tadoussac, Quebec. Late-1800s stereograph view; courtesy of Special Collections, University of Vermont.*

areas of Missouri, Illinois, Louisiana, and Mississippi. Some of these regions were largely settled by French-speaking Acadian refugees evicted between 1755 and 1764 after the British conquest of New France from areas that are now Nova Scotia, New Brunswick, and Prince Edward Island.

One of the earliest documented examples of house with a recessed gallery is the "Planter's Cabin" (figure 1.22) near Baton Rouge, Louisiana, that was probably built in the late 1780s.[37]

An outstanding example of a preserved French-Creole structure is the Nicolas Janis

Figure 1.22. *A deeply recessed gallery extends across the front of this "Planter's Cabin," probably built in the late 1780s near Baton Rouge, Louisiana. Historic American Building Survey photograph, 1978, HABS la14.*

Figure 1.23. *The Nicolas Janis House, circa 1790, in Sainte Genevieve, Missouri, features a double-pitched gable roof that extends over the surrounding galleries. Historic American Buildings Survey photograph, 1937, HABS MO,97-SAIGEN,5-2.*

Figure 1.24. *Louis Bolduc House, circa 1793, in Sainte Genevieve, Missouri.*

House (figure 1.23), which was built about 1790 in Sainte Genevieve, Missouri, with a double-pitched gable roof that extends over the recessed galleries that surround the core of the building.

The Louis Bolduc House (figures 1.24 and 1.25) in Sainte Genevieve, Missouri, built around 1793 by a French Creole family, also features a broad wraparound gallery beneath a double-pitched hipped roof. This building was restored between 1956 and 1958 by the National Society of Colonial Dames to its original appearance, based on physical evidence.[38]

Of the prevalence of houses with galleries in Mississippi, one traveler wrote in 1835: "The dwelling, like most in Mississippi, was a long, wooden, cottage-like edifice, with a long piazza, or gallery, projecting from the roof, and extending along the front and rear of the building. This gallery is in all country-houses, in the summer, the

Figure 1.25. *West rear gallery of the Louis Bolduc House in Sainte Genevieve, Missouri. Historic American Buildings Survey photograph, 1985, HABS MO,97-SAIGEN,6-31.*

Figure 1.26. *A breezeway (or "run") passes through the center of the Cooper-Breasley House in Mobile, Alabama, a dogtrot constructed in 1830. Historic American Buildings Survey photograph, 1937,* HABS ALA,49-MOUV,2-3.

Figure 1.27. *View inside the dogtrot breezeway of the Caldwell-Hutchison Farm, circa 1800, in Abbeville County, South Carolina. Historic American Buildings Survey photograph, 1980,* HABS SC,1-LOWN.V,4-7.

lounging room, reception room, promenade and dining room."[39] The term *gallery* (or *galerie*) is also applied to the multistoried and cantilevered wood and cast-iron galleries typical of the French Quarter in New Orleans and elsewhere in the Mississippi Valley region discussed below.

DOGTROTS

A variation of the recessed porch plan is the dogtrot house, developed as a folk housing form during late eighteenth and early nineteenth centuries in rural areas of the American South and southern Appalachians. To provide enhanced cooling, dogtrots originally featured an open breezeway (also known as a run or hall) passing through the middle of the house. This breezeway would typically connect with recessed porches on the front and possibly the rear.

An example of a dogtrot house with an open breezeway connecting to a front recessed loggia porch is the Cooper-Breasley House (figure 1.26) in Mobile, Alabama, constructed in 1830.[40] A house of hand-hewn

logs with a dogtrot that dates from about 1800 is located on the Caldwell-Hutchison Farm (figure 1.27) in Abbeville County, South Carolina.[41]

DUTCH INFLUENCES

The recessed front porch is not unique to the history of the American South or to traditions of New France, however. Through his careful analysis of landscape paintings and other artistic works, art historian Joseph Manca presents evidence that porches had been widely used architectural features in Old World cultures and that those with roofs supported by wooden posts were a late-medieval tradition brought to the New World by Dutch settlers in the Hudson River valley. He also makes the important point that we cannot rely only on surviving physical evidence of this history, as most of the earliest examples of porches in North America from the first period of European settlement have been lost.[42]

Recessed porches and stoops were featured on some houses built by generations

Figure 1.28. *The Dyckman House in New York City, built about 1783 and restored as a museum in 1916, features raised, full-length porches recessed beneath the curved eaves of both its front and rear gambrel roofs. Historic American Buildings Survey photograph, 1934, HABS NY,31-NEYO,11-1.*

Figure 1.29. *A curved Dutch gambrel roof extends over porch decks on the Johannes Van Nuyse House, built sometime before 1806 in Brooklyn, New York. Historic American Buildings Survey photograph, 1934, HABS NY,24-BROK,3-2.*

of Dutch-descended families in the region around New York that had been settled as New Netherlands during the 1600s. Reputed to be the last eighteenth-century Dutch farmhouse surviving on Manhattan Island, an important example of a house with a full-length recessed porch is the circa 1783 Dyckman House (figure 1.28) in New York City. Restored in 1916 by descendants of the Dyckman family, this National Historic Landmark is now open to the public by the New York City Parks Department.[43] The distinctive form of the Dyckman House, with its curved gambrel roof extending over its recessed porches, served as a prototype design for the many Dutch Colonial Revival houses that became popular in the United States during the early twentieth century.

Another surviving example of a Dutch farmhouse with a recessed porch space formed beneath the broadly overhanging eaves of its curved gambrel roof is the Johannes Van Nuyse House (figure 1.29), built sometime before 1806 in Brooklyn,

New York. Its sheltered porch decks on the front and rear lack any support posts—a design that shares similarities with the French galleries of Quebec. Also known as the Van Nuyse-Magaw House, the building is now listed as a landmark by the New York City Landmarks Commission.[44]

The recessed front porch also became a form associated with bungalows and Dutch Colonial Revival–style houses during the twentieth century, as discussed below.

STOOPS AND PERRONS

As early as the mid-1600s, some buildings in Dutch-settled areas of New York and New Jersey featured small, front-entrance porches that were being called "stoops." With open steps and raised landings that were often flanked by benches, stoops formed intermediate, quasi-public outdoor spaces that straddled private and public realms. Many of these stoops were entirely open above, but on some buildings protection from sun and the weather was provided

Figure 1.30. *The 1642 Stadt Huys of New Amsterdam, New Netherlands, was shown with a stoop of steps protected by a small gable roof at its front entrance in this view from* Harper's New Monthly Magazine, *published in 1854. Simpler stoops protect the entrances of the flanking buildings.*

by hoods or by simple gable or shed roofs supported by posts or extensions of the main roof eaves.[45] Sometimes called "roofless porches," stoops, which may have a few steps or a run of stairs leading to a deck that provides access from ground levels, typically serve as both physical and symbolic transitional entry spaces to buildings.

A view of the 1642 Stadt Huys (figure 1.30) of New Amsterdam, New Netherlands, published in 1854 in *Harper's New Monthly Magazine*, shows a prominent stoop with raised steps and a small gable roof at its front entrance.[46]

The term *stoop* comes from *stoep*, the Dutch word for step or raised platform, and indeed this building feature was common in Holland in the seventeenth century. An example was recorded in the well-known 1654 painting of two people on a stoop by the Dutch painter Ferdinand Bol, titled in French: *Couple à la balustrade d'un perron.*[47] *Perron* is a related archaic architectural term that is still occasionally used in English, especially in Britain, to describe a flight of

ascending steps and platform in front of a raised building entrance.[48] This comes from the French word with the same spelling, which is also used to describe the steps and raised platform, typically of stone, that might be at the base of a monument or at a building entry.

In his 1749 description of Albany, New York, Swedish botanist Peter Kalm observed stoops formed by extended roof eaves (as translated into English):

> Most of the houses are built in the old Frankish way, with the gable-end towards the street, except a few, which were recently built in the modern style. . . . The front doors are generally in the middle of the houses, and on both sides are porches with seats, on which during fair weather the people spend almost the whole day, especially on those porches which are in the shade. The people seem to move with the sun and the shade, always keeping in the latter. When the sun is too hot the people disappear. In the evening the verandas are full of people of both sexes; but this is rather troublesome because a gentleman has to keep his hat in constant motion, for the people here are not Quakers whose hats are as though nailed to the head. It is consider[ed] very impolite not to lift your hat and greet everyone.[49]

During his travels to the United States in 1788, the French writer Jacques-Pierre Brissot de Warville observed in Philadelphia, "[a]t the door of each house are placed two benches, where the family sit at evening to take the fresh air, and amuse themselves in looking at the passengers. It is certainly a bad custom, as the evening air is unhealthful, and the exercise is not sufficient to correct this evil, for they never walk here: they

Figure 1.31. *The front stoop on the Frederick Crounse House, built in 1802 in the town of Guilderland in Albany County, New York, features wooden steps and side benches on a platform sheltered by a projecting hood. Historic American Buildings Survey photograph,* HABS NY,1-ALTA.V,1-3.

supply the want of walking, by riding out into the country."[50]

An outstanding example of a front stoop with side benches is on the Frederick Crounse House (figure 1.31), built in 1802 in Albany County, New York.[51]

In his satirical book *A History of New-York from the Beginning of the World to the End of the Dutch Dynasty, by Diedrich Knickerbocker*, first published in 1809, the New York writer Washington Irving provided a description of Peter Stuyvesant, the colonial governor of New Amsterdam, who "received the common class of visitors on the *stoop** before his door, according to the custom of our Dutch ancestors." The 1828 edition of this text included the following footnote: "*Properly spelled stoeb: the porch commonly built in front of Dutch houses, with benches on each side."[52] In another description of Peter Stuyvesant, Irving wrote of some functionaries, who "found him, according to custom, smoking his afternoon pipe on the 'stoop,' or bench at the porch of his house. . . ."[53]

A picturesque depiction of a colonial Dutch stoop in New Jersey also was included in Washington Irving's satirical story "Communipaw": "Instead of cold marble porches, with close-locked doors, and brass knockers, he sees the doors hospitably open; the worthy burgher smoking his pipe on the old-fashioned stoop in front, with his 'vrouw' knitting beside him; and the cat and her kittens at their feet, sleeping in the sunshine."[54]

Noah Webster's *An American Dictionary of the English Language* offered by 1830 this definition of a stoop: "*In America*, a kind of shed, generally open, but attached to a house; also an open place for seats at a door."[55] In the New York area, the word *stoop* has also been used to refer to a covered porch or piazza, as in this 1835 description of an "old Dutchman" whose dwelling faced Staten Island: "He would often sit at the close of a summer afternoon, upon his stoop, or piazza, and point out the beauties of that surpassing landscape, which was spread out, like a vast picture, before him."[56]

A very precise description of a wooden stoop was included in architect James Gallier's *American Builder's General Price Book and Estimator*, published in New York in 1836: "Front stoops from 3½ to 5 feet high, with ramp and knee rounded rail, square balusters, the sides inclosed with boards tongued and beaded, all firmly fixed complete."[57] For this stoop, Gallier listed a price of sixteen dollars for the materials and nine dollars for a journeyman's labor. He also estimated that a simpler stoop with "straight rails framed into newels" could be built for fifteen dollars in materials and eight dollars for labor.[58]

Informal attributions of Dutch origins of porches and stoops (or "stoups") in northeastern North America were supported by comments of Catharine Parr Traill, an

English emigrant who wrote of her experiences in Upper Canada in the 1830s. This region of Ontario had been settled between the 1770s and 1790s by thousands of United Empire Loyalists who carried traditions of vernacular language and building forms as they fled from New York, New Jersey, New England, and other rebellious American colonies in response to the political uprisings that led to the American Revolution and the subsequent confiscations of their "Tory" properties. With regards to her plans for her own house near Peterborough, Ontario, Traill used the English and Canadian spelling, *verandah*, but also recognized the alternative Dutch-American-Canadian vernacular term as she wrote of her plans in 1836 in the *Backwoods of Canada*:

> When the house is completed, we shall have a verandah in front; and at the south side, which forms an agreeable addition in the summer, being used as a sort of outer room, in which we can dine, and have the advantage of cool air, protected from the glare of the sunbeams. The Canadians call these verandahs "stoups." Few houses, either log or frame, are without them. The pillars look extremely pretty, wreathed with the luxuriant hop-vine, mixed with the scarlet creeper and "morning glory," the American name for the most splendid of major convolvuluses. These stoups are really a considerable ornament, as they conceal in a great measure the rough logs, and break the barn-like form of the building.[59]

Of a visit to an army officer's home nearby, she observed: "Dinner was laid out in the stoup, which, as you may not know what is meant by the word, I must tell you that it means a sort of wide verandah, supported on pillars, often of unbarked logs; the floor

Figure 1.32. *Front stoops on Gothic Revival–style summer cottages of the 1860s provided quasi-public seating spaces along Trinity Avenue at the Wesleyan Grove Meeting Association on Martha's Vineyard, Massachusetts. Courtesy of Special Collections, University of Vermont.*

is either of earth beaten hard, or plank; the roof covered with sheets of bark or else shingled. These stoups are of Dutch origin, and were introduced, I have been told, by the first Dutch settlers in the states, since which they have found their way all over the colonies."[60]

Through the nineteenth century the words *stoop*, *porch*, *veranda*, and *piazza* were all generally used to describe either a roofed or unroofed building entrance with steps, especially in the New York area. John Brodhead's *History of New York*, published in 1853, noted that the word *stoop* referred to "the steps at the entrance of a house" and that the term was "still in familiar use among the descendants of our old Dutch families."[61] George Woodward also equated verandas and stoops when describing the features of a rustic cottage in his 1868 book on

Figure 1.33. *This mid-nineteenth-century front stoop in the Chelsea neighborhood of New York City features sandstone steps, railings of wrought and cast iron, and a recessed entrance with Italianate-style double doors.*

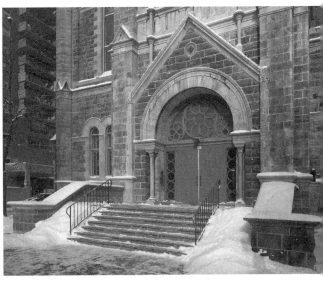

Figure 1.34. *A perron of limestone provides an extended outside entrance space for the Immaculée-Conception Church in Montreal, built between 1896 and 1898.*

architecture. "The veranda, or front stoop, is made with cedar posts and trimmings, but has a plank floor and tight roof."[62]

The following sequence of excerpts from diary entries written by a teenage girl in Yonkers, New York, between September 1864 and June 1866 offers a series of short glimpses of how front stoops could even support nineteenth-century courtship rituals:

I sat on the front stoop this evening for a short time but did not say one word to Mr Grau.

. . . this morning we walked up to the big gate and Grau and I sat on the front stoop till twelve o'clock.

. . . I dressed and went down on the front stoop. Mr Grau came home

early and sat there a while too, talking with me.

. . . when we came home Mr Grau and I made up and sat together on the front stoop till quite late.[63]

In Quebec French, the word *perron* is also commonly used to describe a stoop or small entry porch, especially one with a solid base, in contrast to a *galerie*, which is used to describe a full-length porch or veranda.[64] Such *perrons* serve as entry stoops for religious, institutional, or residential buildings.

By the early twentieth century, the meaning of the term *stoop* had narrowed in English-speaking areas of North America, at least among those concerned with using appropriate building terminology.

Figure 1.35. *Similar to a stoop, this perron with curved limestone steps leads up to the raised front entrance of an Art Nouveau–style residence in Montreal.*

Distinguishing between the terms *stoop* and *porch*, *Audels Carpenters and Builders Guide* of 1923 provided the following explanation: "A careful distinction should be made between these terms and the word stoop which means an uncovered platform at the door of a house, having usually steps with baluster guards and sometimes seats at the sides. A stoop is virtually a primitive porch without a cover, however the objectionable practice of using the word stoop for porch is inexcusable."[65]

Linguistic geographer Hans Kurath, who studied the regional dialect applications of the word *stoop* to describe a small porch, noted a concentration of its usage in western New England and in areas of New York State and northern Pennsylvania in the 1930s.[66] A similar study conducted in the 1960s in Cleveland, Ohio, found that among respondents aged sixty-five and older, about 65

percent used the word *stoop* instead of *porch* to describe "a small porch, often with no roof," but that the word *porch* was selected to describe this building feature by more than 70 percent of those respondents between forty and sixty-five years of age.[67]

Today, the word *stoop* is still commonly used in the American Northeast, often referring to a covered or uncovered entry with steps and deck that has only enough space for standing, as opposed to a small porch that could also provide enough space for sitting.

SYMBOLIC STAGES

With the dramatic waves of political, technological, economic, and social-psychological changes that occurred in North America (and elsewhere in the world) during the eighteenth and nineteenth centuries, it comes as no surprise that just as much of day-to-day life was being transformed, there also would be a blossoming of new architectural expressions during this period. And with the development of new cultural identities in the United States and Canada, so too, came a proliferation of colonnades, porticos, porches, piazzas, and verandas on North American homes, inns, hotels, churches, schools, and on various other buildings of commerce, service, government, and faith.

In his book *Vernacular Architecture*, folklorist Henry Glassie has discussed how changes in common architectural forms may be seen as indicators of changes in broad social conditions. For example, during the 1760s period of social tension in the Chesapeake Bay region, the floor plans of many houses were changed by the addition of partitioned entry halls that added a physical space of security and protection from whomever might enter from the outside, rather than having exterior doors open directly

Figure 1.36. *A tetrastyle Corinthian portico graces Whitehall, the residence of the colonial governor of Maryland, built in the Georgian style in 1765 in Annapolis. Historic American Buildings Survey photograph, 1936, HABS MD,2-____,5-11.*

Figure 1.37. *Added in the late 1770s, a colonnade faces a scenic view of the Potomac River on President George Washington's mansion, Mount Vernon, in Fairfax County, Virginia. As shown in this early 1900s postcard view, eight square Tuscan columns support an entablature and extended roof surmounted by an open balustrade of painted stickwork in a Union Jack motif. The small porch on the side entrance at the left was removed in 1932.*

into parlor living spaces, as was common before.[68] This observation also may provide some hints about why porches, porticos, and piazzas became so popular during the following decades, especially during the American Revolution and, later, as profound tensions over the abolition of slavery grew in the young United States.

Cultural historian John E. Crowley has posited that the construction of porches and piazzas in the mid-eighteenth century in Europe and in colonial eastern North America reflected a fundamental shift in attitudes towards domestic comfort and convenience, as well as serving as a symbolic display of social status. In support, he traces the adoption of porches for military buildings, especially by British colonial regiments, and their use by officers as symbolic stages on which they could demonstrate elevated authority, class, and privileges.[69]

A noteworthy example of such a residential building with a grand classical portico built as a symbolic stage for a person of power and prestige is Whitehall (figure 1.36), the Georgian-style home built between 1765 and 1769 in Annapolis, Maryland, for Horatio Sharpe, the colonial governor of Maryland. With its four colossal fluted columns in the Corinthian order supporting a steeply pitched pediment, this deep portico commands an extraordinary view over Chesapeake Bay. In keeping with the classical Corinthian order, the cornices of the portico are enriched with modillions. This feature is also carried to the cornices of the house walls. William Anderson is believed to be the architect of Whitehall, but records indicate that architect William Buckland may have been responsible for the architectural detailing.[70]

In Virginia, General George Washington added a large colonnade to his Georgian-style home, Mount Vernon (figure 1.37),

Figure 1.38. *A two-tiered front portico supported by Doric columns on the base and Ionic columns on the balcony projects from the front of the Manoir de Salaberry in Chambly, Quebec.*

by the 1780s to provide a shaded space on the side of the house that overlooks the Potomac River. The use of square columns instead of formal round ones gives the building a somewhat improvised vernacular appearance, but the iconic form of Mount Vernon is widely recognized by the public. Long referred to as the piazza, one visitor described it as "a lofty portico, ninety-six feet in length, supported by eight pillars, [which] has a pleasing effect when viewed from the water."[71] Also, a small porch on a side entrance was added in 1822, but it was removed by the Mount Vernon Ladies Association in 1932.[72]

The Manoir de Salaberry (figure 1.38) in Chambly, Quebec, is an important Canadian example of a Palladian-style mansion featuring an impressive front portico that has served as a prominent display of status, even though some suggest this portico was a later addition.[73] This stone mansion was constructed between 1814 and 1816 for Charles-Michel d'Irumberry de Salaberry, the legendary French Canadian hero of the

War of 1812, who led the Canadian Voltigeurs' victory in the Battle of Châteauguay that thwarted a planned American invasion of Montreal.[74]

Government House, also known as Fanningbank, the historic residence of the lieutenant governor in Charlottetown, Prince Edward Island, serves as another important Canadian example of a nineteenth-century North American colonial government building with porches that reflect the transition from traditional Palladian classicism to the Picturesque. Designed in the early 1830s by a local architect, Isaac Smith, the two-story, hip-roofed mansion initially featured an impressive front portico supported by four colossal Ionic columns.[75]

Within three years of its 1834 completion, however, two shallow, single-story verandas supported by Tuscan columns were added flanking the front portico and wrapping around the sides, as can be seen in figure 1.39. These side colonnade verandas were apparently constructed at the behest of a new lieutenant governor without prior approval by the appropriate legislative committee, resulting in words of "disapprobation" recorded in the journal of the colonial House of Assembly.[76] In 1838, the outside of the wooden building was painted, with a sanded finish applied to the columns and cornices. In 1843, painting and repairs were made to the "Porch," the "Colonade," and the "Veranda." The seams in the wooden floorboards were caulked, as the deck of a boat would be, with oakum, then puttied and painted.[77]

Now painted all white, Fanningbank appears as something of a hybrid cross between a staid Georgian mansion and a Victorian seaside resort. Indeed, its unusual form may prompt some casual observers to suspect that the building may date from the

Figure 1.39. *Government House, also known as Fanningbank, in Charlottetown, Prince Edward Island, was constructed in 1834 in the Georgian style with a prominent Ionic front portico to serve as the residence of the lieutenant governor of this British colony, which joined in confederation with Canada in 1873. As shown in this early-twentieth-century postcard view, the wraparound colonnade verandas with Tuscan columns were probably added in 1837.*

Figure 1.40. *A two-tiered Doric colonnade lines the facade of the Old Stone Barracks, 1838, in Plattsburgh, New York. Detail from Historic American Engineering Record photograph, 2000,* HAER NY-326-32.

late nineteenth century, when eclectic Classical Revival features combined with wraparound verandas were common on grand hotels of this scale. But rather than dismissing Fanningbank as an architectural oddity, one might better consider this building as an important example of how fundamental tensions between traditionalism and innovation

were being played out in building designs and construction during the 1830s. The Georgian-style form with the colossal front portico was certainly by then "old school" conservative, whereas the wraparound colonnade verandas were decidedly more current in concept and form, even if still dressed with respectable classical details and columns.

Grand multistory colonnades were also being used to display military authority in the United States during the 1830s. An especially impressive example fronts the 1838 United States Army barracks (figure 1.40) on the grounds of the former Plattsburgh Air Force Base in Plattsburgh, New York. These stone barracks have two-story Doric wooden colonnades covering the entrances of long rows of separate living spaces.[78]

Similar implied symbolic messages of elevated stature conveyed by this architectural form may help explain why porticos, colonnades, and porches were adopted as notable character-defining features on other government buildings, state and provincial capitals, court houses, city halls, public houses, churches and other religious buildings, taverns, and resort hotels, as well as on the houses of prominent political figures, mansions of wealthy merchants and aristocrats, and on the plantation homes of prosperous planters in the antebellum American South.

More than just architectural embellishments for display, grand porticos and colonnades also became symbolically associated with a wide variety of social activities and porch life customs during the early nineteenth century. The following account, from a letter written in June 1812 by a thirty-four-year-old socialite and author, Margaret Bayard Smith, describes the delightful transformation of a "piazza" in Washington, D.C., for a special birthday party: "The Piazza was soon transform'd into a bower,—every hand was busy,— Mrs. Clay, Mr. Smith and all. When the sun was completely excluded, the Pianno was placed at one end of the large piazza and the sopha at the other, and a table on which the big bowl (which is used only on grand occasions) the birth day cake crown'd with lilies and roses and fruit was placed, and we drank punch, and eat cake, till they all felt in a good humour for dancing."[79]

Sixteen years later, reflecting on her visit in August 1828 to Montpelier, the Virginia plantation home of the former U.S. president James Madison, Margaret Bayard Smith again described how the grand portico that had been added to this other mansion around 1797 could fit into social rituals. "After dinner, we all walked in the Portico, (or piazza, which is 60 feet long, supported on six lofty pillars) until twilight, then retreated to the drawing room, where we sat in a little group close together and took our coffee while we talked."[80]

To help clarify proper usages of the words *portico* and *piazza*, the following definitions were offered in 1841: "A *Portico* is an erection over the entrance to a building, and is often made greatly ornamental, while its useful purpose is to shelter the door. A *Piazza* is a walk under a roof supported by pillars."[81]

ENGLISH AND AMERICAN PIAZZAS

Early colloquial English use of the word *piazza* to describe an arched loggia or a colonnade on a building facing a square was actually a corruption of the Italian word of the same spelling that is used to describe a square or plaza (as in the famous Piazza San Marco in Venice). Although its use in England has been traced back to the late 1500s, rather than describing an open square, the word *piazza* became popular in London in 1631 to describe the arcades recessed into the building facades that faced the open square of Inigo Jones's famous Covent Garden Piazza development.[82]

Soon, the word *piazza* was being used in the English colonies of the New World as well. In 1699, when the General Assembly of colonial Virginia passed a resolution calling for the construction of a new capitol in Williamsburg, it specified that the building should be constructed with two wings "joined by a Cross Gallery of thirty foot long and fifteen foot wide" and "raised upon Piazzas and built as high as the other parts of the building." Subsequent changes in the plans, however, resulted in an arcade being constructed in 1751 between the two wings of the Williamsburg capitol.[83]

From various published sources and travelogues and a few documented examples, we know that open porches that were being called *piazzas* had become common features on many houses and taverns in New England, the mid-Atlantic region, and the American South by the 1700s. In the 1740s, for example, observations were published written by an English traveler who wrote the following after seeing an especially impressive wooden house for orphans on a plantation near Savannah, Georgia: "A kind of Piazza-Work surrounds it, which is a very pleasing Retreat in the Summer." Piazzas were also regularly being mentioned in advertisements and articles in colonial American newspapers. In March 1749 a lease announcement in Benjamin Franklin's *Pennsylvania Gazette* described a "very commodious house" with a "large piazza to the south and east fronts." An April 1750 auction notice in the same newspaper described a three-story house in Philadelphia that had "a good brick kitchen behind, with a communication between it and the house by a piazza 10 foot wide." In 1756 a house in New York to be sold at "publick vendue" had "a piazza on the back part of the house." Another notice from 1761 described a farm for sale in the "Province of East-New-Jersey" with a "piazza round the house." And in 1764, a "commodious dwelling-house" with a "handsome balcony in front" and a "piazza the whole length of the house and kitchen ten feet wide" was advertised in Savannah's *Georgia Gazette*.[84]

Another well-known early reference to a colonial American piazza was recorded in a 1771 letter from Boston artist John S. Copley to his half-brother, Henry Pelham, that included a reference to a "peazer." When Pelham complained that he did not know the meaning of the word, Copley replied that it described a structure that he intended to attach to his house with a roof supported by three or four posts with a "Chinese enclosure about three feet high" between and a good floor at the bottom, that would be "so cool in Sumer and in Winter break off the storms."[85]

Some eighteenth-century writers used the term *porch* to describe the same building feature, however. Englishman Isaac Weld Jr., for example, observed the prevalence of full-length porches on houses in rural Virginia in his book that recounted his travels in North America between 1795 and 1797: "In front of every house is a porch or pent-house, commonly extending the whole length of the building; very often there is one also in the rear, and sometimes all around. These porches afford an agreeable shade from the sun during the summer."[86] Weld also observed that in Maryland during the 1790s: "The quarters of slaves are situated in the neighborhood of the principal dwelling-house, which gives the residence of every planter the appearance of a little village,

just the same as in Virginia. The houses are for the most part built of wood, and painted with Spanish brown; and in front there is generally a long porch, painted white."[87]

By the 1790s, piazzas were becoming so commonplace in the newly independent United States that knowledge of vernacular American piazza designs was even traveling back across the Atlantic to England. In his book of sketches of country houses, English architect John Plaw showed his interpretation of American cottages with piazzas, reportedly based on the design of a house that he had seen near New York City. In his 1795 description of these English designs for "American Cottages," he wrote: "These double cottages are built (on the plan and in the style of some in America) at Trowley, near Feversham, in Kent, by Colonel Montresoto. I saw them after they were completed, and for their extreme singularity have introduced them in this work: the East, West, and South aspects have a piazza round them; and the major part of the external appearance, together with the roof, is covered with plain tiles. The general declivity of the roof is well calculated to throw off rain or snow."[88] Plaw's design featured piazzas extending about six feet beyond the outside walls on three sides of the houses. Their sloping roofs connected seamlessly with the main gable roofs, while the wraparound side sections had sloping roofs that projected beyond the walls of the gable ends. Arched spandrels between the simple posts of Plaw's piazzas also provided hints of arcades.

Although porches are now often thought of as settings to be used mainly for leisure activities, piazzas and verandas also have long served as places for household work and domestic chores. In his "Legend of Sleepy Hollow," first published in 1819, Washington Irving described the many pieces of household equipment that would be kept on a farmhouse piazza in New York State's Hudson River valley: "It was one of those spacious farm-houses, with high-ridged, but lowly-sloping roofs, built in the style handed down from the first Dutch settlers; the low projecting eaves forming a piazza along the front, capable of being closed up in bad weather. Under this were hung flails, harness, various utensils of husbandry, and nets for fishing in the neighboring river. Benches were built along the sides for summer use; and a great spinning wheel at one end, and a churn at the other, showed the various uses to which this important porch might be devoted."[89]

In 1828, James Fennimore Cooper described the attached piazza on the home (figure 1.41) of the former New York governor, John Jay, in Katonah, Westchester County, New York:[90] "The house itself was partly of stone, and partly of wood, it having been built at different periods; but, as is usual here, with most of the better sort of dwellings, it was painted, and having a comfortable and spacious piazza along its *façade*, another common practice in this climate, it is not without some pretension externally; still its exterior, as well as its internal character, is that of respectable comfort, rather than elegance, or show."[91]

In his 1828 travelogue, British visitor Captain Basil Hall acknowledged the local use of the word *piazza* to describe what he found on typical houses in rural Georgia. Shown in figure 1.42 is a sketch of one that he produced using a camera lucida, a lensed drawing aid that was a precursor to photographic cameras. He described his picture thus: "The building represented here is what is called a frame house, being made of timbers squared and fastened together, and afterwards covered with planks at the sides and ends,

Figure 1.41. *The John Jay House in Katonah, New York, has been restored to its 1820s appearance with a shed-roofed attached piazza extending across its south facade. Detail from Historic American Buildings Survey photograph, 1961, HABS ny17.*

while the roof is either boarded or protected with shingles, a sort of wooden slate two feet in length, and six inches wide. Almost all the houses in that part of the country have verandahs, or what they call piazzas."[92] Houses similar to the one sketched by Hall still stand in the American Southeast coastal region. An example of a vernacular cottage at the Snee Farm in Charleston County, South Carolina, that was probably built in the 1820s was documented by the Historic American Buildings Survey (figure 1.43).[93]

One should not assume that the practice of constructing piazzas on houses was restricted to the American South during this period, however. Indeed, in 1835 a newly built cottage with piazzas caught the attention of a traveler on a steamer while passing Bucksport, Maine on the Penobscot River: "There are several beautiful houses; one in particular, about halfway between the lower and upper street, built in the cottage style with a piazza on two sides, attracted my attention; it appeared to be quite new, and was painted white with green blinds."[94]

In 1838, Caroline Howard Gilman, a

Bostonian by birth who became a popular nineteenth-century American writer, revealed how a piazza could provide a fluid boundary space for feelings, connections, and separations in antebellum plantation culture of the American South.

The family at the Elms were effectually roused even before the shouts of the children had been heard. From time immemorial, a small field-piece had been kept solely for Christmas; and it was the privilege of their negroes (for there is some little peculiarity on every plantation) to place this cannon in the piazza of the dwelling-house, and fire it at early dawn. Mighty were the shoutings that followed this martial detonation.

The people at Roseland had no cannon; but, as a substitute, they commenced a salute with the combination of every noise they could make by the agency of tin and brass, aiding their rude music. One set of people would have been sufficient to drive Morpheus in a panic from our pillows; but from both plantations united, the clamor was prodigious.

Dancing commenced in the piazza and on the lawn soon after the firing of the cannon, nor was it suspended a moment by the presence of the whites.

Mamma and I and our friends had been busy the day previous in cutting the turban-handkerchiefs, and arranging the woollen caps and other articles which were to be presented.

After breakfast the people withdrew from the piazza, and we took possession while they came up in *gangs* to receive their gifts.[95]

Another traveler's candid description of the role of piazzas in Southern plantation life was published in the 1830s:

Figure 1.42. *Sketch of a house with an attached shed-roofed front piazza in Riceborough, Georgia. With the main-floor level rising eight steps above the ground, this piazza offered its inhabitants a superior view of its surroundings and shade from the sun.* Captain Basil Hall, Forty Etchings from Sketches Made with the Camera Lucida in North America in 1827 & 1828 *(1828); Rare Books and Special Collections, McGill University Library.*

Figure 1.43. *Very similar to the Riceborough, Georgia, house sketched by Captain Basil Hall, this vernacular cottage at the Snee Farm in Charleston County, South Carolina, was probably built in the 1820s. The chamfered posts and turned balusters on the attached front piazza suggest it may have been altered slightly during the late nineteenth century. Historic American Buildings Survey photograph, 1990, HABS SC,10-MOUP.V,2-5.*

A huge colonnaded structure, crowning an abrupt eminence near the road, struck our eyes with an imposing effect. It was the abode of one of the wealthiest planters of this state; who, like the majority of those whose families now roll in their splendid equipages, has been the maker of his fortune. The grounds about this edifice were neglected; horses were grazing around the piazzas, over which were strewed saddles, whips, horse blankets, and the motley paraphernalia with which planters love to lumber their galleries. On nearly every piazza in Mississippi may be found a wash-stand, bowl, pitcher, towel, and water-bucket, for general accommodation. But the southern gallery is not constructed, like those at the north, for ornament or ostentation, but for use. Here they wash, lounge, often sleep, and take their meals.—Here will the stranger or visiter be invited to take a chair, or recline upon a sofa, settee, or form, as the taste and ability of the host may have furnished this important portion of a planter's house.[96]

This traveler also offered an especially detailed description of a well-furnished porch (or gallery) on another antebellum Mississippi plantation:

I once called on a planter within an hour's ride of Natchez, whose income would constitute a fortune for five or six modest Yankees. . . . The planter was sitting upon the gallery, divested of coat, vest, and shoes, with his feet on the railing, playing, in high glee, with a little dark-eyed boy and two young negroes, who were chasing each other under the bridge formed by his extended limbs. Three or four noble dogs, which his voice and the presence of his servant, who accompanied me to the house, kept submissive, were couching like leopards around his chair. A litter of young bull-headed pups lay upon a blanket under a window opening into a bedroom, white with curtains and valances; while a domestic tabby sat upon the window-sill, gazing musingly down upon the rising generation of her hereditary foes, perhaps with reflections not of the most pleasing cast. A hammock, suspended between an iron hook driven into the side of the house and one of the slender columns which supported the sloping roof of the gallery, contained a youth of fourteen, a nephew of the planter, fast locked in the embraces of Morpheus; whose aid-de-camp, in the shape of a strapping negress, stood by the hammock, waving over the sleeper a long plume of gorgeous feathers of the pea-fowl—that magnificent bird of the south, which struts about the ground of the planter, gratifying the eye with the glorious emblazonry upon his plumage by day, and torturing the ear with his loud clamours by night. A pair of noble antlers was secured to one of the pillars, from whose branches hung broad-brimmed hats, bridles, a sheep-skin covering to a saddle, which reposed in one corner of the piazza, a riding whip, a blanket coat or capote, spurs, surcingle, and part of a coach harness. A rifle and a shot-gun with an incredibly large bore, were suspended in beckets near the hall entrance; while a couple of shot-pouches, a game-bag, and other sporting apparatus, hung beside them. Slippers, brogans, a pillow, indented as though recently deserted, a gourd, and a broken "cotton slate," filled up the picture, whose original, in some one or other of its features, may be found in nearly every planter's dwelling in this state.[97]

An 1854 account of the daily social customs and evening rituals associated with the use of piazzas in Pineville, South Carolina, reported:

A portion of the afternoon was always devoted to sleep. Every piazza was furnished, with long benches, and these formed the rude beds on which the gentlemen invariably indulged in the luxury of the siesta.

The siesta over, and whilst the sun was still high above the horizon, the kettle would bubble for the evening refection, and hot tea and cakes would be offered to refresh those whose heavy sleep rendered some refreshment necessary. This early evening meal, of course, indicated that supper would close the labours of the day. And now the active duties of the day being over, and every family having refreshed themselves with tea or coffee, social life commenced. Every one came to tea prepared either to make or receive visits.

Bonnets and hats were articles of female dress which were entirely ignored in the Pineville evening visits. In attire a simple elegance prevailed. Young ladies usually dressed in white; the aged were clad in graver colours. Visits were unceremonious. The guests were received in the piazza. No one ever expected to be invited into the house, and persons might spend a season in social intercourse with the people, without seeing the interior of any house but their own. Sometimes chairs were offered to the visitors, but, more generally, the long benches with which the piazza was furnished, were the only seats. . . .

But though the visiting was done at night, and the piazza the reception room,

the company did not sit in the dark. In front of the house, a fire of lightwood formerly, in later times of pine-straw, was kept constantly burning. The reasons for this practice were manifold. It diffused a cheerful light over the otherwise dark and gloomy lot. The smoke, too, was supposed to be conducive to health; and the light certainly attracted night flies and moths from the inferior lights of the dwelling. Around these fires the children would sport. Each little fellow would take a pride in having a little fire of his own; the larger and more daring would show their courage by leaping through the flames. Around its cheerful blaze time seemed to fly on golden wings. It was literally light to the dwelling, and a house without its yard fire appeared desolate and sorrow-stricken.[98]

VERANDA(H)S

By the early 1700s, the term *verandah* had been imported to England from India, where variations of the word were being used in Hindi and Bengali to describe roofed open shelters that extended along the fronts and sides of bungalows. Some speculate that word may even have been introduced earlier by Portuguese or Spanish explorers, who used the word *varanda* to refer to a balustrade or balcony.[99]

Although in most cases the words *piazza* and *veranda* were used to describe the same open architectural feature in North America during the nineteenth century, a nuanced analysis suggests that *piazza* was the earlier and more generalized term commonly used along the eastern seaboard of the United States. The word *verandah*, however, was used initially by British writers, and then adopted in Canada and in the United States (where it eventually was commonly spelled without the final *h*) to describe these open structures on houses designed in the Gothic Revival, Italianate Revival, and other Victorian-era styles that had been imported from Britain and continental Europe. As an essential character-defining feature of the picturesque English ornamental cottage (or the *cottage orné,* as called by those fond of borrowing terms from French), the veranda had become the focal point of both architectural design and domestic leisure activity. With rustic or trellised columns providing support for vines and climbing plants, the veranda thus served as a visual and physical connection between the building and its surrounding gardens and natural landscape. As with projecting awnings and balconies, verandas also provided designers with means to enliven the appearances of building facades by creating expressions of depth with ever-changing contrasts of light and shadow.

Such English examples as the published works of architects Robert Lugar, John B. Papworth, P. F. Robinson, and John Claudius Loudon, demonstrated that interest in the veranda as a key feature of picturesque villas and ornamental cottages grew on both sides of the Atlantic during the late eighteenth and early nineteenth centuries. And while some designs for houses with verandas were described as "American" in England, soon such house designs with verandas were being popularized back in North America by such influential English architects as John Plaw, who moved in 1807 to Prince Edward Island, and by Gervase Wheeler and Calvert Vaux, who migrated to the New York area of United States several decades later. Together, the works of these English architects helped to add an air of sophistication and refinement to perceptions of the veranda in North America.[100]

Although several decades would pass

before the public in the United States would relax its dependence on the ordered traditions of classical architecture epitomized by Federal and Greek Revival–style porticos and colonnades, in England during the first two decades of the nineteenth century, great progress was made in the development of Picturesque designs for cottages and villas intended to help connect buildings with surrounding landscapes, especially by using light verandas with trellised supports for vines and climbing plants.[101]

English architect John B. Papworth, who had worked with John Plaw in London, noted this trend in his description of a Picturesque veranda suitable to town residences in his influential pattern book, *Rural Residences, Consisting of a Series of Designs for Cottages, Small Villas, and other Ornamental Buildings,* first published in London in 1818:

> No decorations have so successfully varied the dull sameness of modern structures as the *verandah,* the *lengthened window* and the *balcony*; they have produced an intrinsic elegance, and have done much to overcome the architectural prejudice supported in this country, which very unphilosophically adopts the proportion of windows applicable to a clear and warm climate, in one not quite so liable to the effects of light and heat. . . .
>
> It is not improbable, that at some future day the verandah and piazza will form a considerable architectural beauty in this metropolis, and that they will be constructed in a way suitable to the nature of our climate.[102]

Papworth also included in this pattern book a design for a "Cottage orné designed for garden scenery and grounds of undulating forms" (figure 1.44). Of this charming dwelling, Papworth commented, "This building is designed to harmonize with garden scenery, and to afford a degree of embellishment by its verandahs and the variety of shadow which they project, that would be greatly desirable where the landscape is not composed of very interesting features."[103]

By the early 1800s, full-length front verandas had become common features of rural houses in upstate New York. English traveler Lt. Francis Hall, for example, included the following description in his *Travels in Canada and the United States in 1816 and 1817*: "Houses of wood, roofed with shingles, neatly painted, with generally from four to six sash windows on each floor, two stories high, and a broad veranda, resting on neat wooden pillars, along the whole of the front: such is the common style of house-building through the whole State."[104]

E. A. Talbot, Esq., another English traveler, also found piazzas and verandas to be worth mentioning in his description of Rochester, New York, written in 1823, the year that the recently built village on the shore of Lake Ontario was connected via the Erie Canal to the Hudson River and to East Coast markets: "The houses are built of brick, and neatly painted red and pointed out with white; this embellishment, with Venetian blinds, piazzas, verandas, balconies, &c. gives the village a very delightful aspect, and designates the inhabitants as tasteful, enterprising, industrious, and opulent; but, I believe it is more owing to other qualities than to their opulence."[105]

Other travelers commented on the prevalence of verandas on houses built in rural Canada by the 1820s and 1830s. A European tourist recorded, for example, the following account of a summer 1837 visit to a farmhouse that was built by an Irish immigrant family in 1827 in Upper Canada, near what is now Mississauga, Ontario:[106]

> In the evening it was very sultry, the sky was magnificently troubled, and the clouds came rolling down, mingling, as it seemed to me, with the pine tops. We walked up and down the verandah, listening to the soft melancholy cry of the whip-poor-will, and watching the evolutions of some beautiful green snakes of a perfectly harmless species, which were gliding after each other along the garden walks; by degrees a brooding silence and thick darkness fell around us; then the storm burst forth with all its might, the lightening wrapped the whole horizon round in sheets of flame, the thunder rolled over the forest, and still we lingered—lingered till the fury and the rain began to fall in torrents; we then went into the house and had some music.[107]

Verandas (also known as galleries, as discussed above) that were built to wrap around several sides of houses were also commonly found in the American South by the early nineteenth century, as Captain Basil Hall observed near Mobile, Alabama, in 1828: "This mansion, which in India would be called a Bungalow, was surrounded by white railings, within which lay an ornamental garden intersected by gravel walks, almost too thickly shaded with orange hedges, all in flower. From a light, airy, broad verandah, we might look out upon the Bay of Mobile."[108]

In 1852, Lewis F. Allen offered in his book *Rural Architecture* a discussion on how house designs for plantations in the antebellum American South differed from farmhouse arrangements elsewhere in the country. He also provided descriptions of the various functions supported by verandas and

Figure 1.44. *A "cottage orné designed for garden scenery and grounds of undulating form." The formal symmetry of Papworth's design was softened by climbing vines on the front columns and by the diagonal lattice design of the veranda at the right end of the cottage. On the second story, open balconies with metal railings flanked the hip-roofed projecting bay in the center. John B. Papworth,* Rural Residences *(1818); Rare Books and Special Collections, McGill University Library.*

porches in the American South during this period, as in the following description of a model design for a plantation house in the Italianate style with a large veranda wrapping around the front and the sides:

[I]t may be remarked, that no feature of the house in a southern climate can be more expressive of easy, comfortable enjoyment, than a spacious veranda. The habits of southern life demand it as a place of exercise in wet weather, and the cooler seasons of the year, as well as a place of recreation and social intercourse during the fervid heats of the summer. Indeed, many southern people almost live under the shade of their verandas. It is a delightful place to take their meals, to receive their visitors and friends; and the veranda gives to a dwelling the very expression of hospitality, so far as any one feature of a dwelling can do it. No equal amount of accommodation can be provided for the same cost. It adds infinitely to the room of the house itself, and is, in fact, indispensable to the full enjoyment of a southern house.

The side front in this design is simply a matter of convenience to the owner and occupant of the estate, who has usually much office business in its management; and in the almost daily use of his library, where such business may be done, a side door and front is both appropriate and convenient. The chief front entrance belongs to his family and guests, and should be devoted to their exclusive use; and as a light fence may be thrown off from the extreme end of the side porch, separating the front lawn from the rear approach to the house, the veranda on that side may be reached from its rear end, for business purposes, without intruding upon the lawn at all.[109]

As the nineteenth century progressed, with new patterns of identity and engagement emerging in the North American consciousness, porticos, loggias, piazzas, and verandas also became increasingly

Figure 1.45. *Asher Benjamin included this veranda design, enriched with Grecian forms that could be made of cast iron or wrought iron, in his 1839 pattern book,* The Builder's Guide.

prominent features of the domestic residential architectural vocabulary. Various explanations have been offered to explain why these appeared at so many locations scattered across settled areas so abruptly, but the dispersed pattern of this emergence makes it difficult to support any theories based on simple cultural diffusion from a single geographical source. Instead, we might consider the dispersed emergence of these types of porches to be a physical reflection of broad changes in human perspectives and ways of life that transcended the traditions of specific cultural groups during this period of profound social change.

Curiously, this period corresponds so closely with the long reign of the famous British monarch Queen Victoria (from 1837 to 1901) that both the era and its buildings are often characterized as "Victorian." Although a transition in Britain had started decades earlier toward Picturesque ornamental cottages, Romantic villas, and architectural styles based on revivals of ancient styles of building, the shift away from well-ordered

architectural classicism in the United States was perhaps most strongly influenced by the writings of one man: A. J. (Andrew Jackson) Downing. In 1836, this twenty-one-year-old nurseryman and soon-to-be-famous author from Newburgh, New York, suggested appropriate romantic and picturesque designs for country residences should have "harmony of expression with their landscape" in an article published in *American Gardeners Magazine*, questioning "whether the Grecian, with its open colonnades, so delightful under a warm sky, is as suitable for a northern climate like ours, as the Gothic, with its thick walls and comfortable apartments."[110]

Downing also suggested that a country residence should both fit with needs and harmonize with the landscape of its site. With regards to the suitable architectural style for a country residence, he suggested, "There can scarcely be a more appropriate, agreeable and beautiful residence for a citizen who retires to the country for the summer, than a modern Italian villa, with its ornamented chimneys, its broad *verandah*, forming a fine shady promenade, and its cool breezy apartments."[111] His reference to the verandah (often using the British spelling with an *h*) as an appropriate feature of the Italianate style of architecture served as one of the first notices of a trend spawned in Britain that would soon sweep across North America with the coming Victorian era.

Even the aging American architect Asher Benjamin included illustrations of verandas in his next-to-last pattern book, *The Builder's Guide*, first published in 1839. These shallow verandas with curved hipped roofs and richly embellished with Grecian foliate enrichments made of cast or wrought iron closely followed the general form of a veranda adapted to a balcony that the English architect, John B. Papworth had shown in his *Rural Residences* pattern book, first published in 1818 and republished in 1832.[112] In promoting the use of iron as a suitable material for verandas, balconies, railings, and brackets, Benjamin noted, "The fact, that cast iron is produced in most parts of this country, and at a cost so low as to place it within reach of all, the great amount of its yearly consumption, and the facility with which it may be wrought into the most beautiful shapes, render it an object worthy of attention here."[113]

By the 1850s, the veranda had become an expected part of nearly every rural Canadian and American home, and for next several generations its use became a ritual fixture of domestic life (especially for women, children, and the aged) that stretched across virtually all social and economic circumstances.

But functional and protective needs alone cannot entirely account for the dramatic rise in popularity of constructing verandas on rural and suburban dwellings. One must also consider the broad range of

Figure 1.46. *The apparent lack of paint on the shallow, flat-roofed front veranda suggests that it may have been an addition to this circa 1850s house in Eugene, Oregon, that was otherwise painted a conservative white. Circa 1860s carte de visite photograph.*

Figure 1.47. *A long lanai that wraps around this 1850s plantation house on Kauai Island, Hawaii, combines indigenous and colonial forms of building adapted for a tropical climate. Historic American Buildings Survey photograph, 1982, HABS HI,4-LIHU,1-5.*

social influences and cultural changes that occurred during this period, including the great westward migration across the United States and Canada, and the colonization of lands beyond, including such tropical locations as Hawaii, where the deep lanai (figure 1.47) has served as an extended outdoor living space that merges indigenous Pacific Islander traditions with North American building forms.[114]

And so just as we may hear both local innovations and echoes of distant cultures in the vernacular variations of accents and vocabularies of spoken languages and dialects, so too may a very complex web of cultural influences account for how such vernacular building features as porches have been developed, constructed and used.

As porches and verandas could provide visitors with graceful venues for accessing quasi-private spaces, nineteenth-century poets, novelists, and travel writers often found these to be convenient places for setting scenes and introducing characters.

For Harriet Beecher Stowe, the veranda provided a convenient place to develop impressions of several characters and to set key story events in her influential abolitionist novel, *Uncle Tom's Cabin*, published in 1852. Stowe's sentences provide quick glimpses into some typical mid-nineteenth-century veranda activities and their related furnishings. But on a symbolic level, these verandas also served as stages for the dramatic tensions that would soon tear a nation apart, as reflected in these following three separate excerpts from the novel:

It was Sunday afternoon. St. Clare was stretched on a bamboo lounge in the verandah, solacing himself with a cigar. Marie lay reclined on a sofa, opposite the window opening on the verandah, closely secluded, under an awning of transparent gauze, from the outrages of the mosquitos, and languidly holding in her hand an elegantly bound prayer-book. . . .

St. Clare rose up and walked thoughtfully up and down the verandah, seeming to forget everything in his own thoughts; so absorbed was he, that Tom had to remind him twice that the tea-bell had rung, before he could get his attention. . . .

Tom sat down in the verandah. It was a beautiful moonlight evening, and he sat watching the rising and falling spray of the fountain, and listening to its murmur. Tom thought of his home, and that he should soon be a free man, and able to return to it at will.[115]

As today, a lack of consensus generally extended over the precise architectural terminology associated with piazzas, verandas, and porches during much of the nineteenth century, but a New York author, J. J. Thomas, attempted to clarify a subtle difference in meaning between the two words *piazza* and *veranda* in the 1860s by providing the following definitions:

Piazza, usually, a covered walk on one or more sides of a building, supported on one side by pillars. It is used nearly synonymously with veranda, although the latter properly implies more shade and seclusion, a veranda often having lattice work in front. . . .

Veranda, a covered walk on the side of a building, of an awning-like character, with slender pillars, and frequently partly enclosed with latticework. It is usually understood to be more secluded than a piazza. An arbor veranda is where the roof is merely a frame covered with foliage.[116]

In her 1873 novel, *Palmetto-Leaves*, Harriet Beecher Stowe also wrote of various domestic uses of the veranda in Florida: "Our little cottage looks like a rabbit's nest beside the monster oaks that shade it; but it is cosey to see them all out on the low veranda,—the

Professor with his newspapers, the ladies with their worsteds and baskets, in fact the whole of our large family,—all reading, writing, working, in the shady covert of the orange-trees."[117]

In addition to Harriett Beecher Stowe, other Victorian-era American authors used verandas as convenient places to introduce new characters and to provide settings for action in their stories. Here, for example, is a passage from John William De Forest's 1872 novel, *Overland*: "After a time the two men went down to a shady veranda which half encircled the house, and found Mrs. Stanley taking an accidental siesta on a sort of lounge or sofa. Being a light sleeper, like many other active-minded people, she awoke at their approach and sat up to give reception."[118]

FASHIONABLE RETREATS AND FINAL RESORTS

By the early 1800s, colonnades, piazzas, and verandas became popular amenities for taverns, stagecoach inns, public houses, hotels, and spas in North America. By offering a protected sheltered space with views, these could serve as gathering spots for boarders and travelers, as shelters for gatherings of arrival and departure, as promenades, and as places to sit, to be seen, to dine, or for quiet retreats. Although some porches were simple functional additions to existing buildings, many served highly nuanced webs of domestic social interests, behaviors, and appearances, much in the way that articles of clothing could be worn not just for comfort, but also for display. Indeed both by their presence and by their use, porticos, porches, piazzas, and verandas offered unmistakable symbolic associations with hospitality, comfort, and leisure.

Informal competitions even developed

Figure 1.48. *Built in 1800 with long front piazzas, these connected cottages of Paradise Row are some of the earliest buildings at the Greenbrier Resort at White Sulphur Springs, West Virginia. Historic American Buildings Survey photograph, 1974, HABS WVA,13-WHISP,1B-2.*

among summer resort hotels through the nineteenth century to provide the largest, longest, or the tallest piazzas and colonnades, especially at such fashionable retreats as those located in upstate New York, in the Berkshires of western Massachusetts, in the White Mountains of Maine and New Hampshire, at the mineral springs near the Allegheny Mountains of West Virginia, and elsewhere. Many of the most famous early-nineteenth-century North American resorts were initially built as health spa retreats that emphasized the supposed curative powers of local waters. At some, drinking copious amounts of the spring water was thought to promote a cure, whereas at others cold-water bathing and soaking was thought to help restore health.

At West Virginia's White Sulphur Springs, even one of the famed mineral springs was sheltered by a bathhouse piazza.[119] Featuring long piazzas, the nearby connected cottages of Paradise Row (also known as

Bachelor's Row) at White Sulphur Springs are among the earliest surviving buildings at the Greenbrier Resort.[120] Other notable nineteenth century resorts that evolved from cure spas to luxury resorts during the mid-nineteenth century included Red Sulphur Springs in what is now West Virginia, Saratoga Springs in New York, and Beersheba Springs in Tennessee.

Of the famous Congress Hotel at Saratoga Springs, built in 1811, Harriet Otis wrote in her diary in July 1819 about its "showy" piazzas and how their use fit into the daily routines of guests:

> Did I describe Saratoga? After riding many miles through a country which deserves little other appellation than that of a pine barren, you descend suddenly upon the village, quite prettily built, consisting of about one hundred houses, chiefly white, in one street, the lodging-houses making quite a showy appearance from their length and high piazzas. Ours is two hundred feet in length, two stories, the pillars that support the piazza the whole height of the house.
>
> . . . The routine of the house is regular. At five o'clock the whole household is in motion; raps at the chamber doors, with "Ma'am, your bottle;" "Sir, your boots," resound from one end of our long entry (which is a perfect whispering gallery) to the other. Then everybody equips themselves, rather en déshabillé, either for the shower bath, the warm bath, or the springs. It is a pretty sight to see the multitude of pilgrims that resort at this early hour to our spring,—the Congress,—which is so near us it seems to belong peculiarly to us. After drinking what seems to me immoderately, our inmates either walk the piazza if it is warm and fair,

> as if for dear life; or the hall if it is cold and foul, for an hour; then prepare for breakfast.[121]

A British traveler also described the behavior of guests on piazzas at the hotels of Saratoga Springs while on tour in 1823: "There is no sort of ceremony observed at the most fashionable houses; for as soon as a gentleman has satisfied his appetite, he rises from his seat, and, waking out in the Piazza, begins to smoke his cigar."[122] In 1828, another British voyager, Captain Basil Hall, described the piazza of the Congress Hall resort hotel at Saratoga Springs as follows: "The hotel in which we found ourselves lodged at the Springs of Saratoga, was of great magnitude, as may be inferred from the size of its verandah or piazza in front, which measured eighty paces in length, and twenty five feet in height."[123]

Although the artistic exaggeration of the scale of the colonnade of the Congress Hall is obvious in the 1838 engraving published in London in *American Scenery* (figure 1.49), the following quotation, also from a British perspective, offers another taste of the prevalent American social rituals then associated with using this grand liminal space:

> Congress Hall has for many years held the palm of fashion among the rival Hotels of Saratoga. It is an immense wooden caravanserai, with no pretensions to architecture beyond what is seen in the drawing, and built with the sole view of affording the average accommodations of packed herrings to an indefinite number of persons. The roominess and liberal proportions of the Colonnade are one of those lies of architecture common to the hotels of this country. The traveller passes from the magnificent promise of the outside, to a chamber ten feet by four. . . . After

tea, the gentlemen who dressed for dinner and "undressed" for their drive, dress once more for the evening, and the spacious Colonnade is thronged with five hundred guests of the house, who pace to and fro for an hour, or, if it is a ball night, till the black band have made an orchestra of the tables in the dining-room, and struck up "Hail, Columbia!" . . . and, as the triumphant music returns a second time to the refrain, the lady Patroness enters on the arm of the gentleman with the most stock in the Bank, followed in couples by all the gentlemen and ladies who intend to dance or play wall-flower. . . . [T]he beaux who were interrupted in their declarations by the last chassé, (if they wish to go on with it,) lead their partners to take the air and a cold,—perhaps a heart,—on the Colonnade; and at eleven, champagne goes round for the ladies, and the gentlemen take "summat to drink" at "the bar;" after which the candles burn brighter, and everyone is more agreeable.[124]

A fancy piazza could certainly help shape one's first impressions of a resort hotel, such as was reflected in the following 1830s account of approaching by night the large hotel (that stood until 1917) at Red Sulphur Springs in Monroe County, now West Virginia:

Our driver quickened his speed as the distance before us diminished, and when we reached the Red Sulphur just after night had drawn his somber curtains around the silent hills. Our first impression of this spring, were very favorable: the effect was exceedingly imposing. On our arrival the whole establishment had been lighted up, and from every range of buildings, streams of light were pouring across the

area. The large hotel presents at any time a beautiful appearance. The whole building has a light and airy piazza connected with each story, and on the flank of the edifice most conspicuous on approaching the spring, the upper floor is open and surrounded by a balustrade. The first story of this building contains a large dining room, connected with which is a drawing and reading room. When we approached, these piazzas were all lighted up, and from the doors and windows of the halls and apartments of the hotel, the chandeliers were pouring forth their brilliant streams. Two long and handsomely set tables were visible through the doors of the dining room, and every thing had the aspect of comfort and even of luxury. The lower piazza was thronged with cheerful groups of visiters, eagerly awaiting the arrival of our coach, which on that evening was rather behind its usual time.[125]

But in contrast with his initial enthusiastic reaction, the tone of this traveler's descriptions of the Red Sulphur Springs resort soon sagged after he become somewhat better acquainted with other guests after his first night at the establishment:

The Red Sulphur, though but lately improved for the comfortable accommodation of visiters, has been for years known as a place of considerable resort by pulmonary patients. The company bears much more the aspect of sickness, than that of other springs. Their death-like countenances can be seen on every hand; and the deep hollow cough, which is heard almost incessantly, has at first a tendency to affect the sympathies and to throw an air of melancholy over the feelings. Many in the last stages

Figure 1.49. *Slender Tuscan columns wrapped in flowering vines lined the long colonnade of Congress Hall at Saratoga Springs, New York. The artistic exaggeration of the scale of the colonnade is obvious in this engraving.* W. H. Bartlett, American Scenery (1838); Rare Books and Special Collections, McGill University Library.

Figure 1.51. *The main building of the Beersheba Springs Hotel in Grundy County, Tennessee, was built between 1855 and 1856 with a sixteen-bay, two-story front veranda with square posts. First developed near a spring thought to promote good health from medicinal waters, this secluded resort became a retreat for wealthy families. Detail from Historic American Buildings Survey photograph, 1936, HABS TENN,31-BERSP,1-1.*

Figure 1.50. *Filled with guests and staff, a three-story colonnade veranda wraps around three sides of the circa 1835 Clarendon House in Clarendon Springs, Vermont. Detail from a circa 1880s stereograph; courtesy of Special Collections, University of Vermont.*

of consumption, are taken to the Red Sulphur as the final resort, and many, during almost every season, find their long, last home, among the hills near the Red Sulphur.[126]

Many other hotels offering water cures or developed near less famous mineral springs also featured prominent piazzas and verandas for use by their guests. Indeed such long piazzas and verandas could be considered important character-defining features of this type of property. Examples include the Clarendon House (figure 1.50) in Clarendon Springs, Vermont; the Beersheba Springs Hotel (figure 1.51) in Grundy County, Tennessee; and the Wesselhoeft Water Cure hotel (figure 1.52) in Brattleboro, Vermont.[127]

Sprawling verandas helped to shape impressions of other mid-nineteenth-century resort hotels. Of a late summer visit to the

Figure 1.52. *The Wesselhoeft Water Cure hotel in Brattleboro, Vermont, advertised in 1867 that it offered its boarders "a wide piazza 800 feet in length affording a welcome shade in warm and a retreat for exercise in stormy weather." Courtesy of Special Collections, University of Vermont.*

Figure 1.53. *A gentleman relaxes alone on a shallow seaside resort porch with a refreshing beverage, as seen in this illustration from the June 1854 issue of* Harper's New Monthly Magazine. *The simple but durable porch bench on which he reclines appears to be constructed of wooden planks, but the wooden side chair with a cushioned seat upon which he rests his feet would probably have been brought to the porch from indoors. The simple, square-section spindles and the smooth rails of the balustrade are typical of the period. The only embellishment to the woodwork appears to be a thin bead incised along sides of the top railings.*

Isles of Shoals off the New Hampshire coast, Nathaniel Hawthorne, for example, recorded in his journal in 1852:

> We landed at Appledore, on which is Laighton's Hotel,—a large building with a piazza or promenade before it, about an hundred and twenty feet in length, or more,—yes, it must be more. It is an edifice with a centre and two wings, the central part upwards of seventy feet. At one end of the promenade is a covered piazza, thirty or forty feet square, so situated that the breeze draws across it from the sea on one side to the sea on the other, and it is the breeziest and comfortablest place in the world on a hot day. There are two swings beneath it, and here one may sit or walk, and enjoy life, while all other mortals are suffering.[128]

A British traveler, Charles Richard Weld, observed in his 1855 book *Vacation Tour of the United States and Canada*, that unlike at hotels in Germany, where visitors would move "in the direction of the hills" after dinner was served, for vacationers in Saratoga, New York, "to see each other and to be seen is evidently the main object." As Weld further observed, "Accordingly, the ladies, in their gay attire, with their beautiful hair uncovered by bonnet or cap, promenade in the galleries and through the main street from hotel to hotel; some of the gentlemen, meantime, being seated in very remarkable attitudes in the verandahs, from whence they enjoy commanding views of the ladies; while others seek the billiard-rooms or shooting-galleries."[129]

Glimpses of nineteenth-century hotel-porch etiquette and manners may be found in books and articles, especially those written by and for women. One author of an 1870 book, for example, raised questions about "the rights of persons occupying rooms on the ground-floors of hotels, and boarding-houses, with windows opening upon the piazzas of the same," asking, "When a gentleman (?) draws a chair in front of the window, and with his heels on the pillar of the piazza, and his head close to your window, lights an odious pipe, and commences filling your room with its vileness, compelling your immediate retreat, because he prefers the spot opposite to your window to the smoker's end of the piazza: in such case, is it in order for one to request his speedy exit?"[130]

Figure 1.54. *By the mid-1860s, the Grand Union Hotel at Saratoga Springs, New York, advertised itself as the largest hotel in the world. Much of this exclusive resort's social life thrived along its huge Italianate-style verandas. The tall veranda posts reflect a highly stylized version of the Italian Renaissance Revival designs, with chamfered edges relieving the corners of square sections and a profusion of exaggerated moldings and scrolled embellishments. Detail from circa 1870s stereograph.*

Figure 1.55. *Socializing on a veranda at the White Sulphur Springs summer resort in West Virginia. Engraving from* Harper's New Monthly Magazine *(August 1878); courtesy of Special Collections, University of Vermont.*

Figure 1.56. *Grand verandas line the Fiske House resort hotel (built in 1882 and destroyed by fire in 1907), and adjacent summer cottages overlook the sea at Old Orchard Beach, Maine, in this early 1900s postcard view.*

In *Etiquette: The American Code of Manners*, Mary Elizabeth Wilson Sherwood observed in the 1880s that "[a] lone hotel, which brings people into very close juxtaposition, is the very hot-bed of gossip. The idlers have nothing to do but to talk of the busy ones. . . . Young ladies have no idea of the group of moody, jaundiced men of the world who sit at the smoking end of the piazza and say dreadful things of women."[131] But she also allowed that "[i]t is quite proper at a watering place to speak without an introduction to those whom you meet every day. Gentlemen should always raise their hats to their fair fellow-boarders, and the acquaintance of ladies on a hotel piazza can hurt no one. The day the party leaves the hotel, that day the acquaintance can cease if the people so choose."[132]

Similar accounts describe the supporting roles of the verandas and galleries at West Virginia's White Sulphur Springs, where according to one account published in 1916, "The business at the White Sulphur is pleasure. And this is about the order of proceedings: A few conscientious people take an early glass at the spring, and later patronize the baths, and there is a crowd at the post-office; a late breakfast and longing on the galleries and in the parlor; politics and old-fogy talk in the reading-room and in the piazza corners; flirtation on the lawn. . . . The idea seems to prevail that a summer resort ought to be a place of enjoyment."[133]

The informal competition among resort hotels to build the largest and grandest verandas continued through the nineteenth century into the early twentieth century. In an era before mechanical air conditioning, such verandas provided opportunities for patrons from urban areas to enjoy cooler and cleaner air during the hot summer months. Many of these hotel verandas were constructed facing scenic views to

Figure 1.57. *The Mount Washington Hotel opened as a mountain spa resort in 1902 in Bretton Woods, New Hampshire, with 352 rooms and a huge, two-tiered veranda. This hotel was declared a National Historic Landmark in 1986.*

Figure 1.58. *Built in 1872 with a 22-foot-high, 250-foot-long "grand piazza" in the Italianate style overlooking Schroon Lake in the New York Adirondacks, the Leland House was destroyed by fire in 1914.*

encourage sitting and dining. For patrons, daily routines would include time to sit on the porch, both to see others and, of course, to be seen. Even during evenings and when weather was inclement, verandas could also serve as promenades for guests.

Most prominent among these hotels with grand verandas were those built as destination resorts by railroad companies in scenic seaside, lakeside, and mountain locations in the United States and Canada. While the Italianate and French Second Empire architectural styles had been popular for large resorts hotels built between the 1860s and the 1880s, coinciding with changing tastes in domestic architectural design from the 1890s through the 1910s, the Queen Anne style was followed by the Colonial Revival and Neoclassical Revival style for many resort hotels.

As most of these grand hotels were constructed at least partially of wood, tragically many of the structures were lost to fires. Other factors that contributed to the widespread decline, neglect, and closings of these grand resort hotels with their magnificent verandas included the reduced patronage associated with the economic hardships

of the 1930s Depression, the shift to automobile travel, and the resulting decline of the railroads, especially in the United States. The Leland House (figure 1.58), built in 1872 in Schroon Lake, New York, for example, was destroyed by fire in 1914, only to be replaced on the same site by the Leland Hotel, built the following year in the Colonial Revival style with a grand two-story colonnade and porte-cochere. Unfortunately, in December 1938, this grand hotel also was lost to fire.[134]

SUMMER PLACES

Although by the early nineteenth century a few resort hotels in North America had built separate buildings to serve as overflow space for guests during peak seasons, later it became fashionable in many resort areas for the wealthy and socially connected to build their own separate "cottages." These would invariably be equipped with verandas. As the Victorian era progressed, growing numbers of North American families in the middle-income range were also able to acquire such summer cottages in resort areas. In the Berkshires of western

Figure 1.59. *Guests relax on the large corner veranda of Riley's, a circa 1890s summer boarding house overlooking Glen Lake near the Adirondacks in New York.*

Massachusetts, for example, the town of Lenox became known as a cottage retreat as early as the 1830s. By 1880, it boasted more than thirty-five summer cottages and over twice as many in 1900.[135]

In addition to the Berkshires, some other famous nineteenth-century summer cottage resort communities included New-port, Rhode Island; Poland Springs, Bar Harbor, and Old Orchard Beach in Maine; and Long Island, Tuxedo, Lake George, and the Adirondacks in New York. Cottage re-sort communities were also established in many other areas of North America, includ-ing Weirs Beach on Lake Winnipesaukee in New Hampshire; Rice Lake in Ontario; along the coasts of New Brunswick and Nova Sco-tia; and near the various hot springs of West Virginia.

In his popular 1865 pattern book on coun-try house designs, George Woodward of-fered the following recommendations on such summer cottages located in rural locations:

The place designed simply for a summer residence for the citizen, who is obliged to be at his office or counting room daily, bating the few weeks of summer vaca-tion, need not be so complete in its ap-pointments and arrangements, as the permanent country residence. One es-sential condition, however, in this case is, that there shall be room enough, with ample verandahs, and shaded gravel walks, which will afford opportunities for open air exercise in all states of the weather. There is nothing, perhaps, that interferes so essentially with the citizen's enjoyment of the country, as the want of facilities for out door exercise. It is too hot or too dusty to ride or walk, before the shower, and after its refreshment has come, it is too wet and muddy. Spacious verandahs, shaded with vines, and well-made walks, always firm and dry, bor-dered with shrubbery, or overhung with trees, will give us "ample scope and verge enough."[136]

Figure 1.60. *A store porch with plain posts, plank floors, and shallow-pitched roof covered the sidewalk in front of this mid-nineteenth-century brick commercial block on Church Street in Burlington, Vermont. Courtesy of Special Collections, University of Vermont.*

Figure 1.61. *The "most public place" of many communities has been the front porch of the village store, as suggested in this illustration by A. B. Frost. Note the poster being tacked to the wall at the left.* Harper's New Monthly Magazine *(July 1880); courtesy of Special Collections, University of Vermont.*

MOST PUBLIC PLACE

As the porch craze swept across the continent with the Westward movement through the canal era, the Gold Rush, and the railroad era, porches and verandas were being attached to not only nearly every commercial building, store, hotel, rooming house and tenement, but also to most governmental, institutional, and religious buildings. By the 1860s and 1870s, it had become common in some commercial districts of towns and cities to have porches connected in continuous lines to cover sidewalks. Such store porches could provide transitional spaces to provide shelter for patrons, as well as to display a variety of wares.

In addition to providing space for the display of available merchandise and walls for advertising available items, porches on some quasi-public buildings were considered the "most public place" in a community, and thus perhaps the most suitable location for posting public announcements and legal

notices. A law that had been enacted by the State of New York by 1792, for example, required "[t]hat every ferryman shall paste upon a board and hang up in the porch of each respective ferry-house, or at the most public place there-in, a table fairly written or printed of the rates or prices of ferriage as established by this act."[137]

Porches have also long served as convenient focal points for informal exchanges, gatherings, and social connections in both urban and rural areas. On general stores, hotels, post offices, and transportation facilities especially, they have acted as liminal, quasi-public realms, functioning as neutral territories that facilitate contacts between people who might otherwise be unlikely to engage in any other settings. Indeed, the concept of "piazza manners" was well recognized by the 1880s.[138]

Moreover, a string of late-nineteenth-century U.S. presidential campaigns used the home front porch symbolically, as staged

Figure 1.62. *The shady front porch of a village inn could provide a relaxed, quasi-public space for residents and travelers alike to gather in Waynesville, North Carolina, as shown in this illustration.* Harper's New Monthly Magazine *(August 1880); courtesy of Special Collections, University of Vermont.*

Figure 1.63. *President William McKinley posed in a rocking chair on his front porch in Canton, Ohio, for this campaign photograph taken in July 1900, just months before his reelection.*

settings for speeches and photographs to imply connections with the ordinary populace.

PUBLIC INTIMACY AND PECULIAR PRIVACY

The widespread presence and use of porches, stoops, and verandas during the nineteenth century thus had prompted the establishment of new sets of acceptable domestic behaviors, rituals, and etiquette norms as this building feature became a pivotal part of home and social life, as well as a setting for new leisurely and religious pursuits during the Victorian era. Indeed, as liminal spaces straddling the predictable constraints of domestic life and the tempting opportunities and risks of the outside world, these porches could sometimes also provide Victorians with new opportunities for a sort of "public privacy" that combined availability with respectability. Historian Dona

Brown, who has documented the presence of such quasi-private spaces in the arranged closeness of cottages at nineteenth-century religious meeting camps, has aptly described this as "a peculiar kind of privacy."[139]

Three prominent examples of camp meeting associations were located at Martha's Vineyard off the coast of Massachusetts, Weirs Beach on New Hampshire's Lake Winnipesaukee, and Ocean Grove on the Atlantic shore of New Jersey. As a reflection of their Christian religious commitments, many residents chose the Gothic Revival style for their seasonal camp meeting cottages. Many of these were built to replace original camp tents and were later modified with prayer porches and veranda additions that could serve as transitional spaces for leisurely and religious pursuits.[140]

North Americans' love for porches only grew stronger as the second half of the nineteenth century progressed. More than a

Figure 1.64. *Full-width doors are opened to create a recessed seating area for prayer gatherings that combines functions of summer home, prayer porch, and yard with public intimacy at Wesleyan Grove Meeting Association on Martha's Vineyard, Massachusetts. The fanciful ornamentation of this 1860s "Swiss Gothic" cottage features a projecting gable screen and a cross-buck balcony railing on the "pulpit porch." Courtesy of Special Collections, University of Vermont.*

mere architectural appendage, the veranda of the home or hotel had become an established setting for new types of domestic and public behavior and social connections. Released from the confinement of furnished interior rooms, verandas provided residents with opportunities for exercise under cover, social liaisons, and entertainment.

Yet verandas also could provide connec-

tions with the out-of-doors, surrounding landscapes, and the world beyond. By the 1870s, some even felt nostalgia for the porches of earlier times, as reflected in the lyrics of the 1871 song "The Old Cottage Porch":

> Ah! well do I remember, the rustic porch of old,

Figure 1.65. *This circa 1870 Gothic Revival–style summer cottage at Ocean Grove, New Jersey, featured bracketed verandas with balconies on both gable ends. Stereograph; courtesy of Special Collections, University of Vermont.*

With seats and trellis work, which could
    love's tale unfold,
Perchance it is destroyed, some gaudier
    takes its place,
Or time has done its work, no porch the
    door doth grace,
Its seats of knotted oak, its trellis so green
    and white,
Which greets the morning sun, reflecting
    back its light,
Are scattered far and wide, their forms
    destroyed and gone,
The dearest Cottage porch, to me the
    only one.[141]

Perhaps United States President Rutherford B. Hayes best summed up Victorian-era feelings toward porches when he recorded in his journal in 1873: "The best part of the present house is the veranda. But I would enlarge it. I want a veranda with a house attached!"[142] This sentiment was echoed two years later in 1875 by E. C. Gardner, who wrote in his book, *Homes, and How to Make Them*: "No sooner do we get nicely fortified with furnaces, storm-porches, double windows, and forty tons of anthracite, than June bursts upon us with ninety degrees in the shade. Then how we despise our

Figure 1.66. *The front porch of this small summer cottage in Milford, Massachusetts, provides the setting for a humorously posed stereograph depicting Victorian-era courtship rituals. Courtesy of Special Collections, University of Vermont.*

Figure 1.67. *Shaded by a striped canvas awning, retired president Rutherford B. Hayes and his wife, Lucy Webb Hayes, relax in 1887 on the expansive Italianate-style veranda with chamfered posts at their home at Spiegel Grove in Fremont, Ohio. Rutherford B. Hayes Presidential Center.*

contrivances for keeping warm, and bless the ice-man! We wish the house was all piazza, and if it were not for burglars and mosquitoes, would abjure walls and roof and live in the open air."[143]

Whether by sitting in chairs or on benches, or even by reclining on hammocks or daybeds, occupants of porches and verandas could comfortably reside alone or together in pairs or groups within partial sight and earshot of others, including those passing on the street, providing socially discreet opportunities for public access and social exchanges that might otherwise be impossible to achieve during the Victorian era. A sixteen-year-old, for example, confided in her private diary in 1881, "While I was sitting alone on the front porch, saw Max Black coming up the street with a tall stranger with a jaunty, military cap on his brown hair, a blue suit with scarlet stripes and brass buttons, brown eyes and a heavy brown mustache. 'Who in the name of wonder,' I exclaimed under my breath."[144]

Of course by night, opportunities for social engagements and courtship rituals on porches and verandas broadened, as reflected in the following passage from the 1884 novel *The Rise of Silas Lapham* by William D. Howells: "When they went out on the veranda to see the moon on the water, Penelope led the way and Irene followed. They did not look at the moonlight long. The young man perched on the rail of the veranda, and Irene took one of the red-painted rocking-chairs where she could conveniently look at him and at her sister, who sat leaning forward lazily and running on, as the phrase is."[145]

For poets, the porch could even serve as a metaphor for some of life's transitions, as in this excerpt from 1889:

Under the porch!—
  Gleamed her white dress in shade
  Through the half-opened door;
    Then came her little face
    Nearer my own,
      Under the porch.[146]

Figure 1.68. *The elaborate verandas and balconies of the Stick style and the Queen Anne style provided Victorian-era Americans with new opportunities for social engagements, as shown in this amusing illustration. H. Hudson Holly,* Modern Dwellings *(1878); Rare Books and Special Collections, McGill University Library.*

Symbolically, the outward expression of front porches with steps connecting directly to a sidewalk or a street could certainly provide a welcoming alternative to the hard abruptness of the typical North American vernacular house designs of earlier generations that had unprotected front doors on flat walls. Indeed, the combined openness and frontal location of many Victorian-era verandas could provide easily accessible intermediate territories between public and private realms. But more than just providing a zone of protection, this transitional space could also invite engagement, making possible dignified, but not obtrusive means of approach and social contact. With the main formal entrance to the house opening onto the veranda, occupants could gracefully greet guests or strangers in a protected quasi-public space raised up to the level of the house beneath a sheltering roof, without actually inviting visitors into the privacy of their home.

While verandas and porches could thus

Figure 1.69. *Through their proximity and openness, porches and verandas could provide informal neighborly connections across landscaped yards in Victorian American suburbs. Frank J. Scott,* Suburban Home Grounds *(1870).*

provide the public with more graceful means to access private domestic spaces, they also could provide home occupants with discreet, but socially acceptable, access to public realms. By allowing shrubs, vines, or lattice to provide subtle screening, degrees of openness, privacy, or even intimacy, could be strategically regulated in various areas of a veranda. Designed for comfort and relaxation, such verandas on homes

could even provide opportunities for solitary dozing or napping in contemplative solitude.

For some women, children, older persons, and perhaps the lonely, the veranda could provide a welcome alternative from the confines and isolation of the house. This opportunity for partial access to the outside world was especially important for those living in rural or suburban areas before the advent of telephones, radios, televisions, and easy transportation. The front veranda could even serve as a metaphorical stage (or perhaps even a pedestal of sorts) upon which one could connect with the outside community from a physically elevated position within the constraints of prevailing social customs.

The sense of security and comfort that verandas could provide their users can be found in the words of some writers of novels and short stories. But for some people, the porch also served as but an extension of the confines of loneliness. Consider, for example, the role that the veranda plays in following excerpt from Sherwood Anderson's *Winesburg, Ohio*, a short story cycle about the life of a solitary man, written in 1919:

> Upon the half decayed veranda of a small frame house that stood near the edge of a ravine near the town of Winesburg, Ohio, a fat little old man walked nervously up and down. . . . Now as the old man walked up and down on the veranda, his hands moving nervously about, he was hoping that George Willard would come and spend the evening with him. After the wagon containing the berry pickers had passed, he went across the field through the tall mustard weeds and climbing a rail fence peered anxiously along the road to the town. For a moment he stood thus, rubbing his hands together and looking up and down the road, and then, fear overcoming him, ran back to walk again upon the porch on his own house.[147]

Coinciding with a wave of nostalgia-driven recollections of early generations' stories of plantation life, the celebration of traditional porch uses as outdoor living spaces grew especially strong in the American South during the early twentieth century. One author who focused on recording

Southern porch traditions was the novelist and folklorist, Professor Dorothy Scarborough of Columbia University. In the foreword of her book *From a Southern Porch*, written in 1919, she observed, "The porch is the soul of the house. Poor and spiritless indeed is the structure which lacks it. . . . Imagine going right into a house, with no gracious lingering on a porch! Such procedure outrages all the amenities of life. True gentility is inseparable from a porch. Somewhere in the past of every country soul will be found a benignant porch, stretching its influence over the years."[148]

Scarborough confessed to be a "porcher," who would rather do nothing during the "long, delightful summers" at her sister's home in Richmond, Virginia, than to "sit on a porch by the side of the road and watch the world go by."[149] Of this pastime, she noted:

> Porching, in the real sense of the word, cannot be done in the gregarious rockers on hotel piazzas, where idle women crochet industriously and embroider linen and the truth about their neighbors. On the contrary, it is a high calling apart. In the South the porch is the true center of the home, around which life flows on gently and graciously, with an open reserve, a charming candor. One does not stay inside the house more than is absolutely necessary, for all such pleasant occupations as eating and sleeping, reading, studying, working, and entertaining one's friends are carried on some companionable piazza or other. There are porches to meet all needs, all moods, and all hours. As the sun travels, one migrates from porch to porch, though there are some widely shaded verandas that are inhabitable at all times. With numberless

Home

HOME reflects character. More, it moulds character. Home is the image of thought, exposed, inviting the gaze of the world. As your home is, so are you. Then make your home as *you* want to be—in good taste, dignified, ennobling, to be admired. But see to it that it is also beautiful, comfortable and durable.

Home charm is not measured in dollars and cents—selection is more potent than expenditure in its achievement. It is surprising how inexpensively beauty, comfort and durability can be built into homes with the right kind of woodwork.

Somewhere in these pages is a design which peculiarly expresses your individuality. May the finding of your choice multiply the pleasure of the search.

Figure 1.70. *By the 1920s, symbolic connections between the porch and concepts of home and individuality were being recognized in advertising literature, such as this illustration in a millwork catalogue featuring a caption that noted, "As your home is, so are you."* Building with Assurance, Morgan Woodwork Organization *(1921).*

porches upstairs and down, one can always find solitude if one wishes, or discover some congenial soul to talk or be silent with.[150]

Scarborough also recognized the special roles that porches could contribute to feelings of home as liminal places that straddled the realms of privacy and community:

> The porch is an ideal place, for it is essentially a part of the home, yet a part of the outdoors as well. One's personality expands with the far outlook. The hermit who lives in the woods is not so utterly cut off from his fellows as is the cliff-dweller in the city, who lives too near to man to know him or be known. The ideal place for living is the porch, where one may see his fellow-mortals in reason, yet be much alone. To be in the home, yet in the open, to be close to all pulsing life of man and of nature, and yet to be alone at will,—that is the blessedness of porch-life.[151]

More recently, other scholars have explored liminal qualities of porches. Sue Bridwell Beckham, for example, has provided glimpses into some of these realms, especially from perspectives of gender, class, and race in the American South in her 1998 essay, "The American Front Porch: Women's Liminal Space." She also has made the case for the need for more research, noting "the architectural history of porches is most significant for its invisibility."[152] Folklorist Jocelyn Hazelwood Donlon has explored the concept of the liminality of porches, as well, in *Swinging in Place: Porch Life in Southern Culture*. This interdisciplinary study examines how even in recent times, porches have served both as transitional spaces and as boundary zones between private and public realms, especially within social and community contexts of generation, class, race, gender, and sexuality.[153]

PHOTOGRAPHIC GLIMPSES OF PORCH LIFE

Just as advances of science and industry during the second half of the nineteenth century helped to strengthen economic conditions for an expanding middle class, technological advances, namely, the development and growth of photography, also profoundly influenced how the visual evidence of day-to-day life during these times was recorded. For the study of the history of porches and how they have been used, it is fortuitous that this early photography required abundant light to expose the large photochemically sensitive plates. With most interiors being too dark for even the most patient subjects to hold still long enough for the proper exposures, more brightly lit porches become favored settings for photographic portraits of individuals and groups, family gatherings, children, babies, and pets.

In addition to large-format cabinet photographs that might be mounted on stiff cardboard backings suitable for display on a wall and the small *carte de visite* photographs (see figure 1.46) that became popular from the 1850s through the 1870s, imagery of porches was also captured in the popular stereograph pair cards that could be viewed through special viewers to provide three-dimensional perspectives.

Although most porch portraits from the nineteenth century were produced by professional photographers operating from studios or as itinerant travelers, by the 1890s, amateur photography had become a pursuit of those with leisure time and financial means. Eastman Kodak's Folding Pocket Camera, introduced in 1906, helped bring

Figure 1.71. *A closed casket on a Queen Anne–style veranda, circa 1910. Note the black mourning bows fastened to the porch posts near the ends of the casket.*

photography to even the middle class, with a negative the same size as a postcard. As bright lighting was needed to expose the film in these cameras at shutter speeds fast enough to reduce blurring from the slightest movement of subjects, postcard portraits were often taken outdoors—and porches provided convenient settings. The result was a huge number of images of people posing on porches during this turn-of-the century period.

Many of these late-nineteenth- and early-twentieth-century porch portraits reflect stiff, self-conscious commemorative poses, often of feigned leisurely activities; however, some do provide glimpses into the personalities of the subjects, while also revealing the mundane ephemera of domestic porch life a century or more ago. Less common are contemporaneous porch photographs that recorded people at work, such as carrying out the domestic chores that were often relegated to the back porch.

Porches also provided spaces for solemn occasions, especially during the nineteenth and early twentieth centuries, when the practice of holding wakes and memorial services in honor of those who had passed away were still affairs held often at the homes

of the deceased. For practical reasons the porch might be used, especially when it may have been difficult or impossible to display the body and casket indoors in smaller homes, or when it was expected that many people might wish to share condolences with the grieving. Photographic postcards of these sad occasions were sometimes distributed for commemoration.

The approval by the United States Post Office in 1907 of divided-back postcards that allowed both the address and a short message to be written on one side launched what has been called the golden age of postcards. Within the first year, more than 600 million postcards were sent. Many of these were "real photo" postcards, consisting of black-and-white photographs taken with a Kodak Folding Pocket Camera and printed by the Eastman Kodak Company on postcard-size photo paper bearing the AZO and Velox trade names on the back.[154]

Advances in high-quality color inks and printing techniques in Austria and Germany during the late nineteenth century that could not be matched by American printers led to a prolific influx of color postcards into the United States and Canada between about 1907 and the early 1910s. One common type of German-made postcard bore a "Litho-chrome" trademark. In 1909, at the urging of American printers, the U.S. Congress imposed a tariff on imported postcards. Within a short time, very few of the German-printed color postcards were being sold in the United States. This ushered in an era of domestically produced color postcards, characterized by white borders, which flourished during the 1910s and the 1920s. Eventually the postcard fad waned, but we are left with a wealth of surviving imagery of people and their lives on porches from the early twentieth century. Among

Figure 1.72. *A broad veranda skirts two sides of the Garnet Inn near Lake Winnipesaukee in Center Harbor, New Hampshire. Postcard printed in Germany, bearing a postal cancellation date of 1911.*

Figure 1.73. *For summer guests at the Mount Kineo House, which opened in 1884 on the shore of Moosehead Lake in Maine, the piazza could serve as a hub of daily social life, as shown in this circa 1910 postcard view. The hotel's brochure boasted, "For a morning promenade the hotel piazza, fifteen feet wide and eight hundred feet long, offers ideal opportunity." Note the simple Italianate-style scroll-sawn brackets on the chamfered posts that support the piazza roof and the painted wooden floorboards.*

Figure 1.74. *This white-border postcard with a typed message on the back, dated November 20, 1920, shows patrons dining on the porch of the Tacoma Hotel in Tacoma, Washington, which opened in 1885, but was destroyed by fire in 1935.*

the most popular subjects for postcards were those showing resort hotels, casinos, and country clubs.

During the Depression years of the 1930s, the U.S. government inaugurated the Historic American Buildings Survey (HABS) to document important buildings, using high-quality, large-format photographs, measured drawings, and written historical information. Now combined with the Historic American Engineering Record (HAER) and the Historic American Landscapes Survey (HALS), this collection, housed in the United States Library of Congress, comprises more than thirty-eight thousand structures and sites, making it one of the most extensive records of the built environment in the nation.[155]

Another extensive photograph collection that documents the lives of Americans and their surroundings (including porches) between 1935 and 1944 is the Farm Security Administration–Office of War Information Photograph Collection. Also archived in the Library of Congress, this government photo project recorded more than 171,000 images. Many of these FSA/OWI images are now accessible to the public on the Internet, as are many from the Historic American Buildings Survey through the Library of Congress.[156]

Figure 1.75. *Supported by rough logs, the rustic front porch of an old country store in Gordonton, North Carolina, provided an informal quasi-public space for a Sunday afternoon gathering of men in July 1939. Dorothea Lange, photographer, Farm Security Administration, Office of War Information Collection, U.S. Library of Congress.* LC-DIG-fsa-8b33922.

CASINOS AND CLUBHOUSES

At casinos, country clubs, yacht clubs, bathing clubs, and bathhouses, a broad range of social activities have long been supported by prominent verandas, piazzas, and porches. First, it should be remembered that before the twentieth century, the term *casino* commonly was used to describe a range of buildings intended for such leisure uses as dance halls, social clubs, theatres, and restaurants, without implying any gaming or gambling activities. Typically sited in scenic locations, these late-nineteenth- and early-twentieth-century casinos often featured broad verandas and sun porches.

During the turn-of-the century period, many streetcar companies in North America sought ways to boost ridership and to extend the areas served by their lines by creating destinations at parks, beaches, and other attractions. Some even invested in the construction of facilities at these destinations, including auditoriums, dance halls, restaurants, and casinos. Many, such as the Roger Williams Park Casino (figure 1.76) in Providence, Rhode Island, and the Cape Cottage Casino (figure 1.77) in Cape Elizabeth, Maine, featured prominent porches. In addition to providing sheltered spaces for promenades or sightseeing, some country club porches were used as outdoor dining rooms (figure 1.78) that could be used seasonally and as weather allowed.

SCREENED PORCHES

With the widespread availability of wire screening during the late nineteenth century, porches could be enjoyed in areas plagued

Figure 1.76. *The Roger Williams Park Casino in Providence, Rhode Island, was built in 1896 in the Colonial Revival style. It featured a two-story, semicircular portico and a wraparound veranda crowned by a balustrade parapet that provides views to the surrounding park grounds. A café originally served the public on the main floor. A large ballroom on the second floor opened to a balcony above the veranda.*

Figure 1.77. *Ringed by verandas providing views of Casco Bay, the Cape Cottage Casino in Cape Elizabeth, Maine, was built by the Portland and Cape Elizabeth Railroad in 1898 to replace an earlier casino at this site that was lost to fire. With its two-story Neoclassical portico in the Ionic order and the surrounding colonnade in the Doric order crowned by a wooden balustrade, this is an outstanding example of the Colonial Revival style of architecture.*

Figure 1.78. *This circa 1910s view of a Bridgeport, Connecticut, country club shows how a porch could be decorated for fancy luncheons and dinners. Note the dozens of Japanese lanterns hanging from the ceiling, the turned Queen Anne–style porch posts at the right with a striped canvas awning behind, and the network of heating pipes beneath.*

with mosquitoes, flies, and other nuisance flying insects, especially in rural and forested areas and during evenings. Shielded from the persistent annoyances of flying pests, screened porches became popular for summer napping or sleeping by the early twentieth century, especially when constructed for privacy on the second story of houses. Screening also encouraged the furnishing of porches with tables and chairs for summer dining and hammocks and swings for other leisure activities. In addition to their private and public social use, porches came to be regarded as places for healthy living.

Although coarsely woven cheesecloth, linen, and horsehair gauze had long been used for window screening and for protecting beds from flying insects, one of the first suppliers of iron wire gauze for window screening was the Gilbert and Bennett Manufacturing Company of Redding, Connecticut, which first marketed this product in the early 1860s.[157]

Dozens of patents were issued over the next decade for mosquito-bars, mosquito-nets, and mosquito-screens that could be attached to windows and blinds.[158] Although this iron screening was painted (typically black), the iron wire tended to rust quickly. As low-carbon soft steel that could be drawn into wire became available by the late 1880s, it replaced iron for producing screening and other manufactured wire-cloth products.

By the early 1900s, more durable screening woven of galvanized steel or bronze wire was introduced to the market, which when combined with the development of large looms, made it possible to produce screening that could span large areas for use on porches. The galvanized screening typically was painted to delay rusting. Although more expensive than galvanized, bronze screening lasted much longer. Over time, bronze

Figure 1.79. *Wire screening was installed inside posts and railings on this summer camp. Just visible below the turn-of-the-century forty-five-star American flag, and at the corners of the porch at the right, are slatted wooden shades that could be adjusted with cords and pulleys to provide varying amounts of privacy or protection from sun and rain.*

tarnishes from bright metal to dark brownish green, as do old pennies.

The use of wire screening to create large comfortable porches that could serve as outdoor rooms was reflected in this suggestion from 1908: "I would suggest the advisability of screening in the entire veranda with panels of fine wire netting, in localities where mosquitoes are prevalent early in the season. Later in the season the screened-in veranda will be free from the fly nuisance—an advantage one can hardly afford to ignore when the annoyance attendant on dog days is considered."[159]

Screened porches have also served household utilitarian purposes. In 1915, the U.S. Department of Agriculture issued a *Farmer's Bulletin* with the following advice:

For summer in the Northern States and for all the year use in the warmer regions of the country, there should, if possible, be a screened porch opening off from the kitchen on the side which is not exposed

Figure 1.80. *The wraparound veranda on this house built in 1895 in Montpelier, Vermont, features a large, screened sitting space on the side, with wood-framed screens installed inside the turned porch posts and above the clapboard-covered parapets (also called half-walls or knee-walls). The open part of the veranda on the right has a balustrade with turned balusters.*

are
led
and
nd, if
tside
nto the
er a
s can be
ge and
rarily,
e kitchen
duced and
in will be
screens can
indow sash
made use of

was intro-
its corrosion-
resista͟ ͟cost, it became the most popular type o͟ indow and porch screening by the 1950s. Two types of aluminum screening have been commonly produced: that with bright metal wire and a more popular variety made from dark gray anodized aluminum. Fiberglass screening, introduced in the 1970s, has become a common alternative to aluminum screening on porches today. This is mostly produced of woven fiberglass yarn coated with dark filament plastic for durability and to minimize the visibility of the screening when looking through it from the inside.[161]

CURE PORCHES AND SLEEPING PORCHES

Bolstered by recognition that poor indoor air quality could aggravate symptoms of people suffering from tuberculosis, the debilitating respiratory disease that was a leading cause of death in the nineteenth century, a standard treatment at many homes, hospitals, and sanitaria during the late nineteenth and early twentieth centuries was for patients to rest outside on "cure porches" through day and night—even bundled under mounds of blankets in winter.

Based on a principle developed in Germany that prolonged exposure to fresh air could be an effective treatment for tuberculosis patients, the Adirondack Cottage Sanitarium in the village of Saranac Lake, New York, was founded by Dr. Edward L. Trudeau in 1884. Later known as the Trudeau Sanatorium, this facility soon became one of the best-known tuberculosis treatment retreats in North America. As word of the benefits of its open-air treatment method spread, the "cure porches" became common features of the hospitals, rest homes, and cure cottages in the village of Saranac Lake and elsewhere by the early twentieth century.[162]

Figure 1.81. *First- and-second story "cure porches" with rows of operable windows may be found on many former cure cottages and rest homes in Saranac Lake, New York.*

Some sanatoriums featured porch appendages that were lined with large, operable windows where patients could go or be moved to take sun and air. Other facilities specifically constructed for the treatment of tuberculosis provided even bedridden patients with screened (and sometimes shuttered) porches that served as virtual outdoor bedrooms. On these cure porches, less ambulatory patients could rest in the fresh air day and night in special cure chairs. Similar to a chaise lounge, but with an adjustable backrest that could be raised to nearly vertical position to help patients breathe, these lightweight wooden cure chairs featured thick cushions, broad flat side arms, full-length leg rests, and casters for easy movement.[163]

One patient at the Trudeau Sanatorium in Saranac Lake, New York, recalled in an article written in 1917:

As a general rule, on coming to the Sanatorium, one goes into the Medical Building for a period of a week. There all the diagnostic tests are made, and the patient is under close observation by doctor and nurse. He takes no exercise except to go to meals in the next building, and spends practically all his time in the "cure chair," as the long reclining chair is called. At the end of this time, he is moved to a cottage. . . .

The porches, so important a part of the cottage, for here most of the time is spent, are spacious and sunny, with ample room for the cure chair, and at night, the bed. Each patient's room opens directly onto the porch and the bed may be rolled in and out at will.

The cottage life is the distinctive characteristic of Trudeau and that which, above all, makes life here so livable. The small, intimate cottage groups are conducive to congeniality, friendship and good times, on the one hand, and to that privacy which every one of us requires at times. On the porch with me, were a teacher and a young fellow just out of college, both of them very interesting and enjoyable, both good story tellers, and we spent many pleasant hours there together "on the cure."[164]

Soon, cure porches became common features of sanatoriums and tuberculosis treatment hospitals being built across North America. One type that became popular was the lean-to design that featured an open porch on the front with an overhanging roof and walls on the sides and the back that were fitted with slat blinds that allowed air circulation but also afforded protection from the sun and weather. The design was soon modified by enlarging the space with another enclosed lean-to at the back that could provide space for patients to place reclining chairs in front of their beds. Connecting the patient wings was a heated space

Figure 1.82. *Two wings of screened cure porches served patients at the Iowa State Sanitarium in Oakdale, Iowa.*

Figure 1.83. *Metal privacy screens mark the sleeping porch on the rear east side of this early-twentieth-century bungalow in Tucson, Arizona.*

with toilets, bathing facilities, and dressing rooms.[165] An example was the Iowa State Sanitarium (figure 1.82) in Oakdale, Iowa. With a capacity of forty patients, this "lean-to" type of sanatorium measured 240 feet long and 24 feet deep. The screened porches were 12 feet deep.[166]

A report on tuberculosis hospital and sanatorium construction published in 1911 offered detailed recommendations on porch construction:

Usually the exposure of the porches should be south-east rather than due south in temperate climates, for since the lean-to has become popular it has been found that the air in the porches with direct southern exposure often gets exceedingly hot, and sometimes unbearable during the middle of the day and the early afternoon, in the summer months, causing the patients great discomfort. . . .

The front of the porch is usually protected by canvas curtains hung on rollers, Japanese matting, glass and sash windows which can be raised and lowered, or glass doors which can be opened

and closed. The rear and end openings are generally protected by sliding windows known as the "barn-door" shutter, ordinary glass and sash windows hung at the side or from the top, or a frame covered with canvas hung on hinges or on a pivot.[167]

For the home treatment of tuberculosis, a report published in 1915 by the New York State Department of Agriculture recommended: "Porch sleeping offers one of the best and simplest methods of treatment. Almost every country house has a porch or veranda which may be utilized for this purpose."[168]

With dry air, comfortable climate and more than three hundred days of sunshine annually, by the 1910s, Tucson, Arizona, and other communities in the American West also became popular retreats for tuberculosis sufferers and those seeking better health. Whether used for treatments or just for comfort, porches designed for sleeping were built on some Southwestern homes through the 1930s. Typically located on the ground floor toward the side or rear of the house in

Figure 1.84. *A screened sleeping porch extends from an upper story over the entrance of a large porch on a house in Washington County, New York.*

this hot arid climate, these sleeping porches were usually fitted with privacy screens and rows of windows that could be opened or closed to adjust the amount of ventilation.[169]

By the early twentieth century, before home air conditioning was common, home porches were favored places to sleep in many other areas of the United States and Canada, not only on hot summer nights, but even during other times of the year for those seeking the fresh air to promote a good night's rest or perhaps to help strengthen their health. Indeed during the sleeping porch craze of the 1910s, one Indiana company even offered a line of woolen "camp and sleeping porch blankets" that offered "real warmth and extra durability."[170]

In temperate climate regions, these sleeping porches were typically located on an upper story adjacent to a bedroom or on the side or the rear of a house for privacy. In an article about porches published in *House Beautiful* in 1905, the author observed, "In seashore or country houses which are seldom used in winter, the two-storied porch is often a delightful feature—the 'upper deck,'

so to speak, serving as an outdoor sleeping apartment in sultry weather, and always a retreat for a quiet afternoon nap."[171]

Gustav Stickley, a promoter of Craftsman-style of furniture and bungalows, described a sleeping porch in his book *Craftsman Homes* in 1909: "Just above the sun room is an open-air sleeping room of the same size and general arrangement, except that it has no fireplace. On this upper porch a balustrade is replaced with a solid parapet made of the wall of the house. Like the sun room, this sleeping porch can be glassed in when necessary for protection during driving storms. But under ordinary circumstances no protection from the weather is needed even in the winter, as nothing is better for the average housed-up human being than sleeping out of doors under plenty of covers."[172]

A sleeping porch was even constructed on the roof of the White House in Washington, D.C., in 1909 as a space for President William Howard Taft and his family to escape from the heat of summer nights. Accessible from the third floor, this temporary screened porch structure was replaced with a "Sky Parlor" sun room in 1927, which was again replaced in 1952, during the Truman administration's reconstruction of the building, with a solarium surrounded by a private rooftop promenade.[173]

By the 1910s, sleeping porches had become expected amenities on comfortable new suburban houses and desired additions to many older homes. The creation of an upper-story loggia in a corner room was one way that a sleeping porch could be created, as one health advocate suggested in 1912: "Where a spare room can be used for the purpose, a simple and effective method of making a permanent open-air sleeping loggia is to remove the walls of the two outer sides of a corner

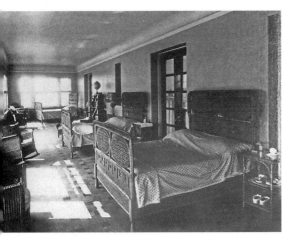

Figure 1.85. *Circa 1916 view inside a sleeping porch on the James A. Allison mansion in Indianapolis, which could sleep six people. Historic American Buildings Survey photograph,* HABS IND,49-IND,23-8.

room. The lower portion of these walls three feet high from the floor should be left standing to serve as a parapet, and a post or pillar placed at the corner and at other points if necessary, to support the roof. The ceiling and remaining walls should be protected against the weather by paint and coach varnish, or other waterproofing material."[174]

For planning bungalows with sleeping porches, the Philadelphia-based architect C. E. Schermerhorn recommended in 1915:

It is often desirable to provide a permanent sleeping porch in connection with one or more bedrooms, for sleeping in the open air is both attractive and beneficial. A permanent sleeping porch, to be convenient, should have an entrance from a bedroom, and when possible from a hall; also proper exposure and protection from varying weather conditions. The interior finish and floors should be of such a character as to be least injured or defaced by dampness or exposure to the sun's direct rays. Complete screening, together with casement or removable sash is advised.[175]

But the construction of sleeping porches was not limited to providing a private space for just a single bed. Indeed, many early-twentieth-century sleeping porches could be used by numerous sleepers. The one at the James A. Allison mansion (figure 1.85) built in 1914 in Indianapolis, Indiana, for example, had enough space for six people sleeping in single and double beds.[176] And at Iowa State University, a sleeping porch suitable for "fifteen to twenty men" was built on the second floor of a Colonial-style fraternity house in 1916.[177]

So important had sleeping porches become by 1917 that an article in *Scientific Monthly* observed: "Sleeping-porches are a comparatively recent invention. Their increasing use bears witness to the fact that we are wisely paying more and more attention to hygiene. For climatic reasons the sleeping-porch can be used only during the summer-time in the northern portion of the United States, but elsewhere it can be used to advantage throughout the year. In Los Angeles it is difficult to sell or to rent a dwelling that does not have at least one sleeping-porch."[178]

Some challenges of how to best incorporate sleeping porches into new designs and how to best add them to existing houses were addressed in an article titled "The Sleeping Porch Problem," published in *House Beautiful* in 1917:

When one builds a country or suburban home of his own, the manner of present-day living makes him demand sleeping-porches as among the essentials of health and comfort. Nor will anyone deny their desirability in summer at least, whatever his views on year-round outdoor sleeping. Thus the owner, whose house was erected five or ten years ago, eventually

Figure 1.86. *Two matching screened sleeping porches were added in 1937 as dormers projecting above Colonial Revival–style porticos on the Holman-Hamilton House in Aurora, Indiana. Historic American Buildings Survey photograph, 1938,* HABS IND,15-AUR,1-3.

discusses sleeping-porches with his architect, or oftener with his carpenter, either to save expense, or because he considers the matter too insignificant for an architect to undertake.—And so the unfortunate affair usually begins.[179]

The author then offered suggestions on how sleeping porches could be integrated into the design of existing houses and provided examples of such structures designed by architects in various regions of the United States. The approaches included adding screened dormers with projecting pediments or flat or shed roofs; recessing screened spaces into a sunny corner or into the wall of the house to form a loggia; and screening a corner of a patio and extending the house with a two-story portico or colonnade, divided in half horizontally.[180]

As "home economics" became a course of study for women in high school and at institutions of higher education during the early twentieth century, the benefits of sleeping porches were mentioned in some textbooks that made recommendations about house planning. The following advice was offered in 1923, for example, in *House and Home, A Manual and Textbook of Practical House Planning*:

> The sleeping porch, which affords the benefits of sleeping in good, fresh air, and the comfort of a warm room to dress in, is in use in many parts of the country. Where the winters are severe, or where winds are high, sleeping porches should be enclosed with windows which may be closed on one or all sides as the weather necessitates. The sleeping porches we see do not always add to the beauty of a house, but by planning them so they do not project beyond the walls of the house, by having the openings not over large, and by making the porches themselves small, they will add character and interest to the dwelling. In planning them care must be taken that the dressing rooms with which they connect are not robbed of air and sunlight.[181]

Although upper-story porches are often called sleeping porches, ground-floor porches have also long been used for sleeping during very hot weather or when extra space was needed for guests, especially at vacation cottages and camps. Describing the design of a summer cottage, an article published in *Popular Science* magazine in 1918 proposed "[a] front porch 8 by 18 ft., which by the use of screens may be turned into a sleeping porch. Rear porch almost as large capable of the same use."[182]

One way to provide privacy and shade while controlling the amount of ventilation into a sleeping porch was to install durable curtains. Founded in 1912, the Aeroshade

Figure 1.87. *Aerolux wooden sleeping porch curtains could be rigged with the tops lowered for ventilation and with center posts designed to prevent the curtains from being blown in heavy winds. Courtesy of Aeroshade, Inc.*

Figure 1.88. *Enclosed with small-paned sashes from floor to ceiling, daylight fills a side porch on a Vermont farmhouse, photographed in the late 1800s. Courtesy of Special Collections, University of Vermont.*

Company of Waukesha, Wisconsin, has produced a line of Aerolux sleeping porch curtains, designed for use around the year, for example. Constructed of basswood splints woven with cotton twine, these curtains were typically hung with cords so that they could be raised or lowered by means of pulleys and cleats. In its promotion of these sleeping porch curtains that could "make an ideal all-the-year-round sleeping room on any porch," the manufacturer observed:

> Open air sleeping is the greatest of tonics. After a night's rest in the open air one awakens refreshed, invigorated, ready for the day's work or pleasure. One in good health should sleep out-of-doors to prolong life and add to his powers for accomplishments; in poor health to increase his powers for resisting disease. Open air sleeping is the one undisputed remedy for weak lungs as well as other ills.[183]

Such shades that could allow both ventilation and privacy have uses that extend beyond comfortable sleeping. As one person

observed of roll-down wooden porch shades in *Good Housekeeping* magazine in 1907, "An interesting feature is the fact that, while persons on the inside can see everything going on outside, it is impossible for passers-by to look in. This affords absolute privacy, and my lady can entertain or serve luncheons there in perfect seclusion. Miss 'Sweet Eighteen' may receive her girl friends or callers with the assurance that there will be no inquisitive gazing from neighboring porches or the sidewalk."[184]

PORCH ENCLOSURES AND SUN PORCHES

Removable enclosures around entryways and small porches became common during the nineteenth century in cold regions for winter protection, as well as for added security and as convenient spaces for storing snow shovels, buckets of sand for icy walks, and other winter items. Some enclosed porches could even serve as small greenhouses for starting plants in the spring.

The practice of enclosing entire porches

with window sashes to transform them into living spaces, however, became increasing common during the twentieth century. In 1910, book and magazine editor Henry Saylor commented:

> It is a very strange thing, when you come to think of it, that we Americans have, in the main, been perfectly satisfied to give up the use of our porches for the greater part of every year. In no other country in the world has the porch been accepted as such an indispensable part of home life as in the United States. We spend upon it the greater part of our waking hours from June through September—not to mention the increasingly great use we make of the porch in our sleeping hours as well. And yet, when the cooler days and chilly evenings of October come around we give it up with scarcely a murmur, and take refuge in the darker, less cheerful and less healthful portions of our homes on the other side of the front door. One would think that our Yankee ingenuity would long ago have devised some means of getting around our climate in this regard, and yet the instances where this has really been done are so few as to be actually noteworthy.
>
> And the strangest part of it all is that the solution of the problem is so very easy. In the mosquito infested parts of the country it has long since become the customary thing to do to enclose the whole porch, or a portion of it, with screens to keep out the insects, yet the enclosing of the same space with glazed sash in winter to keep out the cold—or, to be more accurate, to keep in the warmth—is remarkably uncommon.[185]

In addition to offering suggestions on how such enclosed porches could be con-structed on new houses, Saylor provided advice on how to add winter sash to existing porches so that they could be easily removed in the spring. To facilitate the changeover to the insect screens, both sets could be held in place with screws or brass turn-buttons. Small panes were recommended for the winter sash, as some breakage of glass would be "almost certain to occur when the sash are being taken down or put in place." The system of adaptation worked best on porches built with solid half-walls and square posts, but even older verandas with turned balusters and columns could be adapted with the installation of small strips of wood, to which the sash or screens could be fastened. These stops could be mounted on the porch floor and the ceiling so that the sash and screen panels could align on the inside of the balustrades.[186]

The benefits of glazing a portion of a porch were noted by home decorator Lillie Hamilton French in 1903, but with the following precaution: "Now and then the corner of a country piazza is enclosed with glass, so that a summer dining-room is made; but when this is done, it must not be supposed that what at times is called 'a sun parlor' has been created. Every one who has been to certain resorts knows what a hideous place a 'sun parlor' may be,—nothing more or less, in fact, than a sitting-room near the street and open to the gaze of every pedestrian."[187]

With proper solar orientation and the careful filling of gaps and cracks, such enclosed porches could become suitable sun porches that could to be equipped with rugs and furnishings, and perhaps even heating. Many of these enclosure projects resulted in the eventual loss of use of the open porch, however. For some, efforts to tighten up the new sunroom for continuous winter

Figure 1.89. *A turn-of-the century example of a combined enclosed and open porch is seen on the corner of this vernacular Colonial Revival–style house in Charlotte, Vermont. The open porch section with turned Queen Anne–style balusters and posts extends to the east-facing front of the house on the right, while the glazed porch section on the left corner, with square posts and solid paneled half-walls, connects with the rear west-facing kitchen door.*

Figure 1.90. *Sun porch of Beinn Bhreagh, the Alexander Graham Bell estate on Cape Breton, Nova Scotia. Circa 1915 photograph by Wm. Notman & Son (detail). McCord Museum v8366.*

use made it impractical to undo all the work each spring. Eventually many such porches were thus converted into interior spaces. Thus, in a predicable pattern manifested in neighborhoods across North America, many open porches became permanently enclosed. This trend was nourished by the increasing levels of dust and noise from streets and roads caused by the growing numbers of automobiles and trucks being used during the 1920s and 1930s.

A July 1935 *Popular Mechanics* magazine article even offered detailed instructions on how to convert open porches into enclosed spaces with humorous references to requests from a wife and hints from a mother. The article suggested starting by pulling up the existing porch floor that would have been pitched for rain drainage, and replacing it with a new level floor. The open porch railings were to be replaced with solid half-walls with bevel siding nailed on the outside and plasterboard installed on the inside. Other tasks would include adding new support posts, as well as mullions and casings for new windows and doors to fully enclose the porch space.[188]

Sun porches, which could be easily closed off from the heated areas of a house, and sunrooms, which were more fully integrated rooms with banks of windows, thus became common on both new and existing homes during the first part of the twentieth century in the United States and Canada. A noteworthy Canadian example of a sun porch was built for inventor Alexander Graham Bell's estate home, Beinn Bhreagh, in Cape Breton, Nova Scotia.[189] A circa 1915 photograph of Beinn Bhreagh (figure 1.90) by Wm. Notman & Son shows this sun porch enclosed with

Figure 1.91. *The sun porch on Henry and Clara Ford's Fairlane estate was built in 1915 in Dearborn, Michigan, to serve as a private, intermediary space between indoors and out.*

large-paned wooden sash windows and furnished with wicker chairs, a billiard table, potted plants, and a telescope.[190]

Another example is the sun porch that industrialist Henry Ford and his wife Clara had built in 1915 on the rear of their mansion, Fairlane (figure 1.91), in Dearborn, Michigan, to overlook a view of the estate's landscaped grounds and the Rouge River. Separated from the interior spaces of the house by heavy walls and doors, this private sun porch was constructed with casement windows, durable floor tiles, and radiators for steam heating.

Even for modest new house designs, a clear shift from open porches toward enclosed sun porches continued during the early twentieth century. Indeed, nearly all of the two-story Colonial Revival–style house designs shown in the 1926 Sears, Roebuck *Honor Bilt Modern Homes* catalogue featured a sun porch or a sunroom. The materials and plans for a sun porch cost $329 for a ten-foot by twelve-foot model with a flat roof and rooftop balustrade that would

be suitable for adding to a larger residence. A $279-model with a shallow hipped roof and no balustrade was offered for single-story homes.[191] Also, when *Popular Mechanics* published a house design in 1929 billed as "America's Most Popular Plan," one of the first features mentioned in the article was the sun porch, which could be placed on the side, rear, or front.[192]

For many households, the urge to use their enclosed sun porches for storage was irresistible. Sheltered from the weather, they could easily become convenient repositories for seasonal furniture, snow shovels, firewood, and many other items that would not need to be kept indoors. For some, the spring would bring a dilemma of finding space for all the things that had accumulated through the winter months. Sooner or later however, the temptation to just leave things in place through the summer months would trump the prospect of annually cleaning out the enclosed porch and taking down the window sash. A common result was the gradual conversion of sun porches into unheated storage, and thus the loss of an open summer porch. Back porches were especially prone to these incremental changes.

The advent of aluminum combination screens and storm windows during the 1950s and 1960s encouraged these conversions even further, to the point where in some neighborhoods nearly every porch was enclosed and few open porches remained available for summer use. Although some observers may be tempted to criticize this trend as eroding architectural integrity and some may even seek ways to use local preservation regulations to prevent building owners from making these conversions, such attitudes also may stoke anger and resentment.

In his insightful book *How Buildings Learn*, Stewart Brand argued that most

Figure 1.92. *Evidence of incremental changes to this house provides insights into layers of its history. The sign over the entrance by the flag reads "1857." Whereas the gable-front orientation, heavy corner-boards, and eaves trim are design elements typical of the late Greek Revival style, they are combined with contemporaneous 1850s Italianate-style elements, including the section of the veranda on the right with its chamfered posts and brackets, and the paired, arched windows in the gable wall above. The low railing on the right section of the veranda appears to be a later addition, however, probably dating from the 1880s, as indicated by the fancy cutout design motif of the fretwork. This railing projects forward of the veranda eaves, providing more floor space in front of the bay window. The apron beneath the floor of this section has lattice screening installed on the diagonal. The section of the veranda on the left side, however, appears to have been added circa the 1890s, as indicated by its Colonial Revival–style Tuscan columns, the shingled parapet railing, and the horizontally oriented lattice screening of its apron. A vertical joint between the cornice frieze boards marks the transition between these two sections. The community where this house is located, St. Johnsbury, Vermont, became the shire town of its county in 1856, shortly after the arrival of the railroad in 1850. As a manufacturing center, the town's fortunes then grew steadily through the Victorian era, indirect evidence of which may be reflected by the various porch additions on this house.*

building alterations stem from a natural human instinct to adapt surroundings incrementally to changing needs, especially when it is easy to visualize these changes. For porches, these step-by-step alterations may include adding windows, tightening foundations, and even installing heat for year-round use, so that eventually the porch becomes part of the interior space. Rather than just dismissing later additions and alterations to buildings as unfortunate detractions from the original building design, Brand suggests that when incremental changes are viewed as layered evidence of the process of adaptation they can provide subtle indications of historical changes in social and cultural aspirations. These alterations and additions also may reveal incremental changes in the needs of the occupants and how they have used a building.[193]

CHANGING ATTITUDES

Although porches continued to serve as prominent features on many popular designs of homes built in North America, the transition to the twentieth century brought profound changes in how a new generation viewed their lives, and these changes in turn influenced how they saw their homes. In contrast to the older term *piazza*, even the word *porch* took on a new range of meanings at the start of the century, as reflected in the following excerpt from an article that appeared in *House Beautiful* magazine in 1904:

> The porch of today is in reality an outdoor room, where a large part of the family life is spent. It serves as an informal breakfast-room, and as a convenient place for an impromptu luncheon. It is the ideal spot for afternoon tea.
>
> The porch has brought about the downfall of the piazza, and threatens to rob both living-room and dining-room of their original prominence. . . .
>
> The great advantage of the porch over the piazza is its seclusion. The architect has made a special point of this. The piazza faced the street or driveway, so that privacy was impossible. The publicity of the piazza has been a theme for cartoonists at home and abroad. It has been associated with all that was ostentatious in American life, and with American high voices and bad manners. The porch is so situated that passers-by are unaware of its existence, and where callers may come and go and never catch a glimpse of it.

Figure 1.93. *The replacement of original porch posts and balustrades with these manufactured steel substitutes is an example of an incremental alteration intended to reduce maintenance costs, but it is also a modification that has changed the character of the porch, the building, and even the neighborhood.*

> The piazza is a purely American institution, the porch we have borrowed from our English cousins. It is a preparation for the English garden wall and several other things that will come in good time. It is a step in the right direction. It shows a growing reverence for privacy and for home life.[194]

In 1905, *Canadian Architect and Builder* also featured an article that commented on the shift away from "the old fashioned habit of sitting on the front steps in hot weather" in city homes: "But a porch in the same position, close to the street is no great gain; especially when the street has rails upon it and has reached high development of a three minute service. Here the porch is not the poetical feature it might be in a village. It suggests not fresh air of summer and the quiet moonlight nights but the crude disturbances of the trolley car. A rush and roar every minute and a half, followed by a cloud of dust that spreads wide and settles on everything. The proper place for sitting in connection with a city house is at the back."[195]

A shift from the Victorian era's obsessions with outward appearances and fancy embellishments toward the Progressive era's more functional perspectives, restrained displays, and a growing thirst for privacy was also reflected in the following observation from 1914:

This business of living out-doors has brought about a change in our ideas of house building. We have actually found it desirable to drop Show and embrace Comfort. From boxlike houses with no porches at all, or porches so narrow as to be useless, we have jumped to an embarrassment of porches.

We were once content with a long front porch where we sat in six green rocking chairs with six turkey-red tidies at our backs, and gossiped as the neighbors passed. And we sat in our best clothes, and busied ourselves with company sewing—lace or embroidery or such. We didn't take the darning basket to the front porch. We didn't even go there in the morning. The porch was reserved for afternoons and good clothes. We sometimes had a back porch, but that wasn't intended to be enjoyed; it was a place for churns and milk-cans and fuel and so forth. The cook didn't think of sitting there.

In short, most porches were then ugly and meaningless excrescences, built for show.[196]

House Beautiful, in an article titled "Back Yard *versus* Front Porch," picked up this anti–front porch campaign in 1922 by observing that "the increase in motor traffic, the dust and proximity to other houses tend to make the front porch less desirable each year."

The front porch is not only an architectural feature, but a state of mind, peculiar to a definite American period. . . . Idleness, curiosity about one's neighbors, and chatter did not, to be sure, enter the world with the front porch, but they flourished with it. . . .

The front porch grew up with golden oak, brass beds, and bird's eye maple furniture. America, catching her breath after strenuous pioneer days, wished to settle down for a breathing-spell, in a neighborly fashion, and watch the activities around her. . . . Golden oak and brass beds are disappearing. The front porch grows passé, but it cannot pass as quickly as those less permanent features. It will go gradually as the cult of the back yard grows. Those who have front porches will cease to use them much, but they will not ruthlessly abolish them. . . .

Porches are good enough for rainy days, but even then one prefers them turned away from the trivial drama of the street with its hucksters and milkwagons and gossip, to the serenity of trees and flowers in the back yard.[197]

The same issue of *House Beautiful* also included an article called "Placing Our Houses on the Small Lot," which showed four site plans for homes with either rear or side porches—but no front porches—on lots ranging from forty to eighty feet in width. The author observed: "The front porch, once the favorite outdoor living-room, is becoming a thing of yesterday. Fashion, figuratively, and the automobile, quite literally, have consigned it to dust, and the philosophy of its passing is an intriguing subject much written upon. Once it was an escape from an unsightly back yard; now we are escaping from it in turn to discover that back yards are just as charming as we make them."[198]

Both of these 1922 articles emphasized changing attitudes toward privacy and public space. Thus as it became less desirable for families to gather on the front porch, the orientation of porches was shifted to the side or to the rear of houses, where more seclusion could be found. Another result of these changing attitudes was that many front porches were removed entirely by homeowners to "restore" or to "clean up the lines" of their older houses.

Evidence of the trend to remove narrow Victorian-era piazzas can be found in textbooks written for high school girls as early as 1913, when household arts education professors made the following recommendations to future "home makers": "A dignified two-storied house with fine gambrel roof is made commonplace by a straight, narrow piazza stretching across the front. Remove such a piazza. Add a square porch in front, or possibly at the end, and the change is wonderful."[199] The following year a Pratt Institute School of Household Science and Arts instructor of design echoed this sentiment: "Aside from their ugliness, it is recognized that large porches standing across the front of the house afford little privacy, and they also darken the adjoining rooms. A porch needs vines and shrubbery to relieve the bare skeleton of its structure. One built at the side or rear of the house, shielded from the street by trellis or shrubbery, is a much more intimate and practical luxury than when in direct view from the street."[200]

After the shortages of World War I, the economic prosperity of the early 1920s brought a brief wave of renewed optimism to much of North America. Along with the social changes of the so-called Roaring Twenties, came many changes in fashions of dress and architecture styles. At first, the front porch lingered as a feature of the various nostalgic Colonial Revival–based styles, including the Dutch Colonial and Pennsylvania Colonial variations. Many Dutch Colonial–style houses were built with bold gambrel roofs that extended over full-length, recessed front porches. On this type of house, overscaled Tuscan columns typically supported the overhanging upper story.

Although their status was becoming more associated with the ways of the past, many of the functions of porches remained well entrenched in social customs and traditions, especially through their associations with courtship rituals and discreet flirtations. A few popular "college" songs of the 1920s even had lyrics that joked about love on the back porch or on the old veranda.

As the popularity of the broad, open, front porch faded, designs for new porches favored low half-walls instead of open balustrades. Sometimes called parapets, these solid half-walls provided more physical and visual protection for porches. They were typically constructed of the same materials as the walls of the house and were often fitted with scuppers (figure 1.94), as on boats and ships, to provide drainage off the porch decks. The openings above these half-walls could easily be fitted with insect screens in frames and/or be enclosed with windows.

To be sure, some older house designs with large front porches endured through the 1930s, especially for workers' housing, farmhouses, cottages, and vacation and retirement homes, but the trend for suburban

Figure 1.94. *A scupper opening at the base of a paneled wooden half-wall on a 1930s worker's cottage front porch provides drainage for the gently pitched floor.*

North American homes generally favored exposed front doors with a few steps, small stoops, simple door-hoods, or very modest entry porches.

Coinciding with this shift away from front porch activities came an increased focus on recreational uses of suburban backyards—spaces that previous generations used mainly for such utilitarian purposes as clothes drying, trash burning, and kitchen gardening, or even to accommodate outhouses, carriage barns, storage sheds, chicken coops, hog pens, and wood piles. With tall fences and hedges installed for privacy and security, these new suburban backyards were developed into family refuges with mown lawns, play yards with swing sets and sandboxes for the kids, flower gardens for mom, and perhaps even a workshop for dad in the garage.

Thus back porches, which had been long regarded as service entrances for ice, milk, and grocery deliveries, and as places for such chores as clothes washing, rug beating, chicken plucking, and dog washing during the 1920s and the lean years of the 1930s were slowly transformed into comfortable spaces for leisure and social activities. With the added privacy and security, rear porches also sometimes doubled as outdoor living rooms in regions with mild climates, or seasonally elsewhere.

But with the increased prosperity of the 1950s and 1960s, even these back porches came under threat, as newly constructed backyard patios and private decks became more popular settings for relaxing and entertaining. With a public obsession for progress and a craving for release from the burdens of the past expressed by the antihistoricism of the Modern movement, traditional porches had became worn-out symbols of an old-fashioned, outdated way of life.

With the passage of generations, attitudes often change however, and a substantial revival of interest in porches and their preservation has been growing in many areas of North America in recent decades, as is discussed in the epilogue to this book.

Character, Functions, and Furnishings

Before tracing further how various types and forms of porches have evolved, let us examine some physical qualities that can influence a porch's character, including its functions and associated feelings. First, consider location and orientation, as well as dimensions and layout.

LOCATION AND ORIENTATION

Certainly, the location of a veranda can help to harmoniously connect a house with its setting. Architect Gervase Wheeler noted this synergy in 1867 in his *Homes for the People in Suburb and Country*: "By the side of a river where a grassy lawn slopes to its brink, with woods forming the background, the villa should be designed with long parallel lines, low, and not much broken by irregular heights, wide spreading verandas, overhanging roofs, low walls and few gables towards the river; these will produce a façade that shall appear perfectly in harmony with the scene."[1]

Of course when sheltering entrances of hotels, businesses, and other public buildings, porches typically face public spaces, as do the front porches of many houses, but side and rear porches may offer opportunities for other uses and architectural effects that may be enhanced by the terrain, landscape, and location. Such orientations of porches may also provide opportunities for privacy or for various uses that would not be appropriate for public view.

Although spacious suburban and rural settings may offer opportunities to place houses (and possibly their porches) in their best solar orientation, even houses on small lots may sport porches that are positioned to take advantage of their location and the direction in which they face. For many North American homes, a southeasterly porch orientation is especially desirable for regular summer

Figure 2.1. *The ell-shaped veranda on this Italianate-style villa in Westchester County, New York, designed by Gervase Wheeler, was sited to offer both a sheltered front entrance and side views toward Long Island Sound. Gervase Wheeler,* Homes for the People *(1867).*

use, because it creates a microclimate that offers users both warm morning light and cool afternoon shade, especially in regions where even in midsummer, some mornings may start cool and clear but both temperature and humidity may increase during the day. This southeastern orientation also may provide shelter from prevailing chilly northwesterly winds and protection from the westerly rain squalls of advancing thunderstorms in many temperate regions of the continent. In northern latitudes, where spring and summer mornings tend to be cool and damp (or foggy), and afternoons are sunny and warm (but not too hot), a westerly orientation may invite late-day and evening use, especially where the site provides a pleasant sunset view or when afternoon shadows lengthen as summer fades into autumn.

Deep porches may provide welcome shade in hot, sunny climates, yet porches with excessive depth can become too cavernous or dark to encourage use in their inner reaches unless ceiling heights are substantially increased—but then such loftiness can limit the sheltering effects near the outside edges. Deep porches also limit the amount of daylight that can enter interior rooms directly though windows, so shallow porches, such as the narrow veranda in Napierville, Quebec, shown in figure 2.2, may better serve needs in long-wintered latitudes.

For many persons considering alternative locations for adding a porch to an existing house, the tension between orienting it toward the solar arc or toward a compelling view may present challenging decisions. In his semiautobiographical short story, "The Piazza," Herman Melville's narrator faced such a dilemma in the 1850s when trying to decide on the best orientation for a porch addition to his older house

Figure 2.2. *The southeast orientation of this circa 1880s shallow, bracketed veranda in Napierville, Quebec, allows generous light inside its large, low windows, especially on sunny winter mornings. Also note how the low veranda railings align with the window sills.*

Figure 2.3. *Herman Melville's home, "Arrowhead," in Pittsfield, Massachusetts, as viewed from the northeast in April 1934. By then, the north-facing piazza described in "The Piazza" had been replaced with the deeper Colonial Revival–style porch with Tuscan columns seen above at the right. A small Italianate-style entry porch had also been added on the east front facade at the left. Both of these later porches have since been removed, and a re-creation of Melville's north-facing piazza has been installed by the Berkshire Historical Society. Detail from Historic American Building Survey photograph, 1934, HABS MASS,2-PITFI,1-1.*

in the rural Berkshires of western Massachusetts. Although an easterly or southerly exposure would provide pleasant light and warmth, it was the attraction of the majestic, albeit northerly, distant view of Greylock Mountain, or "Old Charlemagne" as Melville called it, that eventually settled his debate. Beneath the objective reality of the story, where the piazza is seen as a bridge between "coziness" and "freedom," other messages may be embedded, especially as one considers the feelings and psychological states of the narrator (and perhaps the transcendental spirituality of the author) in the following excerpt from the tale:

When I removed into the country, it was to occupy an old-fashioned farmhouse,

which had no piazza—a deficiency the more regretted because not only did I like piazzas, as somehow combining the coziness of indoors with the freedom of out-doors, and it is so pleasant to inspect your thermometer there, but the country round about was such a picture that in berry time no boy climbs hill or crosses vale without coming upon easels planted in every nook, and sunburnt painters painting there. . . .

Now, for a house, so situated in such a country, to have no piazza for the convenience of those who might desire to feast upon a view, and take their time and ease about it, seemed as much of an omission as if a picture gallery should have no bench; for what but picture galleries are the marble halls of these same lime-stone hills?—galleries hung, month after month anew, with pictures ever fading into pictures ever fresh. And beauty is like piety—you cannot run and read it; tranquility and constancy, with, nowadays, an easy chair, are needed. For though, of old, when reverence was in vogue and indolence was not, the devotees of Nature doubtless used to stand and adore—just as, in the cathedrals of those ages, the worshipers of a higher Power did—yet, in these times of failing faith and feeble knees, we have the piazza and the pew.[2]

Figure 2.4. *A group of "easy-chairs" on a deep veranda prompts relaxed conversation while their occupants enjoy the summer view from "the most valuable room in the house." Illustration from Eugene C. Gardner,* Illustrated Homes *(1875).*

DIMENSIONS AND PLANS

Along with orientation, physical dimensions may also influence the character and feelings associated with porches. Tall porticos and shallow porches may serve well as architectural embellishments for show or as passageways or for limited sitting, but many observers have recommended that a porch depth of at least six feet is needed to comfortably support a wider range of domestic uses. In 1850, for example, A. J. Downing wrote of the benefits of a "continuous veranda" on a country house that was "10 feet wide and 80 feet long, which affords a fine promenade at all seasons." He went on to comment, "There are few greater luxuries in a country house in an American summer, such as it is in this latitude, than such a cool and airy veranda—especially if it looks out upon our fine river or lake scenery."[3]

Describing a suitable home for a professor in his 1875 book, *Illustrated Homes*, Eugene C. Gardner offered a sketch (figure 2.4) and the following recommendations on the importance of providing verandas with sufficient depth to permit groups to gather for conversations: "At the east side, where the views are the finest, we want a large square veranda, not a ropewalk, a tantalizing strip of balcony barely sufficient for a man to walk back and forth or a single row of seats, but large enough for a dozen people to group about in easy-chairs without danger of falling off the edges. Summer afternoons this will be the most valuable room in the house."[4]

The shift toward designing verandas with adequate dimensions to serve as comfortable, sheltered outdoor rooms was reflected in an article published in 1908 that recommended the following improvements to country houses:

One of the pleasantest features of a comfortable country home is the veranda. Not the narrow "stoop," which used to be so much in evidence, which was of little practical benefit except as affording some shade for the windows beneath it, but one wide enough to allow the use of hammocks without their excluding large and comfortable chairs, and such other furniture as may be needed to make these outdoor rooms the pleasantest and most used part of the house during the summer season. . . .

I would advise making the veranda at least ten feet wide, and long as conditions will admit of. You will not be likely to have too much space, for the ideal veranda should be roomy enough to accommodate all the family, at one time. There should be a table for books and papers, large enough to answer as a tea table on hot days when eating out of doors is a luxury. . . .

In building a veranda, do not give first consideration to looks. Comfort and convenience should be considered of prime importance. The worth of a veranda is to be estimated by the amount of pleasure that can be got out of it when put to practical use, though, if well built and in harmony with the dwelling it adds much to the appearance of the place. The writer has seen many square, ugly houses made really attractive by the addition of verandas.[5]

In 1909, Gustav Stickley noted the ideal width of a domestic porch in his book *Craftsman Homes*: "The porch at the front of the house is eight feet wide, permitting the use of a hammock and such rustic furniture as is needed for veranda life in the summer."[6] This trend toward creating deep porches to serve as outdoor living spaces for suburban and country houses, rather than as shallow shelters or architectural ornaments, was observed in comments published in 1918: "Time was when the typical country house consisted of an imposing edifice to which a small porch or 'piazza' formed an insignificant appendage. Today the situation is reversed and the home in the country has evolved into a small body of rooms completely surrounded by porches: another illustration of the tail that wags the dog."[7] Note, too, how here the use of the word *porch* was being redefined in the early twentieth century to describe

Figure 2.5. *This deep corner porch on a circa 1900 Craftsman home in Pasadena, California, forms an ample outdoor room that is partially screened by flowering shrubs.*

these comfortable room-size outdoor living spaces, in contrast with the shallower and less well-furnished *verandas* or *piazzas* of previous generations.

With regard to dimensions of porches, Professor Dorothy Scarborough (the "Porcher" mentioned in chapter 1) observed the following advantages to those of great size: "The front porch where I spend most of my time is large enough for an enormous family to enjoy either solitude or society there as they might wish. It is, let us say, fifty feet long and fifteen feet wide. I have never had the inquisitive energy to measure it, but that is about what it looks to be. It stretches the width of the colonial house, with great white columns across the front."[8]

The dimensions of porches can certainly affect their character and potential for uses. Those that measure about twenty-four feet long and about eight feet wide are of a size that is generally suitable to support comfortably a wide variety of uses, including walking, sitting, dining, reclining, and possibly even sleeping. Smaller porches may also accommodate these uses, but with activity zones that overlap. The advantages of roomy porches have recently been recognized by some community planners and "new urban" architects and developers in order to emphasize the vitality of streetscapes as public spaces.[9]

One common plan for full-length porches is to have a passage zone bisecting the space, with defined activity areas on each side. When a passage zone is offset to one side, a larger unified area may be available for various sedentary uses, which can be especially important for smaller porches. In accordance with its use, a passage zone across a well-traveled floor may be marked with mats or rugs for collecting outside dirt. Porch passage zones may also include a stool or bench for changing shoes and boots, and a table or space where grocery bags, luggage, and other such items in transit may be temporarily placed.

Adjacent to a passage zone is often a spot that can be used for the convenient storage of a variety of items for outdoor use—such as a broom, rubber boots, watering can, walking stick, flashlight, insect repellant in summer, and in winter, snow shovels, skis, ski poles, snowshoes, and perhaps a bucket of sand for better traction on icy steps or walkways.

TWINING EDGES

Hanging plants, climbing vines, trellises, and shrubs have long helped to shape the character of verandas and porches by defining their edges and boundaries in what otherwise would be open space. This partial screening may also provide a gradual transition between inside and out that gracefully connects domestic spaces with nature and the world beyond.

Depending on climate and location, several species of vines have commonly been grown on porches to provide partial screening: Dutchman's pipe, with its dense growth of large, heart-shaped leaves; clematis, known for its profuse display of large, bluish purple or white flowers; wisteria, which has climbing woody vines that yield showy cascades of purple, white, or pink pealike blossoms; honeysuckle, of which some species produce elongated bell-shaped yellow, orange, or white flowers; roses, known best for their familiar fragrant flowers and thorny stems; and even grapes.

Given his fervent belief that truth, the "real meaning of architecture," lies in the harmony between the beautiful and the picturesque, A. J. Downing recommended planting various vines to grow on porches and verandas. One design for a cottage included in his *Architecture of Country Houses* (1850) featured an "arbor-veranda" (figure 2.6). Of this he wrote:

[T]here is an air of rustic or rural beauty conferred on the whole cottage by the simple or veranda-like arbor, or trellis, which runs round three sides of the building; as well as an expression of picturesqueness, by the roof supported by ornament brackets and casting deep shadows on the walls. . . .

The *arbor-veranda* of this house is one of its most important features. To build a substantial roof with a veranda of this size round the whole cottage, or round three sides of it, would be too expensive an outlay for most occupants of such a dwelling. This arbor, which is barely a skeleton of such a veranda—being, in fact, only an arbor with rather better poles than usual, would cost little, and would not only be productive of much

Figure 2.6. (left) *Surrounding three sides of a cottage, an arbor-veranda with trellis bars supporting grape vines could provide shade in the summer and sunlight during the winter. A. J. Downing,* The Architecture of Country Houses *(1850); courtesy of Special Collections, University of Vermont.*

Figure 2.7. (right) *With different types of vines entwining each column of his veranda, General Egbert L. Viele wrote in 1878 that he enjoyed a "glimpse of nature from my veranda." Engraving from* Harper's New Monthly Magazine; *courtesy of Special Collections, University of Vermont.*

beauty, but a good deal of profit. We suppose it to be covered with those two best and hardiest of our native *grapes*—the Isabella and Catawba—the most luxuriant growers in all soils—affording the finest shade, and, in the middle and western States, giving large and regular crops of excellent fruit—worth, in the market, from six to twelve cents a pound.[10]

Architect Gervase Wheeler also demonstrated how vines trained to grow on porches could contribute to their rustic character. Of a design for a gatehouse in the country, he wrote in 1850: "The finish of the exterior is in a style of rustic simplicity, such as unornamented construction in the materials at hand would most readily allow. The porch in front is of natural wood, with twining roses and honeysuckles trained over its posts."[11]

Some people have found that vines on a veranda could be a convenient venue for communion with nature in its many forms.

Of this, General Egbert L. Viele wrote in 1878:

My house faces south, and a broad veranda extends around three sides of it—the south, the west, and the east. The roof of this veranda is supported by a number of columns encircled with a different vine, all meeting overhead along wires that extend from column top to column top. Some of these vines have been selected as a permanent home by different families of harmless insects; others are the resort only at night of little winged messengers that select them as the place to make their nests and deposit their tiny eggs, from which in time the progeny emerge to take care of themselves.[12]

But rather than just letting nature have its wild way with the growth of vines on porches, some gardeners have offered suggestions on how such porch vines should be pruned. Here, for example, is some advice published in 1899:

Figure 2.8. *The corner veranda of this Queen Anne–style house features turned posts, a decorated gable, and a spindled valance with diagonals supporting a rich growth of vines. Partially screened by an Eastlake-inspired balustrade formed by rectangular panels with circular cutouts surrounded by spiral stickwork, are a wicker rocking chair and two side chairs. At the left, a canvas hammock with a rectangular frame has a padded mattress and pillows. At the right corner, a small, oval, braded rug for wiping dirty feet is partially hidden by the maple tree in front. Diagonal lattice screen fills the apron beneath. Postcard postmarked: Montgomery, Vt., 1911; courtesy of Special Collections, University of Vermont.*

Pruning Porch Vines.—The object in pruning vines is to keep them neat and vigorous, and not permit a dense mat of growth, excluding light and air from the porch. To accomplish this, it is customary to cut back, in winter, the last season's growth to within a bud or two of the previous year's wood, leaving the stems close to the trellis—referring chiefly, of course, to those vines, like the honeysuckle, that make a thick, branching growth. The tops are usually trimmed off near the porch roof, and the operation is ended. The effect is to produce a strong, dense growth from the tops, giving a top-heavy,

unkempt appearance by mid-summer, but fault in the pruning is rarely recognized then.

The best method of pruning summer-flowering vines, like the honeysuckle and clematis is to cut them down as near the ground as possible, in the winter, allowing the young vigorous shoots to cover the trellis each year, which they will quickly do. In the spring, when the new growth attains about two feet in height, go carefully over them, select four or five of the strongest or as many as may be needed to cover the required space, train them properly on the wires and any unneeded shoots rub off. By the time the shade is needed in summer, the vines will be high enough, and will not have the unsightly bunched appearance of other neglected ones. The clematis is not as strong growing, and if on the same trellis with other vines, should not be cut so low.[13]

The role that vines on porches can play in harmonizing the character of a house with its surrounding gardens was also recognized by one of America's first women landscape architects, Grace Tabor, who observed in 1911, "A Garden is as much the expression of an idea as a poem, a symphony, an essay—a subway, an office building or a gown!" With regard to porch vines, she added, "Primarily a vine is a drapery and should be treated as such. Where it is wanted for shade it should be trained out over a horizontal, awning-like framework or extension to a porch roof, rather than in a dense, vertical wall that closes the porch in from light and air and view."

On the design of suitable supports and care of such porch vines, Tabor advised:

Generally speaking, all porch vines should be provided with a trellis to climb on—and right here let me say that the ornamental possibilities of various forms of trellis are rarely taken advantage of as I should like to see them, and as they very easily might be. There is permanent beauty in a well designed and well constructed permanent support, that frankly takes its place and makes no attempt to hide when the plant which it supports does not conceal it. It is a feature that deserves more consideration than it usually receives.

Strings and chicken wire are not to be despised in their place, but the dignity of heavy-growing and profuse-blooming hardy climbers requires something worthier than these to support it—and this something should always be built. The architecture of a building will usually suggest the form and the design to be adopted, and some architects, indeed, include such suggestions in their elevation drawings for a house.

Vines over a porch, however, whether supported on a trellis or climbing directly on the uprights which sustain the roof, should always follow the lines of construction and should never cross the open spaces between columns or uprights; nor should they be allowed to fill these by hanging over them from above.[14]

SOUNDS

The character of porches may also be shaped by sounds. For example, walking in some neighborhoods, one may pass through a nearly continuous serenade of gentle rings and tings from porch chimes and bells being played by even the faintest of breezes. Combined with those of nature and place, subtle sounds may envelop occupants of a porch space with feelings of comfort and calm. But, of course, with heavy winds, such porch

Figure 2.9. *Perennial vines of Dutchman's pipe on the left side of the veranda and the annual vines trained to grow on strings on the right side provide screening and shade, while also suggesting separate occupancy of the two halves of this circa 1890s duplex house. Queen Anne–style features include turned porch posts, scroll-sawn brackets, and a spindlework valance and balustrades.*

chime music may become more of a disconcerting clamor!

Most auditory signals, however, are not deliberately introduced by the porch dwellers. Sinclair Lewis in his popular novel *Babbitt*, memorably described the banging of a milk truck, the cranking of a reluctantly starting automobile, and the thump of a morning newspaper's delivery that spurred awakening on a sleeping porch in a suburban American neighborhood in the 1920s.[15] Depending on location, time of day, and season of year, other familiar porch sounds may include the ambient background symphonies of calling birds, squirrels, peepers, crickets, katydids, and cicadas, as well as the noises of barking dogs, traffic, trains, sirens, lawnmowers and neighborhood activities, all punctuated by voices near and far, squeaks of hanging porch swings, and slaps of closing screen doors.

Figure 2.10. *Dozens of matching sack-back Windsor armchairs await guests on the piazza of the Grand Union Hotel in Saratoga Springs, New York. Circa 1870s stereograph. Courtesy of Special Collections, University of Vermont.*

PORCH FURNITURE

Although a wide variety of furnishings have long served the needs of porch occupants, several factors have influenced the common types. The two most important characteristics are portability and durability. With the exception of heavy pieces, such as rustic benches and daybeds, most porch furnishings have been lightweight so as to be easily moved to accommodate various uses and to be brought inside for protection from theft and the weather. Indeed, many furnishings such as chairs, tables, and small benches have served functions both indoors and on porches. Other furnishings, such as hammocks and folding chairs, might typically be placed in storage when not needed on a porch.

Although lightweight wooden chairs and settees long have been carried outside for use on a veranda and then returned inside, some types of furnishings have been adapted especially for seasonal use on porches. Lightweight, strong, and comfortable, wooden Windsor chairs have been a popular item. Developed in Windsor, England, in the late 1600s and produced in volume in the American colonies after the 1720s, Windsor chairs became one of the most popular porch and garden seats through the mid-1800s. Indeed, in 1800, General George Washington had thirty Windsor chairs available for use by his guests on the piazza of Mount Vernon.[16]

Traditionally, those intended for such outdoor uses were painted dark green. Constructed of turned spindles and legs, sawn arms, bent backs, and solid seats shaped from wooden planks, the sack-back form of Windsor chairs became a very popular design for porch use, as can be seen in figure 2.10, where they line the piazza of the Grand Union Hotel in Saratoga Springs, New York. Lacking side arms, simpler fan-back Windsor chairs also were also used on piazzas, verandas, and porches, as were Windsor benches and settees.

During the second half of the nineteenth century, manufacturers developed other types of furnishings that were suited specifically for veranda uses. As with the Windsor chairs so popular with earlier generations, lightweight and durable porch furniture made from turned or bent wood continued to be very popular, especially for rocking chairs that were produced in England, Sweden, and America. By the 1880s, the high-backed rocking chair, in particular, with turned wooden frame, woven seating, wide arms, and curved rockers sawn from wooden boards became one of the most common types of furniture on verandas.

Figure 2.11. *A phalanx of high-backed wooden rocking chairs with woven backs and seats lined the veranda of the Hotel Manavista, located south of Tampa in Bradentown, Florida. Note the use of precast concrete blocks with rusticated surfaces for the veranda posts and hotel walls in this early-twentieth-century postcard view.*

Indeed, the verandas of many hotels were lined with phalanxes of tall wooden rockers during the late 1800s and early 1900s. So too, the wooden rocking chair became a fixture on many domestic verandas during this period and later. In time, the sight of a rocking chair on a porch became symbolically associated with the elderly and retirement in popular American culture.

More permanent types of nineteenth-century porch furnishings included built-in seating on Gothic Revival–style porches, such as those that appeared in A. J. Downing's *Cottage Residences*, first published in 1842.[17] These built-in benches are shown in figure 2.12 flanking an entry porch and on a veranda. Downing also showed a rustic settee made from rough branches and/or gnarled tree roots that could be used on a porch or to ornament a garden, as can be seen in figure 2.13.[18]

Architect Gervase Wheeler also included examples of such rustic furniture in his book, *Rural Homes: or, Sketches of Houses*

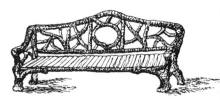

Figure 2.12. *Built-in benches flank the porch entrance at the left and are set beneath the windows of the projecting polygonal bay on the right. A. J. Downing,* Cottage Residences *(1842).*

Figure 2.13. *A rustic seat for garden or veranda use. A. J. Downing,* Cottage Residences *(1842).*

Suited to American Country Life, published in 1851: "So much of effect may be obtained by the careful and artistic placing about the house and verandas of articles of rustic furniture, I have given some specimens of simple manufacture suited to the purpose. The chair here shown is of a simple but durable construction, and admirably suited to the veranda or to the grounds of a summer lodge. It is made strongly and compactly, and the bark is left on, so that it may be in keeping with the appearance and texture of surrounding objects."[19] In his 1867 book, *Homes for the People,* Wheeler included an illustration of a Gothic suburban villa (figure 2.14) with such a rustic seat on the front veranda, which would be a "pleasant resting-place for an after-dinner cigar, in fitting weather."[20]

An especially popular type of rustic wooden porch furniture was produced from hickory saplings and bark. As early as the 1880s, rustic hickory chairs (figure 2.15) were being handcrafted in southern Indiana, North Carolina, and elsewhere in the

Appalachian region. In 1898, the Old Hickory Furniture Company was incorporated in Martinsville, Indiana, which with the help of prolific magazine advertising shipped its products to resorts and homes across the United States during the early twentieth century.[21] A 1903 *Good Housekeeping* magazine ad offered an "Old Hickory Porch Set" combination of chair, rocker, and settee for $7.75, a set of three spindle-back chairs for $4.25, and a set of three rockers for $5.40. Said to be "appropriate for your veranda or lawn," these furnishings were "made entirely of tough white hickory with the bark left on."[22]

Not everyone was pleased with the comfort provided by rustic porch furniture, however. One author observed, "The chief drawback to the rustic chairs and settees is that they often have projecting knobs and angles which, by some malignant fatality, are invariably placed where they will do the most harm. Happily, this defect can be mitigated by judicious cushioning."[23]

With improvements in standards of living and increased amounts of leisure time

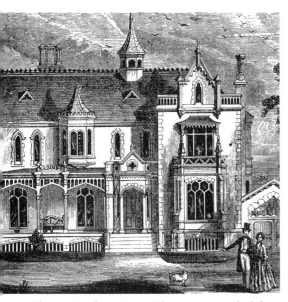

Figure 2.14. *The rustic seat that appears on the left in the center bay of the veranda shown in this detail from a drawing of a Gothic suburban villa was described by the book's author as a "pleasant resting-place for an after-dinner cigar, in fitting weather."* Gervase Wheeler, Homes for the People *(1867).*

Figure 2.15. *A rustic "Old Hickory" rocking chair and a matching armchair with seats and backs of woven bark are displayed in the foreground of this pre-1907 postcard view of the veranda of the Rest House at Rose Hill Park in Altoona, Pennsylvania.*

during the late 1800s and early 1900s, however, some North Americans were able to create more permanent porch environments that could serve as outside living spaces that were well provided with tasteful and comfortable furnishings. In his influential book *Craftsman Homes* (1909), Gustav Stickley addressed the subject of porch furniture:

> Outdoor living and dining rooms, to be homelike and comfortable should be equipped with all that is necessary for daily use so as to avoid the carrying back and forth of tables, chairs and the like, as when the veranda is used only occasionally. It goes without saying that the furniture should be plain and substantial, fitted for the rugged outdoor life and able to stand the weather. Indian rugs or Navaho blankets lend a touch of comfort and cheer, and the simple designs

and primitive colors harmonize as well with trees and vines and the open sky as they do with their native wigwams. Willow chairs and settles seem to belong naturally to life in the garden, and with a few light tables, a book rack or two and plenty of hammocks, the veranda has all the sense of peace and permanency that should belong to a living room, whether indoors or out, that is habitually used by the family.[24]

This trend to furnish porches as comfortable outdoor rooms reached its pinnacle during the first two decades of the twentieth century. An article written in 1918 about furnishing porches of country homes noted these changes:

> A generation or two ago the women of a family would drag their rocking chairs

out from the sitting room to the piazza on warm afternoons, and there sway placidly to and fro, plying industrious needles, until the setting sun, stabbing its sharp lances thru the loopholes in the protecting curtain of woodbine or "creeping Jinny," forced retreat. Occasionally, in the evening, the young folks assembled on the steps to greet the rising moon with the assurance that Nellie was a Lady, or a fervent entreaty to Bring back my Bonnie to Me-e-e. For the remainder of the twenty four hours the piazza was deserted. It did not even have any furniture of its own except for the hammock of netted cord, the brigade of rocking chairs being daily tugged forth crabwise from the house, and as regularly tugged back again before the early dew should dampen their haircloth or patchwork cushions.

Today, what a difference! We eat, sleep, lounge, read, write, knit, cook, receive calls, give teas and auction parties, and even get married on the porch. Once a porch party was a rare and exciting event: now, life in the country is a perpetual porch party with three very capital P's. Moreover, the furnishing of the porch has assumed an importance not surpassed by that of any room inside the house.[25]

In 1914, Ruby Ross Goodnow and Rayne Adams wrote in detail about porch furnishings in a chapter titled "The Pleasure of Porches" in their book *The Honest House*:

The furniture-makers are giving us really charming furniture for out-of-doors, and it is hard to decide just what we will have on our ideal porch. I think there should be a Gloucester hammock of green and white drilling, fitted with green cushions and mattress; a wing-chair of willow with a big pocket for magazines; a large Canton hourglass chair with a tabouret of the same type beside it; a chair built on the lines of the familiar steamer-chair in willow or rattan; a long bench painted dark green (this bench may be eight or ten feet long, and it will serve as a table as well as a seat when there is company); a chest or settle with box seat for tennis-rackets and such; one or more tables of green painted wood or willow; several large jars of green things, and a bird-cage. Surely, if there is ever an excuse for having a bird in a cage, I think one might be excused for having one of those enchanting thrush cages of orange-colored reeds on one's living porch. You needn't have a thrush in it; have any bird you please. The cage itself is such a charming thing that any bird would be happy in it. A wooden settle with a box beneath the seat to hold outdoor things, or a long chest of painted wood, will be found most useful on any living porch. Such a settle or chest offers a great chance to young people who have been studying the applied arts, for here is a fine opportunity to decorate a simple straightaway object with some bold scheme of design and color. Don't allow your porch to become untidy. Have as much freedom and gaiety and informality as you please, but none of the shabby disorder that is so distressing. The cushions, for instance, should be covered with water-proof cloth if possible, and then with whatever you choose—denim, linen or chintz; but the outer covers should be made to button on so they may be washed. Cushions that have faded or "run" in unsightly streaks are unpleasant.[26]

Hammocks have long served as a popular type of porch furnishing for casual resting or for sleeping, especially in hot weather. Said to have been introduced to Europe by Christopher Columbus after observing them in use by the indigenous inhabitants of the Bahamas, these first hammocks were made from woven bark. By the late 1500s, canvas hammocks had been adopted by the British Navy for shipboard sleeping.

In 1845, a woman in her mid-thirties wrote in a letter of her feelings while in a hammock: "I have had my hammock slung on the piazza; I lie and swing there with the baby in the daytime, in the evening alone; while the breezes whisper and the moon glimmers through the stately trees, and am very sorry it was not so while you were here that I might have heard you sing there some happy evening; it is just like being in a cradle."[27] In an 1885 issue of *Life* magazine, a cartoon (figure 2.16) of a couple enjoying veranda life with a hammock appeared with the caption: "Summer at a Fashionable Resort. They do this all day. How refreshed they will be after their stay in the country. They love this simple, out-of-door life, with plenty of exercise. They are New Yorkers."[28]

Simple hammocks are made from a heavy fabric or loosely woven cord gathered at the ends and attached to ropes that connect to secure points (figure 2.17). When used on porches, these supports may be a porch post, roof beam, or a strong hook fastened to a wall. One great advantage of hammocks is that they may be set up or stored away with ease. Hammocks with wooden or metal spreaders at one or both ends (figures 2.18 and 2.19) provide a flatter surface than those without, but what the spreaders add to comfort may be countered by a reduction of stability when in use.

The risks associated with using worn-out hammocks were also well known, but one design developed with reinforcing cord attached to the spreaders was reported in *Good Housekeeping* in 1907: "Modern ingenuity has devised new styles of hammock architecture, as well as in verandas. For instance, in the old-fashioned hammock the cords were fastened directly to the frail 'body warps,' and a few weeks' use so weakened them that consequent disaster was inevitable. But by fastening the suspension cords direct to a sturdy spreader this part of the hammock is the last to go, instead of the first."[29] A disadvantage of falling asleep in public on a porch hammock, removed from the protective confines of a bedroom, is that a recumbent user may be more subject to unwelcomed disruptions (or even pranks!), as seen in an illustration (figure 2.20) published in 1880 in *Harper's New Monthly Magazine*.[30]

Some porches were even designed to provide sufficient space for several hammocks, as this 1904 description of a summer cottage suggests: "The porch in front being twelve feet wide, gives a most desirable place for hanging hammocks."[31]

A type of hammock that became popular by the early 1900s, commonly known as a Gloucester hammock (figure 2.21), was made from heavy canvas stretched over a metal pipe frame with a rectangular back and side panels.[32] In their 1914 book, *The Honest House*, Ruby Ross Goodnow and Rayne Adams wrote of these hammocks: "Gaudy, sagging hammocks of many colors and untidy fringe are also unpleasant, but the modern Gloucester hammock is a comfortable resting-place by day and a bed by night. It is the ideal porch hammock, because the lines are logical, and you are screened while you are resting."[33]

Figure 2.16. *Cartoon of New Yorkers enjoying "summer at a fashionable resort" with a string hammock and Japanese paper lanterns. Life magazine (1885); courtesy of Special Collections, University of Vermont.*

Figure 2.17. *Four people, accompanied by a dog, potted plants, and a bird, enjoy a leisurely summer afternoon circa 1890 on a veranda in Ontario. Furnishings included: from the left, a bentwood chair, a pressback side chair, a folding chair, a bench for houseplants, another pressback side chair, a wicker trunk in the corner, a string hammock, a small pillow on the floor, a metal wheelchair behind, and a small turned-legged side table at the right. McCord Museum MP-1977.76.176.*

Figure 2.18. *One of a series of hammock-themed postcards published by 1909 that used the porch as a setting for courtship tableaus, the caption here reads, "When as steel to magnet, hand seeks hand, As the waves roll softly over the sand." This string hammock with tassels has curved wooden spreaders at the head and foot.*

Figure 2.19. *A shy cat strides away from a row of potted plants as a light afternoon breeze flutters a pair of American flags on the corner of the open veranda that surrounds two sides of the vernacular Gothic-style Cascade House on Lake Dunmore in Salisbury, Vermont. Strung between a post and the wall is a fringed hammock with a pillow and spreader at one end. Other porch furnishings include two cane-backed rocking chairs, an armchair, and two side chairs. A wooden armchair, a wicker rocking chair, and a side chair also are on the small rear side porch off to the right. Courtesy of Special Collections, University of Vermont.*

Figure 2.20. *A jovial prank is played on a victim napping in a hammock on the porch of a seashore club. Illustration in* Harper's New Monthly Magazine *(1880); courtesy of Special Collections, University of Vermont.*

Figure 2.21. *A canvas Gloucester hammock and wicker chairs and table furnish a sun porch in this view.* Building with Assurance, Morgan Woodwork Organization *(1921).*

Figure 2.22. *A wicker "Lady's Comfort Rocking Chair" made of reed, with woven cane on the back and a hardwood frame and rockers, holds a watchful cat. In the background of this porch view are two plant stands and a fringed cloth hammock.*

THE E-Z PORCH SWINGS MAKE FRIENDS WITH EVERYBODY
MADE IN SINGLE AND DOUBLE SIZES. NO CROSS RUNGS TO SIT UPON. NATURAL HEAD REST. RECLINABLE.
MOST COMFORTABLE SEAT MADE. BETTER THAN A ROCKER, EASIER THAN A HAMMOCK.
LIGHT, DURABLE, ECONOMICAL, ADJUSTABLE. FURNISHED COMPLETE
WITH CHAINS AND CEILING HOOKS.

Figure 2.23. *The Benefits of "E-Z Porch Swings" were promoted on this penny postcard mailed in 1911.*

Wicker chairs, divans, tables, tabourets, and ottomans were all popular furnishings for North American porches from the second half of the nineteenth century through the early twentieth century. As early as 1851, architect Gervase Wheeler noted, "On a veranda, such cane lounges, settees, and chairs being light and easily removed would be appropriate. . . . The natural color of cane-work is a light yellow; it is stained

sometimes black, and sometimes left parti-colored, producing a pretty effect."[34]

Although the practice of weaving stalks, twigs, and sticks into baskets and mats has ancient roots, the large-scale manufacturing of wicker furniture in North America was developed in Massachusetts in the 1840s by a shopkeeper, Cyrus Wakefield. He developed lightweight, durable furniture designs mainly using the split stalks (or "cane") and the pliable inside pith (or "reed") of the rattan vine. This inexpensive material, which was being imported on clipper ships from Asia as dunnage for packing cargo, was readily available in the nearby Atlantic seaports. Also, willow bows and various turned and sawn hardwoods were also used as raw materials for this wicker furniture. Established in 1853, the Wakefield Rattan Company of South Reading, Massachusetts, quickly grew to become one of the largest manufacturers of wicker furniture in America. In 1897, the company merged with its longtime rival furniture manufacturer, the Heywood Brothers & Company of Gardner, Massachusetts, to form the Heywood Brothers and Wakefield Company. This firm monopolized the production of wicker furniture in North America for decades.[35] Consumer interest in wicker eventually faded however, and in 1936 the Heywood-Wakefield Company revived itself by launching its now famous and very collectable "Modern Line" of birch home furnishings.

Although the reed and cane were often left in their natural, unfinished state, wicker furniture was also stained and shellacked or painted. According some advice offered in 1914, "The best of all colors for porch furniture, awnings and so forth are white, gray, brown, light green and very dark green. The light green should be the color of green apples, or green peas or lettuce—if you are uncertain of the tone I mean. The dark green should be the soft velvety tone of the evergreen tree—the boxwood, olive, gardenia, japonica, laurel, or any such green. Yellow is a good porch color, properly used. Red is extremely popular, and extremely dangerous."[36]

Another type of furnishing that became strongly associated with porches by the early twentieth century was the porch swing. A 1905 advertisement in the *Spokane Daily Chronicle* described one swing being sold for $22.50 as being "constructed of selected wood and finished in the new fumed oak finish. The upholstering is of plain tapestry and the swing is attached to the roof of the veranda by a heavy cord."[37] A book published in 1917, *Home Labor Saving Devices*, offered a description of how to make an inexpensive oak porch swing in the mission style "with space long enough for two to sit in and broad enough to be used for lounging purposes." For comfort, the author suggested making a pad "of burlap and stuffed with an old discarded quilt." Four chains were then connected to iron fittings on the sides of the swing to suspend it from a porch ceiling.[38] Film buffs may recall a delightful spoof on attempts to sleep outside on a porch swing that was featured in the 1934 comedy *It's a Gift*, starring W. C. Fields.[39]

Classical Order

Any attempt to appreciate the depth of meanings and symbolism associated with classical architectural forms must first start with a review the classical orders and then explore how they have been used through waves of architectural design innovations and revivals. Classical styles of architecture that were fundamentally based on elaborations of the Doric, Ionic, and Corinthian orders were developed first in ancient Greece from about 600 BCE and were refined over many centuries. The ancient Romans modified the proportions and details of these orders during the first five centuries of the current epoch.

In addition to the three ancient orders, two other orders were subsequently added: the Composite order and the Tuscan order. The Composite order is a more elaborate version of the Corinthian that combines elements of the Ionic. The Tuscan order, which was documented in the works of the Roman architect Vitruvius during the first century BCE, has a column similar to that of the Roman Doric, with a simple base (but without the decorative fluting) and a plain entablature that lacks the Doric ornamentation. Because of its simplicity, the Tuscan order has been especially popular for vernacular versions of the various classical revivals. In his 1833 pattern book, *Practice of Architecture*, Asher Benjamin observed, "The Tuscan capital is distinguished by rustic plainness; the Doric by grave simplicity; the Ionic, by graceful elegance; and the Corinthian and Composite, by gorgeous richness."[1]

Whether based on ancient Greek or Roman examples, each of these classical orders is comprised of a horizontal entablature supported by columns that may rest on a pedestal. From the top, the entablature is comprised of a cornice, a frieze, and an

Figure 3.1. *A colonnade of Tuscan columns extends along the facade of the Essex Inn, built about 1810 in Essex, New York.*

architrave. The column also has three basic parts—a capital at the top, a shaft, and a base at the bottom. Greek Doric columns normally have no base; however, very simple bases are sometimes installed for protection. The pedestal, also known as a stylobate, may be omitted, but in its proper form it has a cap (or cymatium), a die (or dado) and a base. It may be solid or arcaded in a Roman form associated with classical designs from the Italian Renaissance.

The simplest of the three main classical orders is the Doric, which can be recognized by its plain capital comprising a series of moldings. On a Roman Doric column, the capital has three parts: the series of moldings at the top is the abacus; the space beneath is the necking; and the lower series of

moldings is the astragal. On a Greek Doric column, the astragal is rendered as an incision around the shaft (or is sometimes even omitted), and the square abacus at the top is supported by a large echinus, a convex molding that has a cross-section based on a segment of an ellipse. Moldings on the Roman orders, however, generally have cross-sections that are based on sections of a circle. The proportions of the various parts of the Greek and Roman orders also differ, with the columns on the Roman versions being more slender.

Greek Doric columns typically are finished with sixteen or twenty elliptical flutes carved deep enough into the shaft to form vertical pointed edges (each called an arris) where the flutes meet. Columns of the other

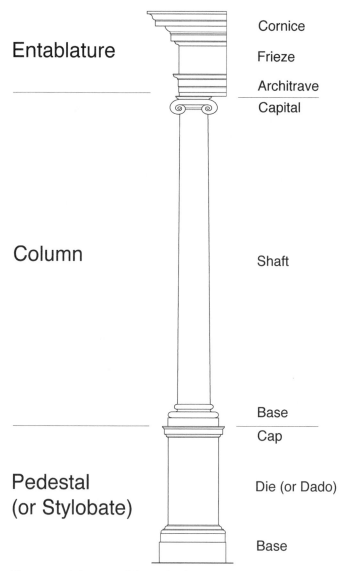

Entablature
- Cornice
- Frieze
- Architrave
- Capital

Column
- Shaft
- Base
- Cap

Pedestal (or Stylobate)
- Die (or Dado)
- Base

Figure 3.2. *Major parts of classical orders.*

orders are rendered either with or without fluting; however, when applied to Ionic and Corinthian column shafts, the flutes are typically cut deeper, in the form of a segment of a circular curve, to leave a flat fillet between each, instead of a pointed arris.

Doric friezes are enriched with triglyphs, slightly projecting rectangular blocks incised with two V-shaped channels and chamfers to produce three vertical lines. Between each

triglyph is a square space called a metope that is sometimes ornamented with carved decorations. On Roman Doric friezes, the metopes may be ornamented with bucrania (ox skulls) dressed with garlands of flowers or husks hanging from the horns. Soffits (the underlying surfaces) of Doric cornices are enriched with mutules, projecting rectangular blocks that are carved to reveal a grid of guttae, the circular bases of

Figure 3.3. *Roman Doric entablature, St. Michael's Church, 1752–61, Charleston, South Carolina. Contrasting with the simple moldings of the capital of the column, the Doric entablature is enriched with triglyphs, mutules, and guttae. Historic American Buildings Survey photograph, 1977,* HABS SC,10-CHAR,8-20.

Figure 3.4. *Fluted cast-iron columns with noticeable entasis line the Greek Doric portico of the main entrance of the Marché Bonsecours in Montreal. Note the prominent triglyphs that ornament the frieze of the entablature.*

truncated cones. A row of six guttae also extends below each triglyph. Decorations are also sometimes applied to the metopes between the mutules along the soffits.[2]

An example of a Doric portico, seen in figure 3.4, covers the main entrance of the Marché Bonsecours in Montreal. This portico was added in 1860 to the large public market building that was started in 1842.[3]

More elaborate than the Doric, the Ionic order has columns crowned with distinctive capitals featuring pairs of spiral-shaped volutes that look somewhat like rolled cushions or scrolls. Unlike the capitals of the

other orders, the Greek Ionic capitals and some Roman Ionic capitals have two separate elevations: faces that display the volute spirals and "baluster" sides that display the pulvinated (convex) form of the volutes, which are constricted in the middle by a set of balteus straps. Ringing the bottom of the Ionic capital, at the top of the column shaft, is a thin astragal that is sometimes enriched as a bead-and-reel molding. Above this astragal between the curls of the volutes is a larger echinus molding that is typically ornamented with an egg-and-dart enrichment.

Classical Order 101

Figure 3.5. *This Ionic capital in the Greek Revival style on the First Presbyterian Church (1835–38) in Princeton, New Jersey, displays an egg-and-dart enriched echinus molding over a thin bead-and-reel astragal ringing the top of its fluted column shaft. The cushionlike rolls of the volutes that face front and rear appear constricted at the sides by balteus straps. Detail from Historic American Buildings Survey photograph, 1964, HABS NJ,11-PRINT,25-5.*

Figure 3.6. *This Scamozzi Ionic capital is on the north portico, from 1829, of the White House in Washington, DC. Detail of Historic American Buildings Survey photograph, 1985, HABS DC,WASH,134-48.*

A variation of the Ionic capital is the Scamozzi capital, which combines features of the Ionic and Corinthian orders. The most noticeable features of this type of Ionic capital are the volutes that roll out at radial angles on all four corners to offer four matching faces. Named for the Venetian architect Vincenzo Scamozzi (1552–1616), who was a student of the famous architect Andrea Palladio (1508–1580), this alternative Ionic capital design became very popular during the Italian Renaissance and was included in various pattern books produced by Scamozzi and others. The presence of the angular Scamozzi Ionic capitals provides a quick hint to the observer that the associated portico or colonnade was not designed in the Greek Revival–style, but rather in one of the Neoclassical styles based on Roman and Renaissance forms. There are exceptions to this rule, however.[4]

The most elaborate of the classical Greek orders is the Corinthian. Its capitals are encircled with three rows of acanthus leaves crowned by a row of small volutes. A simplified and commonly used variation of a Greek Corinthian capital is based on the columns of the porticos on the Tower of the Winds clock structure in Athens, which dates to about 50 BCE. This capital dispenses with the volutes, featuring instead a row of acanthus leaves surmounted by a row of palm leaves, with a square abacus at the top.[5] This design was widely copied after it was included in the portfolio of drawings of ancient monuments by James Stuart and Nicholas Revett in their *Antiquities of Athens*, first published in 1752.[6]

Figure 3.7. (above) *This example of a Greek Revival Corinthian capital is on the Austin Perry House, built before 1841 in Southport, Connecticut. Detail of Historic American Buildings Survey photograph, 1966,* HABS CONN,1-SOUPO,15-3.

Figure 3.8. (right) *Corinthian columns with Tower of the Winds capitals grace the front portico of the John Wheeler House in Burlington, Vermont, designed in the Greek Revival style by Ammi Burnham Young in 1840. As does the design shown in Stuart and Revett's* Antiquities of Athens, *these fluted columns lack molded bases and stand directly on the stone plinth.*

In addition to the characteristic shapes of their features, classical orders are also based on set rules of proportion that determine relationships between the height of a column and the diameter at its base, as well as the proportions in relation to other elements and distances between columns. Even the proper amount of tapering and swelling curvature (entasis) of column shafts varies according to the orders. On all the orders, the height of the columns is typically four times the height of their entablature.

To permit easy scaling to suit the needs of building designers, drawings of orders in pattern books may designate dimensions of classical elements according to a unit of measurement known as an "entablature" or "En," which may be divided into one hundred parts. Another similar proportional measurement system, such as that rendered by the Italian Rennaisance architect Andrea Palladio, uses a "module" that is equal to the radius of a column shaft at its base. These modules may be subdivided into twelve parts. A third system uses "diameters," sometimes expressed as "D" on measured drawings, based on the diameter of the column at the base. In the pattern book drawings of Asher Benjamin, for example, each diameter is divided into sixty equal minutes. The scales and measurements on these drawings are thus shown in diameters and minutes, instead of in feet and inches.[7]

As with the grammar of proper spoken or

Figure 3.9. *Design for a church with a Doric portico. The narrow columns, arched doors, and decorative urns on the tower are typical of the Classical Revival style. Asher Benjamin*, The American Builder's Companion *(1826); courtesy of Special Collections, University of Vermont.*

written languages, correct applications of the architectural orders are based on study and training, and to those with learned perspectives, variances may be seen as errors reflecting the ignorance or lack of training of the designers. Thus, to reduce possibilities of embarrassment or ridicule, architects and builders have long sought guidance from

pattern books on correct designs and proportions for the classical orders.

One of the most influential proponents of the Federal and Greek Revival styles was Asher Benjamin, a New England architect, who at the age of twenty-four, in 1797, published his first book, the *Country Builder's Assistant*. Undoubtedly based on English pattern books of the era, but believed to be one of the first architectural pattern books published in the United States, this simple volume combined succinct discussions of the basic concepts of classical architecture with drawings of the classical Roman orders and architectural details. Through this and his subsequent series of pattern book titles published over the next four and a half decades, comprising more than forty revised editions, Asher Benjamin provided carpenter-builders up-to-date templates for the architectural orders, column capitals, moldings, windows, doors, and various architectural details. Although in every book Benjamin placed his major emphasis on the designs and proportions of the architectural orders, builders were encouraged to apply these patterns to buildings of their own designs. Asher Benjamin therefore offered only a few full building elevations and plans in his books. In the 1826 revised edition of *The American Builder's Companion* (first published in 1806), however, he included a design for a church (figure 3.9) with a front portico in the Roman Doric order and dressed with such Adamesque details as round-topped windows and decorative urns on the clock stage of the steeple.[8]

In his *Practice of Architecture* pattern book first published in 1833, Benjamin even risked offering a design of his own creation for a column and entablature, borrowing elements from the Tuscan, Doric, and Ionic orders, but he prefaced it with the following note:

I am aware that the publication of anything in the shape of an order unless it be really one of the Grecian or Roman orders, is, by persons well versed in architecture, thought to be little less than heresy. Although I am not much disposed to differ with them in their opinion, I have deemed it advisable in this case to depart from it. My reasons for doing so proceed from the fact, that more than one half of all the columns and entablatures erected in country situations, for either internal or external finishings, belong neither to the Grecian nor Roman system. The same fact holds true in relation to our cities and large towns. . . .

I have often inquired the reason for this, from very intelligent workmen, and have often received for answer that the Tuscan order is too massive and plain, the Doric too expensive, and the Ionic too rich, and that they are therefore under the necessity of composing a column and entablature which will conform to the views and purses of their employers.

With these facts before me, no doubts rest in my mind but what it would be better to give a design here of a column and entablature, constructed on scientific principles, and of a character capable of meeting the views and practice above mentioned, than to leave it to be composed by unskilled hands.[9]

PORTICOS AND COLONNADES

A portico is a type of porch supported by classical columns, rather than by posts, pillars, or arches. Through their associations with the ancient orders of architecture, classical porticos and colonnades embody in their trabeated designs of supporting posts and horizontal beams a highly nuanced language of tradition and inference that has been conveyed through Western culture for more than twenty-six centuries. Typically associated with the sheltering of entrances to grand public buildings and mansions, many portico designs are based on the ancient Greek and Roman orders of classical architecture and their revival forms. Porticos

Figure 3.10. *An engaged Ionic portico of the 1780s ornaments the north elevation of The Woodlands mansion in Philadelphia. Detail of Historic American Buildings Survey photograph, 2002, HABS PA,51-PHILA,29-9.*

Figure 3.11. *The Benjamin Conklin House in Cambridge City, Indiana, was built in 1840 with an Ionic in antis portico at the front entrance and a shallow Doric loggia on the second story above. Detail from Historic American Buildings Survey photograph, 1975, HABS IND,89-CAMB,1-1.*

generally possess axial symmetry and repetitive classical forms that may reflect quests for order and perfection in human endeavors.

On some classical buildings, the major parts of the orders may define the proportions and components of both the body of the building and of the portico. Thus, entablatures of both may match; flat pilasters on the walls may correspond to the columns of the portico, and a raised building foundation may correspond to the portico pedestal. Exterior steps or stairways may provide access to the top of this pedestal level.

Classical porticos can be divided into three types: engaged, in antis, and prostyle. With columns, entablature, and pediment connected directly to the wall of a building, the shallowest type is the engaged portico. Providing virtually no shelter, engaged porticos generally offer ornamentation rather than functionality to buildings. An important historic example is the engaged portico on the north elevation of The Woodlands

mansion (figure 3.10) in Philadelphia, which was added to the original 1740s house as part of its expansion in the 1780s.[10]

An in antis portico has a recessed space and its columns extend in a line across the opening in alignment with the flanking walls. A portico or a balcony that is fully or partially recessed into the body of the building is also called a loggia, a noted feature of Renaissance architecture. An example of a Greek Revival–style house with an Ionic in antis portico on the first story and a Doric loggia balcony above, is the Benjamin Conklin House (figure 3.11) in Cambridge City, Indiana.[11]

A prostyle portico projects a row of columns ahead of a wall of a building and is the most common type (figures 3.13, 3.14, and 3.15).

Porticos may be described in classical terms by the number of columns in the row. Thus, when the projecting portico has a row of four columns visible, it is a prostyle tetrastyle portico. When two columns are visible in an opening of a loggia, the portico is distyle in antis.

Other varieties of porticos include the tristyle, with three columns; pentastyle, with five; hexastyle, with six; heptastyle, with seven; octastyle, with eight; enneastyle, with nine, decastyle, with ten; and dodecastyle, with twelve. Even numbers of columns are most common, as this allows for an opening in the center of the row, but porticos with an odd number of columns also do occur.[12]

Even the spacing between columns, or intercolumniation, is regulated by conventions. Whatever number, columns normally are placed to align under the centers of the triglyphs on Doric entablatures. When columns are coupled, they align under adjacent triglyphs. When one triglyph is between, the intercolumniation is monotriglyphic; when two are between, it is ditriglyphic; when three are between, tritriglyphic; and when four are between, the intercolumniation is tetratriglyphic.[13]

The principles of intercolumniation were discussed and illustrated in Asher Benjamin's *The Builder's Guide*, first published in 1839. Although a strict interpretation of the Doric order might encourage a designer to select monotriglyphic or ditriglyphic intercolumniation for large structures, Benjamin suggested some practical considerations for employing this order on smaller buildings. His comments below refer to the drawing from *The Builder's Guide*, shown in figure 3.12, of a Doric portico elevation and plans of four examples of intercolumniation.

In common practice, when the columns are much less than three feet in diameter, they cannot generally be placed nearer to each other than those of No. 3, because the interval between them would in that case be insufficient to enable a person of large size to pass between them freely. Take for instance the example of a piazza to be erected in front of a dwelling-house, whose columns are one foot six inches in diameter. In that case, the distance between the columns, if set in imitation of No. 1 or 2, would be only two feet three inches, which would be about one half of the breadth of the windows of the house; and if they were set in imitation of No. 3, the distance would be four feet one and a half inches, which also would be insufficient. It would be expedient therefore, in such a case, to place three triglyphs over each intercolumniation. It is however to be observed, that when intercolumniation is so extended as to admit three triglyphs over it, it produces a lean and unsolid aspect, by reason of the numerous and massive details of the entablature, which will require the appearance of frequent support. Hence the student will perceive that this order succeeds better, when wrought on a large than on a small scale, and it will be well for him, in cases like above, to use one of the other orders, in which the same nicety is not required in placing the columns.[14]

For all the orders, intercolumniation is generally at least one-and-half times the diameter of the columns at their bases, unless the columns are paired or coupled. This spacing is known as *pycnostyle*. Other intercolumniations are two diameters, systyle; two and a quarter diameters, eustyle; three diameters, diastyle; and four diameters, araeostyle.[15]

Although not commonly used in the either the ancient Greek or Roman orders, the coupling (or pairing) of columns, instead of placing them at evenly spaced intervals,

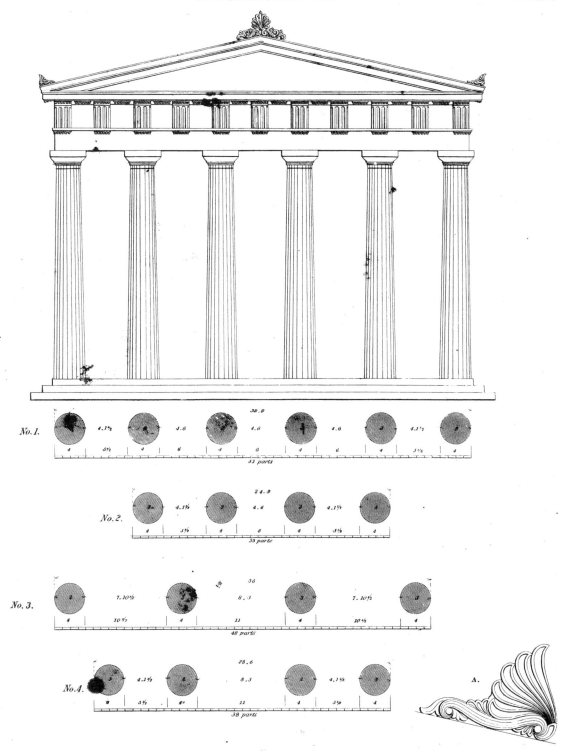

Figure 3.12. *Examples of intercolumniation and a Doric portico were illustrated in this plate. The elevation and first two plans show monotriglyphic spacing, the third plan has ditriglyphic intercolumniation, and the fourth illustrates ditriglyphic spacing over the center and monotriglyphic spacing between the flanking outside columns. Asher Benjamin,* The Builder's Guide *(1839).*

Figure 3.13. *A prostyle hexastyle portico in the Doric order graces the Greek Revival–style facade of Windsor House, built as a hotel in 1840 in Windsor, Vermont. The columns have ditriglyphic intercolumniation, providing enough space between each for two triglyphs in the frieze above.*

Figure 3.14. *A prostyle portico with coupled Tuscan columns shelters the front entrance of the Old Montreal Customs House. This portico was reconstructed to match John Ostell's original 1836 Neoclassical design when the building was enlarged in 1881.*

Figure 3.15. *This prostyle portico with coupled Ionic columns shelters a side entrance on the Greek Revival–style Timothy Follett House, Burlington, Vermont, designed in 1840 by architect Ammi Burnham Young. Surrounding the doorway within are Ionic columns in antis, flanked by simple Doric anta, which are the flat pilasters found at the corners of the walls.*

became something of a novelty among such noted seventeenth- and eighteenth-century architects as Claude Perrault in France and Sir Christopher Wren in England. Since then, many architects have also chosen to dress porticos and colonnades with coupled columns, rather than strictly following the classical rules of intercolumniation.

An example of a prostyle portico with coupled Tuscan columns in Montreal was designed for the Montreal Customs House (figure 3.14) by the English-born architect John Ostell in 1836.[16] For the Timothy Follett House (figure 3.15) in Burlington, Vermont, the American architect Ammi Burnham Young designed a prostyle portico with coupled Ionic columns in the Greek Revival style in 1840.

Both porticos and colonnades are types of classical porches with columns supporting entablatures. Porticos typically shelter doorways, whereas colonnades are constituted by longer rows of columns that sometimes extend along an entire side of a building or structure. Generally, when a row is of six or fewer columns, the term *portico* is applied, and when there are more than eight, the word *colonnade* is used. For a row of eight columns, when they are clustered near an entrance, especially on a gable end, the feature is typically described as a portico, but when the row is a linear feature that extends along the entire length of the building, then it is a colonnade.

When columns extend around the entire perimeter of a building or around an inner court, this is known as a peristyle colonnade. Ancient examples of these include the Parthenon temple on the Acropolis in Athens and the remarkably well-preserved nearby Temple of Hephaestus (figure 3.16), which is also known as the Theseion, built between 449 BCE and 415 BCE.

Figure 3.16. *A peristyle colonnade in the Doric order surrounds the Temple of Hephaestus in Athens. The intercolumniation is monotriglyphic.*

Figure 3.17. *The Pantheon temple in Rome has a prostyle octastyle portico supported by three ranks of eight Corinthian columns. Detail from circa 1870 stereograph, "Roman Antiquities," published by A. F. Styles, Burlington, Vermont. Courtesy of Special Collections, University of Vermont.*

One of the earliest surviving references to a portico comes from the Greek philosopher Socrates, recorded in Xenophon's *Memorabilia*, written about 371 BCE:

"It is pleasant to have one's house cool in summer and warm in winter, is it not?" and this proposition also having obtained assent, "Now, supposing a house to have a southern aspect, sunshine during winter will steal in under the portico, but in summer, when the sun traverses a path right over our heads, the roof will afford an agreeable shade, will it not? If, then, such an arrangement is desirable, the southern side of a house should be built higher to catch the rays of the winter sun, and the northern side lower to prevent the cold winds finding ingress; in a word, it is reasonable to suppose that the pleasantest and most beautiful dwelling place will be one in which the owner can at all seasons of the year find the pleasantest retreat, and stow away his goods with the greatest security."[17]

The Pantheon temple (figure 3.17), a notable surviving building of ancient Rome, has an octastyle portico (or *pronaos*) consisting of three ranks of Corinthian columns constructed about 125 CE during the reign of Emperor Hadrian. The thirty-nine-foot stone columns of this grand porch were carved from gray granite, said to have been quarried in Egypt and shipped across the Mediterranean Sea.[18]

Aside from archaeological examples, much of what is known about classical ancient Greek and Roman architecture and building methods comes from one important surviving book, *De Architectura*, written about 15 BCE by the Roman architect Vitruvius. The rediscovery of *De Architectura* in the Abbey of St. Gallen in Switzerland in 1414 led to the first printed version of this Latin work in 1486. As subsequent translated versions with woodcut illustrations were printed during the 1500s, this work by Vitruvius greatly influenced Renaissance architecture and helped to rekindle interest in classical designs in Europe and beyond, especially as various reprints and translations were again published in the eighteenth and nineteenth centuries.[19] Also known as *The Ten Books on Architecture*, Vitruvius's work included descriptions of Greek and Roman houses that featured peristyles, the rectangular colonnades surrounding interior courtyards. These were proportioned to provide both light into the adjacent inward-facing rooms and ventilated spaces shaded from the sun and rain. Vitruvius specifically recommended that the peristyles, "lying athwart, should be one third longer than they are deep, and their columns as high as the colonnades are wide. Intercolumniations of peristyles should be not less than three nor more than four times the thickness of the columns."[20]

About the design of houses for various groups of Roman citizens, he declared: "For capitalists and farmers of the revenue, somewhat comfortable and showy apartments must be constructed, secure against robbery; for advocates and public speakers, handsomer and more roomy, to accommodate meetings; for men of rank who, from holding offices and magistracies, have social obligations to their fellow-citizens, lofty entrance courts in regal style, and most spacious atriums and peristyles, with plantations and walks of some extent in them, appropriate to their dignity."[21]

Vitruvius also discussed the designs of Greek houses that featured two interior peristyles, one principally for use by men and the other for the women of the household. Of one of these houses, he wrote: "This peristyle has colonnades on three sides, and on the side facing the south it has two antae, a considerable distance apart, carrying an architrave, with a recess for a distance one third less than the space between the antae."[22]

With the blossoming of the English Renaissance, porticos were being added to some religious and civic buildings, as well as to country estate houses of the English aristocracy, as early as the 1650s.[23] Few buildings constructed in the English colonies of North America during the seventeenth century featured porches or porticos, however. Instead, the architectural vocabulary of the colonial First Period, especially in Puritan New England, generally emphasized practicality and austerity, with minimal decoration.

Even on high-style buildings, the ornamentation of this colonial period generally appeared as shallow embellishments applied to grace such features as doorway frontispieces, rather than as open transitional spaces that could surround users in three dimensions. Entry porches more commonly were enclosed with walls, and access was gained through doors, as discussed above. Thus, distinctions between the inside and outside of buildings were clear and definite, just as were the era's public precepts of right and wrong. This traditional medieval attitude was to be challenged by enlightened perspectives that coincided with a growing embrace of architectural classicism during the eighteenth century, however.

GEORGIAN

Coinciding with the ascent of King George I to the throne of the kingdom of Great Britain in 1714, the Georgian architectural style that developed in phases in Britain and its colonies over the following century strongly reflects theoretical foundations that were well suited to this Age of Reason. In accord with Palladian principles, the architectural designs of the Georgian style were logically composed assemblages of discrete architectural components. These components were geometrically arranged on flat walls, in accord with principles of proportion and treatment of details that were based on classical orders.[24] Less ornate than the earlier Baroque style, these fundamental principles of logic and integrity of motifs can also be heard in the classical musical of the era. The Georgian portico might thus be considered an opening movement of an architectural symphony.

During the mid-eighteenth and early nineteenth centuries, classical porticos and colonnades that projected far enough to serve as intermediary liminal spaces started to become fashionable in North America, especially on the grand country homes of the American aristocracy and on civic, academic, and religious buildings. Although the designs were typically constrained by established stylistic protocols, these classical porticos and colonnades marked the launching of a trend that would soon radically alter the appearance of the North American architectural landscape.

One of the oldest surviving country houses with a classical portico in the English-settled areas of North America is Drayton Hall (figure 3.18), located near Charleston, South Carolina. Built between 1738 and 1742 as a country estate house by a wealthy plantation owner, its design reflects the classical symmetry of the English Palladian style. The facade facing the road has a portico with Doric columns on the first story and Ionic columns on the second. This serves as both an accessible, covered entry portico and a protected, elevated balcony. As this portico is recessed, it also could be described as a two-tiered loggia. The projecting gable

Figure 3.18. *A Georgian-style house with a two-tier portico that could also be described as a double loggia, Drayton Hall was built between 1738 and 1742 near Charleston, South Carolina. Detail from Historic American Buildings Survey photograph, 1973, HABS SC,10-CHAR.V,8-4.*

Figure 3.19. *The Redwood Library, 1748–50, Newport, Rhode Island, Peter Harrison, architect. Historic American Buildings Survey photograph, 1970, HABS RI,3-NEWP,15-3.*

above, with its ornamented tympanum, reinforces the grandeur of the building.

The Redwood Library (figure 3.19) in Newport, Rhode Island, constructed between 1748 and 1750, is one of the first buildings erected in the North American British colonies with a portico based on the form of a classical temple. Peter Harrison, a gentleman architect from Yorkshire, England, who moved to Rhode Island after serving as a ship captain and merchant, based his design for the library on a drawing included in a reprint of the *Fourth Book of Palladio*, published in London in 1736.[25] The Redwood Library's prostyle portico features four Roman Doric columns with ditriglyphic and tritriglyphic intercolumniation supporting an entablature enriched with triglyphs and guttae on the frieze and mutules on the soffits of the pediment cornices.

Harrison's 1749 masterpiece, King's Chapel (figure 3.20) in Boston, features a colossal front portico that was completed to Harrison's original design between 1785 and

Figure 3.20. *King's Chapel, 1749, Boston, Peter Harrison, architect. Historic American Buildings Survey photograph, 1961, HABS MASS,13-BOST,55-1.*

Figure 3.21. *St. Michael's Church, 1752–61, Charleston, South Carolina. Historic American Buildings Survey photograph, 1977, HABS SC,10-CHAR,8-15.*

Figure 3.22. *Doric portico with tritriglyphic intercolumniation, St. Michael's Church, Charleston, South Carolina. Historic American Buildings Survey photograph, 1977, HABS SC,10-CHAR,8-17.*

1787. This deep hexastyle portico, which surrounds the base for the bell tower is one of the first classical porticos designed for a church in North America.[26] The columns and pilasters on King's Chapel have Scamozzi capitals. The entablature on the portico is surmounted by a Palladian balustrade with paneled pedestals centered above each unfluted column, interspersed with urn-shaped balusters. Although Harrison's original plan called for a tall spire to be erected on the austere tower base, this was never constructed. It is thus the beautiful Ionic portico that attracts the main attention of the observer.

In contrast to the apposite comfort of the design of King's Chapel, the seemingly impossibly tall 186-foot-high spire on St. Michael's Church (figure 3.21) in Charleston, South Carolina, startles one's attention. Built between 1752 and 1761, St. Michael's has a pedimented tetrastyle front portico with

tritriglyphic intercolumniation (figure 3.22). It is probably the oldest surviving example of this type on a church in North America.[27] The design follows the classical principles of superposition, with the simple Doric order used for the portico and the pilasters on the exterior walls of the church; the Ionic order decorating the first stage of the spire; and the Corinthian order enriching the clock stage above. The restraint of the beautifully executed Doric front portico also helps to unify the design by avoiding visual competition with the highly embellished spire.

Although its architect has not been identified, St. Michael's Church, with the templelike front portico and massive spire rising from the body of the building, shares similarities with St. Martin's-in-the-Field, built between 1721 and 1726 in London. A drawing of that church, designed by the influential British architect James Gibbs, was published in 1728 in Gibbs's *Book of Architecture*. This illustrated pattern book helped disseminate Palladian principles of architecture and influenced the designs of many classical buildings constructed throughout Britain and the British colonies.

A North American example of a Gibbs-inspired Palladian country house built between 1758 and 1762 is Mount Airy (figure 3.23), located in Richmond County, Virginia. With restrained classical formality of the Georgian style, the front facade features a shallow projecting pavilion with a raised entry loggia supported by square Doric piers of limestone.[28]

NEOCLASSICAL: ADAM, FEDERAL, AND CLASSICAL REVIVAL

Compared with the earlier Georgian style, the Neoclassical style architectural designs of the late 1700s and early 1800s in the United States and in Canada were lighter, more graceful, and picturesque. Prominent front porticos served as character-defining features as more attention was given to the separate identities of classically inspired architectural elements that each stood in contrast to taut planes of wall surfaces. Variations of the Neoclassical style discussed below are also referred to as the Adam, Federal and Classical Revival styles.

A sophisticated example of a high-style mansion that reflects the evolution of the Neoclassical architectural style after the American Revolution is The Woodlands (figure 3.24), located in Philadelphia. Between 1788 and 1789, a central pavilion was extended from the existing 1740s house to form a prostyle temple-front portico on the south elevation, complete with Tuscan columns supporting a simple entablature and a pediment detailed with a dentil moldings on its cornice and an ocular in its tympanum.[29]

Figure 3.23. *Mount Airy, built between 1758 and 1762 in Richmond County, Virginia, features a shallow pavilion with a raised entry loggia dressed with square limestone piers and pilasters. Detail from Historic American Buildings Survey photograph, 1971, HABS va45.*

The design of The Woodlands bears many similarities to some works produced by English architect, Robert Adam, who with his brother, James, greatly influenced architectural trends in Britain and beyond after the 1760s. Their works helped to introduce a new approach to design that emphasized the use of classical forms and motifs inspired in part by the amazingly rich archaeological discoveries of ancient Roman architecture and colorful designs found in the buried ruins of Pompeii and Herculaneum. The publication in the late 1770s of the *Works in Architecture of Robert and James Adam* so profoundly influenced architectural design that buildings displaying their approach to Neoclassicism are typically described as Adamesque or Adam style. In the United States this also became known as the Federal style.[30]

Some important public buildings constructed in the United States during the late 1700s and early 1800s include Classical Revival–style works designed by Thomas

Figure 3.25. *The Virginia State Capitol in Richmond, a design offered by Thomas Jefferson in 1786 in the Classical Revival style, is based on the form of a Roman temple. The southwest facade, shown here, features a hexastyle front portico with colossal columns in the Ionic order with Scamozzi capitals. Historic American Buildings Survey photograph, 1988, HABS VA,44-RICH,9-7.*

Figure 3.24. *A prostyle tetrastyle portico with colossal Tuscan columns was added between 1788 and 1789 to The Woodlands mansion in Philadelphia. Historic American Buildings Survey photograph, 2002, HABS pa93.*

Jefferson, the main author of the Declaration of Independence, a governor of Virginia, and the third president of the United States. Working with the French architect, C. L. Clérisseau, the Classical Revival–style design that Jefferson offered in 1786 for the Virginia State Capitol (figure 3.25) in Richmond was based on the Maison Carrée Roman temple in Nimes, France, with an Ionic hexastyle portico providing a grand front entrance. The use of the Scamozzi capitals on the Ionic columns of this portico reflect a change from Jefferson's initial design that was made by Samuel Dobie, the architect-builder who supervised the construction of the building while Jefferson was serving as the minister to France between 1784 and 1789.[31]

The design of the Virginia State Capitol soon became a prototype for many state capitols and other monumental temple-fronted public and commercial buildings, including

the First Bank of the United States (figure 3.26), designed in 1794 in the Classical Revival style by Samuel Blodgett Jr.[32] Its front facade features an impressive hexastyle portico in the Corinthian order, surmounted by a pediment with an ornamented tympanum.

Charles Bulfinch of Boston, one of the most influential architects of the Federal period, made prominent use of portico colonnades supported by arcades in his best-known Adamesque Federal–style public and religious buildings. The Massachusetts State House (figure 3.27), built in Boston to Bulfinch's design between 1795 and 1797, established a precedent for domed capitol buildings with monumental porticos supported by arcades, including the Maine State House, designed by Bulfinch in 1829.[33] Perhaps the most famous of his designs is the Lancaster Meetinghouse (figures 3.28 and 3.29), built in 1816 in Lancaster, Massachusetts. The most identifiable feature of this

Figure 3.26. *A hexastyle portico in the Corinthian order projects from the main facade of the First Bank of the United States in Philadelphia, built in 1794. Historic American Buildings Survey photograph, 1974, HABS PA,51-PHILA,235-5.*

Figure 3.27. *Designed by Charles Bulfinch in the Adam style, the Massachusetts State House was built between 1795 and 1797. Its two-tiered front portico features a colonnade of paired and single Roman Corinthian columns supported by an arcaded base. Historic American Buildings Survey photograph, 1941, HABS MASS,13-BOST,1-8.*

church is its iconic front porch, which combines the form of a classical portico with the arched openings of a brick arcade. This porch is enriched with pilasters and pediment in the Doric order.[34]

On domestic buildings, delicate porticos enriched with carefully executed classical elements and attenuated columns became hallmark features of such high-style American Federal houses as those designed by Charles Bulfinch in Boston and by the talented architect-builder, Samuel McIntire, in the nearby prosperous shipping port of Salem, Massachusetts.[35] An example of Samuel McIntire's work is the 1805 Crowninshield-Deveraux House (figure 3.31). The focal point of the design of the front elevation of this wooden house is its semicircular portico with Tuscan columns, topped by a Palladian balustrade with pedestals above the columns interspersed with turned balusters. Inside the portico is a

typical Palladian door surround with an elliptical leaded glass fanlight above the raised paneled door and leaded glass sidelights. As with many Federal-style houses, these sidelights extend down only as far as the bottom line of the first-story windows.

Another outstanding example of the Adam-influenced Federal style is the Nickels-Sortwell House (figure 3.31), a National Historic Landmark built in 1807 for a ship owner in the Downeast seaport of Wiscasset, Maine. The elegant front portico of this three-story mansion features four slender, fluted Corinthian columns arranged in an unusual stepped-back pattern.[36] The portico cornice is enriched with modillions along the soffit and the balustrade above features stylized lattice screens.

A gradual shift toward an eclectic blending of Neoclassical motifs derived from a range of Roman and Palladian sources via various pattern books can be seen in

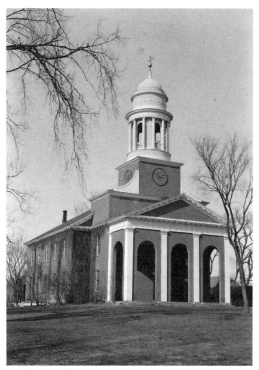

Figure 3.28. *With its distinctive arcaded front porch, the 1816 Lancaster Meetinghouse in Lancaster, Massachusetts, is one of Charles Bulfinch's best-known works. Historic American Buildings Survey photograph, 1941, HABS MASS,14-LANC,1-1.*

Figure 3.29. *View inside the arcaded front porch of the 1816 Lancaster Meetinghouse in Lancaster, Massachusetts. Historic American Buildings Survey photograph, 1986, HABS MASS,14-LANC,1-8.*

important American architectural works produced in the Classical Revival style during first several decades of the nineteenth century. Two grand Neoclassical porticos were added to the White House, the United States president's mansion in Washington, D.C., during the 1820s, for example. These were based on designs developed in 1807 by Benjamin Henry Latrobe, who had been hired as the Surveyor of Public Buildings and Grounds in 1802.[37] The curved south portico of the White House (figure 3.32) that was constructed of Seneca sandstone under the supervision of James Hoban in 1824, serves as a two-tiered porch facing the South Lawn. It connects directly to the main floor of the living spaces. Hoban, an architect who had emigrated from Ireland to the

United States, had developed the original design for the White House in 1792 with a south porch that was never built.

An outstanding example of a portico used to accent the front and rear entrances of a Classical Revival–style dwelling designed in the Palladian tradition is Thomas Jefferson's Monticello (figure 3.33), located on a hilltop near Charlottesville, Virginia. Monticello features two pedimented porticos in the Roman Doric order. The larger prostyle tetrastyle portico is on the west, garden-facing facade. A similar, but slightly recessed portico on the east facade serves as the main public entrance. President Jefferson adapted the design for this house, finished in 1809, from a plan published in 1728 by British architect James Gibbs.[38]

Figure 3.30. *The Crowninshield-Deveraux House, built in 1805 in Salem, Massachusetts, to the designs of Samuel McIntire, features a semicircular front portico with Tuscan columns. Historic American Buildings Survey photograph, 1941, HABS MASS,5-SAL,45-2.*

Figure 3.31. *Four slender, fluted Corinthian columns accent the shallow front portico of the 1807 Nickels-Sortwell House in Wiscasset, Maine.*

Figure 3.32. *The curved, two-tiered, Neoclassical south portico of the White House in Washington, DC, was built in 1824. Historic American Buildings Survey photograph, circa 1992, HABS DC,WASH,134-102.*

A Federal-style house with a distinctive front portico is Tudor Place (figures 3.34 and 3.35) in Washington, DC, built in 1816 for Thomas Peter and his wife Martha Custis Peter, a granddaughter of President George Washington. It was designed by Dr. William Thornton, architect of the United States Capitol and the Octagon House in Washington. This portico on the south-facing elevation of Tudor Place is known as a tempietto.[39] This type of circular portico with a domed roof gets its name from the Tempietto of San Pietro on the Montorio church in Rome, designed in 1502 by Donato Bramante to commemorate the site where Saint Peter was said to have been martyred.[40] A much earlier precedent of a tempietto is the ancient Roman Temple of Vesta (or of the Sibyl) at Tivoli, Italy, constructed between

Figure 3.33. *Thomas Jefferson's Monticello features a prostyle tetrastyle portico in the Roman Doric order on its east facade. Historic American Buildings Survey photograph, 1978, HABS va47.*

Figure 3.34. *This tempietto on Tudor Place in Washington, DC, designed by Dr. William Thornton, was built in 1816. Historic American Buildings Survey photograph, HABS dc91.*

50 and 10 BCE. Andrea Palladio included designs of both the Bramante tempietto and the Tivoli Vesta temple in his *Quattro libri dell'architettura* (*The Four Books of Architecture*). Reprints of Palladio's works were certainly available to architects such as Thornton, who employed the simple Tuscan order for this beautiful "little temple" porch at Tudor Place.

After the Virginia State Capitol and Monticello, another of Thomas Jefferson's ambitious architectural projects was his design for the "academical village" (figure 3.36) at the University of Virginia in Charlottesville. Constructed between 1817 and 1826, it features long colonnades connecting the academic and residential "pavilions" arranged on the east and west sides of a two hundred foot–wide rectangular lawn, with the Rotunda building at the north end.[41] Recent research has revealed that beneath many

Figure 3.35. *View looking out through the 1816 tempietto at Tudor Place in Washington, DC. Historic American Buildings Survey photograph, HABS dc95.*

Figure 3.36. *The University of Virginia's East Lawn "pavilions" are marked by Ionic porticos connected with Doric colonnades. Historic American Buildings Survey photograph,* HABS VA,2-CHAR,1B-2.

layers of white paint, the columns originally were finished with tan stucco and the trim was painted a khaki color.[42]

Although porticos and colonnades graced many Adam, Federal, and Classical Revival–style houses, churches, and other buildings constructed in the early nineteenth century, some casual observers may falsely assume these to be indicative of later Greek

Revival–style works. One example is St. Paul's Episcopal Church (figure 3.37), built between 1820 and 1822 in Windsor, Vermont. Architect Alexander Parris (1780–1852) of Boston designed this brick church in the Classical Revival style.[43] Another example of a late Federal-style temple-front mansion with a full-width classical front portico with six columns in the Doric order

Figure 3.37. *A distyle in antis portico featuring Ionic columns with Scamozzi capitals shelters the recessed front entrance of St. Paul's Episcopal Church, built between 1820 and 1822 in Windsor, Vermont.*

Figure 3.38. *Facing the Hudson River, the Federal-style west elevation of Edgewater, built in 1824 in Barrytown, New York, is dominated by a Roman Doric ditriglyphic hexastyle portico. Historic American Buildings Survey photograph, 1979,* HABS NY,14-BARTO.V,1-3.

Figure 3.39. *Four slender, wooden columns capped by Scamozzi Ionic capitals form a tall, shallow portico on this late Federal–style house built in 1830 in Burlington, Vermont. Single-story verandas with Ionic columns line the flanking wings. The extended front deck with balustrade and the Italianate-style rooftop belvedere are later additions.*

is Edgewater (figure 3.38), built in 1824, overlooking the Hudson River in Dutchess County, New York.

In his 1828 book, *Travels in North America*, British tourist Captain Basil Hall recorded seeing porticos and colonnades on better houses in the Northeast, especially along the Erie Canal in central New York: "In the more cleared and longer settled parts of the country, we saw many detached houses, which might almost be called villas, very neatly got up, with rows of wooden columns in front, shaded by trees and tall shrubs running round and across the garden, which

Figure 3.40. *A Neoclassical hexastyle portico in the Corinthian order fronts the 1847 Bank of Montreal at Place d'Armes in Montreal.*

Figure 3.41. *Very slender colonnettes support an elliptically shaped entry porch on Swanwyck, a rare example of a Regency-style house built in 1820 near New Castle, Delaware. Historic American Buildings Survey, photograph, 1936, HABS DEL,2-NEWCA.V,1-1.*

was prettily fenced in, and embellished with a profusion of flowers."[44] Swedish traveler Carl David Arfwedson also noted in the early 1830s that in Worcester, Massachusetts, "The houses all look new, adorned with colonnades of the Doric and Corinthian order, and surrounded by gardens and trees, which give them alike the appearance of rural and town residences."[45]

One of the most impressive Canadian examples of a mid-nineteenth-century Neoclassical-style commercial building with a Corinthian portico is the Bank of Montreal (figure 3.40), designed by the English-born architect John Wells and built in 1847 at Place d'Armes in the heart of Old Montreal.[46]

REGENCY

Simple porches, porticos, and loggias, as well as more ornate verandas, were also constructed using classical forms on houses designed in the early decades of the 1800s in the Regency style, especially in Canada. Although quite rare in the United States, the

Regency style became popular in Britain after the Georgian era and before the Picturesque architectural styles of the Victorian era. The porches on these Regency-style buildings generally followed Neoclassical inspirations, and thus many shared similarities with those on late Federal-style buildings.

For example, Swanwyck (figure 3.41), a rare example of a Regency-style house built in 1820 near New Castle, Delaware, features an elliptically shaped entry porch supported by very slender colonnettes.[47] In Windsor, Nova Scotia, the Judge Thomas Chandler Haliburton House (figure 3.42), or "Clifton," was built in the Regency style in 1836 with a simple portico with boxed columns.[48]

GREEK REVIVAL

Although ancient Roman architectural orders and motifs had generally served as the basis for classical design through the Renaissance, as well as for the Georgian, Adam, and Classical Revival styles, the rediscoveries of ancient Greek buildings by British

Figure 3.42. *A simple portico with boxed columns protects the entrance of the Judge Thomas Chandler Haliburton House, or "Clifton," built in the Regency style in 1836 in Windsor, Nova Scotia, as seen in this detail from an early-twentieth-century postcard view.*

archaeologists, which were documented in drawings published in 1762 by Nicholas Stuart and James Revett in the *Antiquities of Athens*, led to the development of the Greek Revival architectural style during the mid-1700s. Notable early European examples of the Greek Revival style include Carl Gotthard Langhans's Brandenburg Gate, constructed in Berlin between 1788 and 1791, and Sir Robert Smirke's 1823 design for the main block of the British Museum in London. Although the Greek Revival emerged as the most popular style in the United States by the 1830s, it was one of several architectural styles popular in Europe during this period. As with its direct predecessor, the Classical Revival style, the monumental dignity of Greek Revival style served the symbolic needs of domestic, government, institutional, and religious buildings during this period.

Also well-suited to the democratic aspirations of the new American nation, the public appeal of the Greek Revival style coincided with the great building boom of the canal era and the Westward Expansion. The use of this architectural style for a new generation of public and domestic buildings, even in some long-settled areas, reflects the wealth generated during this period by expanding mercantile trade, by the New England Merino sheep boom (especially in the Connecticut River valley and Vermont's lush Lake Champlain valley), and by the plantation–slave labor system in the antebellum South. Some of the most widely recognized architects who worked in the Greek Revival style in the United States include Robert Mills (1781–1855), William Strickland (1788–1854), Ammi Burnham Young (1798–1874), and Thomas U. Walter (1804–87).[49]

A prominent portico with six squat, Doric columns and an entablature ornamented with triglyphs along its frieze was added in 1817 to the Arlington House (figure 3.43), also known as the Custis-Lee Mansion, in

The Lee Mansion, Arlington, Va.

Figure 3.43. *Arlington House, also known as the Custis-Lee Mansion, in Arlington, Virginia, features a prominent portico with six squat, Doric columns that was added in 1817, as seen in this early-twentieth-century postcard view.*

Figure 3.44. *Fluted Greek Doric columns distinguish the front portico of the Second Bank of the United States, 1818–24, in Philadelphia. Historic American Buildings Survey photograph, 1939,* HABS PA,51-PHILA,223-4.

Figure 3.45. *Funerary portico, Monumental Church, 1812–14, Richmond, Virginia. Historic American Buildings Survey photograph, 1987,* HABS VA,44-RICH,24-3.

Arlington, Virginia. An early example of a Greek Revival-style addition, the portico was designed by George Hadfield, a young English architect invited to the United States to supervise the construction of the U.S. Capitol Building in 1795.[50]

The Second Bank of the United States (figure 3.44) in Philadelphia, designed by William Strickland in 1818, may be the first Greek Revival–style public building in the United States to be based on the Parthenon in Athens. Like the Parthenon, Strickland's building is constructed in the Doric order, but the bank features porticos on its two gable ends, rather than being surrounded by a peristyle colonnade, as is the ancient temple on the Acropolis.

One of the first examples of the Greek Revival style's being used for a portico on a religious building is the Monumental Church (figure 3.45), constructed between 1812 and 1814 in Richmond, Virginia. It was designed by Robert Mills, a Charleston, South Carolina, native who was trained by Benjamin Latrobe, James Hoban, and Thomas Jefferson, and who served as the state architect of South Carolina from 1820 to 1827. Built in commemoration of the tragic deaths of seventy-two people who died in the conflagration of a theater at the site in 1811, the church features a somber funerary portico on its southwest facade. This sandstone portico is cornered by heavy piers with

Figure 3.46. *Featuring tetrastyle Doric porticos set on arcaded bases, the Charleston District Record Building (also known as the Fireproof Building) was built between 1821 and 1827 in Charleston, South Carolina. Historic American Buildings Survey photograph, circa 1977, HABS SC,10-CHAR,64-7.*

Figure 3.47. *An octastyle Ionic portico designed in 1827 shelters the main entrance of Biddle Hall, U.S. Naval Asylum, in Philadelphia. Historic American Buildings Survey photograph, 2003, HABS PA,51-PHILA,577A-27.*

Doric columns standing in antis on each of the three side openings. These columns have fluting only on the capitals and bases. Rather than ornamenting the Doric entablature with triglyphs, the friezes on this portico are decorated with lachrymatorial urns (the vases used for holding tears found in some ancient Roman burial sites). Stone palmette-shaped acroteria stand at the corners of the front pediment.[51]

A public building by Robert Mills with a prominent portico and Classical–Revival features that shows the transition from the Federal style to the Greek Revival style is the Charleston District Record Building (figure 3.46), constructed in Charleston, South Carolina, between 1821 and 1827. Also known as the Fireproof Building, this masonry edifice has two porticos, located on opposite sides of the building. Each has four unfluted Greek Doric columns, surmounted by pedimented parapets above the cornice line.[52]

Another one of the earliest and most important examples of a Greek Revival–style institutional building in the United States is

Biddle Hall (figure 3.47) of the United States Naval Asylum (also known as the Naval Home) in Philadelphia. Designed by William Strickland, this landmark features a prominent central portico and recessed verandas on its side wings (figure 4.42). According to the Historic American Buildings Survey, Strickland based the 1827 design of the front portico of this hospital building on an illustration of the Ionic temple on the Ilissus River included in the 1762 publication of the *Antiquities of Athens* by James Stuart and Nicholas Revett.[53] A December 1829 communication from the architect to the commissioners of the Navy hospital fund reported that the 140-foot-long building was "embellished with a marble portico of eight Ionic columns, three feet each in diameter."[54]

Like the Second Bank of the United States, the Biddle Hall portico supports a pediment with a shallow roof pitch that helps emphasize the width and grandeur of the colonnade. Biddle Hall served as a naval school between 1839 and 1845, and as the headquarters building of the hospital and

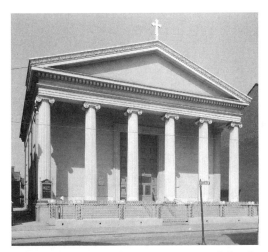

Figure 3.48. *St. Andrew's Protestant Episcopal Church, 1822, in Philadelphia. Historic American Buildings Survey photograph, 1958, HABS PA,51-PHILA,667-1.*

health-care facility for retired naval personnel until 1976, when it was declared surplus government property. Although listed on the Philadelphia Register of Historic Places in 1956, the National Register of Historic Places in 1972, and declared a National Historic Landmark in 1975, the property has since suffered from neglect and fire damage. At the time of this writing, however, plans are under way by a private developer to convert the facility to housing.[55]

The Greek Revival style became a favorite for religious buildings in the United States from the 1820s through the 1850s. Many featured grand-columned porticos on their gable fronts that symbolically formed portals that bridged thresholds between sacred and secular realms. While many architects and builders employed full-width porticos with tall columns supporting a pediment of a gabled roof, some Greek Revival churches were built with recessed loggias or simple engaged porticos. Among the first churches designed in the temple form in the Greek Revival style in the United States were the First Presbyterian Church and St. Andrew's

Protestant Episcopal Church in Philadelphia. These were both designed by the London-trained architect John Haviland, who moved to the city in 1816. St. Andrew's Protestant Episcopal Church (figure 3.48), designed in 1822, follows the form of the ancient Greek Temple of Dionysus at Teos, with a prostyle hexastyle Ionic portico constructed of wood.[56]

Designed in 1836 in the Greek Revival style by architect Thomas U. Walter, the Doric hexastyle portico on Andalusia (figure 3.49) in Bucks County, Pennsylvania, is an important early example of the Greek temple form used on a residence. Andalusia was the home of Nicholas Biddle, who served as president of the Second Bank of the United States.[57]

One of the best-known Canadian examples of a Greek Revival–style residence was Temple Grove (figure 3.50), built around 1837 for Judge John Samuel McCord in Montreal. Located on a picturesque landscaped site on the slopes of Mount Royal overlooking the city of Montreal, this house featured a prominent temple front surrounded on three sides by a Doric colonnade.[58]

The Greek Revival design that Ammi Burnham Young produced in 1833 for the Vermont State House (figure 3.51) in Montpelier helped to establish a national reputation for this architect, born in 1798 in Lebanon, New Hampshire. Based on the ancient Temple of Hephaestus (also known as the Theseion) in Athens (figure 3.16), the temple-front portico of the Vermont State House features six colossal Doric columns, each made from six stacked pieces of white granite quarried on Cobble Hill in nearby Barre, Vermont. Although the building was severely damaged by fire in 1857, Young's Doric portico was repaired and retained as part of the larger replacement building.[59]

Figure 3.49. *A Greek Revival–style portico in the Doric order fronts Andalusia in Bucks County, Pennsylvania, designed by architect Thomas U. Walter in 1836. Historic American Buildings Survey photograph, 1976, HABS PA,9-ANDA,1-11.*

Figure 3.50. *Temple Grove, circa 1837, Montreal. Photograph by Alexander Henderson (detail), 1872, McCord Museum, MP-0000.33.1.*

Figure 3.51. *Vermont State House, Montpelier. The impressive granite Greek Doric front portico was designed in 1833 by Ammi Burnham Young, architect.*

Figure 3.52. *The Boston Customs House, designed in the Greek Revival style by architect Ammi Burnham Young in 1837, as seen in a circa 1905 postcard view.*

Figure 3.53. *Surmounted by a pediment, six Ionic columns line the hexastyle portico on the west facade of the Timothy Follett House, built in 1840 in Burlington, Vermont.*

Ammi Burnham Young also designed the Boston Customs House (figure 3.52) in the Greek Revival style in 1837. It is surrounded by an engaged peristyle colonnade in the Doric order. Two prostyle hexastyle porticos provide grand formal entrances. Between 1913 and 1915, its shallow Roman dome was replaced by a 496-foot-high tower, which became Boston's first skyscraper and remained its tallest building until the 1940s.

Standing like a temple, with its front portico overlooking shipping piers and harbor on Lake Champlain, another prominent example of Ammi Burnham Young's residential work that typifies the Greek Revival style is the Timothy Follett House (figure 3.53), built in 1840 in Burlington, Vermont.

By the 1830s and 1840s, the embrace of the Greek Revival style produced a transformation of the appearance of the built

Figure 3.54. *This detail from a mid-1800s stereograph view of Edgartown, Nantucket Island, Massachusetts, shows a vernacular Greek Revival style–building painted all white except for the dark, louvered blinds. A single-story Doric pentastyle portico dresses the gable end, and a small matching Doric distyle portico shelters a side entrance on the left. Both are crowned with entablatures and balustrades of solid panels and turned balusters. Courtesy of Special Collections, University of Vermont.*

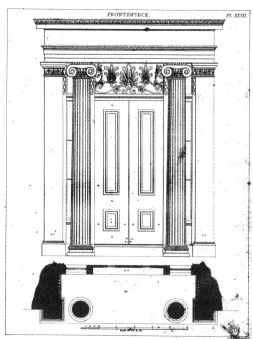

Figure 3.55. *Design for a frontispiece with an Ionic in antis portico. Asher Benjamin,* Builder's Guide *(1839).*

landscape in North America that was noticeable to travelers from oversees. In an 1837 discussion of North American architecture, the English architect John Claudius Loudon observed, "Of late, it has become much the fashion to build country houses in the form of a Grecian temple, with a projecting portico in front, resting on very magnificent columns."[60]

Even Charles Dickens, the popular English author, noted the prevalence of Classical Revival and Greek Revival porticos while traveling in 1842 through New England, where "every house is the whitest of the white; every Venetian blind the greenest of the green; every fine day's sky the bluest of the blue." But according to Dickens, the shallow rows of columns on these buildings seemed built more for visual effect:

"There was the usual aspect of newness on every object, of course. All the buildings looked as if they had been built and painted that morning, and could be taken down on Monday with very little trouble. In the keen evening air, every sharp outline looked a hundred times sharper than ever. The clean cardboard colonnades had no more perspective than a Chinese bridge on a teacup, and appeared equally well calculated for use."[61]

In addition to the influence of architect-designed showplaces, pattern books produced by Asher Benjamin (1773–1845), Minard Lefever (1798–1854), and others also helped to promote the Greek Revival style by offering detailed drawings of portico designs, as well as suggested elevations for various building types. From these pattern books, local carpenters and builders worked

Figure 3.56. *The Governor's Mansion in Austin, Texas, completed in 1856, features a two-story hexastyle portico in the Ionic order, as seen in this circa 1909 postcard view.*

RENAISSANCE REVIVAL

As interest in the Greek Revival style eventually waned in the United States during the 1850s, the Renaissance Revival and Italianate styles soon became popular. As part of the Victorian Picturesque movement, the eclectic designs of the Italianate style soon drifted away from the formal classicism of the earlier styles. Based more on a mixture of Italian Renaissance motifs than on documented examples of ancient Greek or Roman architecture, this new style offered architects more artistic freedom. Although porches were typical features of most Italianate style houses, porticos, loggias, and colonnades were also used on some grand Renaissance Revival–style buildings, especially those constructed to serve residential, governmental, and institutional uses.

Important examples of Renaissance Revival–style buildings with prominent porticos, loggias, and colonnades include Belmont (figure 3.57), a villa built in 1850 in Nashville, Tennessee, and the Galveston Customs House (figure 3.58), built between 1859 and 1861 in Galveston, Texas.[63]

A typical character-defining feature of colonnades designed in the Renaissance Revival and the Italianate styles is the use of arched spandrels between the columns along the entablature. These were sometimes ornamented with keystones at the midpoints of the arches and with decorative moldings. As polychromatic schemes became popular on buildings during the Victorian era, such applied moldings and other architectural details were sometimes accented with colored paints. The Fort William Henry Hotel (figure 3.59), for example, built in the Renaissance Revival style in 1854 at Lake George, New York, featured a majestic Corinthian colonnade with arched spandrels

with building owners to develop fashionable designs for houses, banks, and hotels; for other commercial, civic, and religious buildings; and for additions and alterations to existing structures. Asher Benjamin's *Builder's Guide*, first published in 1839, was especially popular with those working in the Greek Revival style during the 1840s.

The popularity of the Greek Revival style was not confined to New England or the Northeast. Although less common in Canada, many important examples of government buildings, religious structures, and houses—from small vernacular gable-front homes to the impressive colonnaded Southern plantation mansions—were built in this style across the settled areas of the United States through the 1850s.

A well-known example is the Governor's Mansion (figure 3.56) in Austin, Texas, completed in 1856. With a two-story hexastyle portico in the Ionic order supporting an entablature without a pediment, this mansion was designed in the Greek Revival style by the talented local master builder, Abner Cook.[62]

Figure 3.57. *Corinthian columns accent the recessed entrance portico (or loggia) and side projecting porches on the Renaissance Revival–style villa, Belmont, built in 1850 in Nashville, Tennessee. Historic American Building Survey photograph, 1940, TENN-19-NASH,2-2.*

Figure 3.58. *The Galveston Customs House in Galveston, Texas, was built between 1859 and 1861 in the Renaissance Revival style with two-story loggias recessed along the north and south sides and a two-story projecting portico at the west end, all featuring Ionic columns below and Corinthian columns above. Historic American Buildings Survey photograph, 1936, HABS TEX,84-GALV,12-1.*

Figure 3.59. *The majestic Corinthian colonnade with arched spandrels accented by polychromatic moldings provided guests with a grand setting for stagecoach arrivals and departures at the Fort William Henry Hotel, built in the Renaissance Revival style in 1854 at Lake George, New York, as seen in this late 1800s Stoddard stereograph.*

Figure 3.60. *This design for a "Country Home for North or South" featured a prominent colonnade with arched spandrels surrounding the mansion and a projecting semicircular ombra at the front. Gervase Wheeler,* Homes for the People *(1867).*

Figure 3.61. *Reportedly based on plans of a house displayed at the 1876 Centennial Exposition in Philadelphia, this Italianate-style house in Anderson, South Carolina, features arched spandrels between the front veranda posts. Historic American Buildings Survey photograph, 1960, HABS SC,4-AND,6-1.*

Figure 3.62. *This Neoclassical Revival–style porch with balustrades and Ionic columns was added to former president Benjamin Harrison's house in Indianapolis, in 1895.*

accented by polychromatic moldings. This hotel burned in 1908.[64]

In his book, *Homes for the People*, Gervase Wheeler offered several designs for Italianate-style villas featuring colonnades with arched spandrels, including a "Country Home for North or South" (figure 3.60).[65] With keystone-ornamented arched spandrels between the front veranda posts and with turned balusters on the balustrades, the design for an Italianate-style house (figure 3.61) in Anderson, South Carolina, was reportedly based on plans of a house displayed at the 1876 Centennial Exposition in Philadelphia.[66]

NEOCLASSICAL REVIVAL

Although the use of classical porticos and colonnades waned somewhat during the later Victorian era, the rise in popularity of the Neoclassical Revival style during the late nineteenth and early twentieth centuries brought many renewed applications of these classical forms. Some early examples show a continuation of the inventive spirit of the Victorian aesthetic, whereas later works by such architectural firms as McKim, Mead, and White were rooted in a deep respect for formal classical design motifs and proportions.

Thus, when the former U.S. president Benjamin Harrison returned to his circa 1874 Italianate-style home (figure 3.62) in Indianapolis, Indiana, in 1895, he chose the Neoclassical Revival style for building a new large front porch with Ionic columns to replace a small front stoop and the small side porch where he gave some of his famous "front porch" speeches while campaigning for the presidency in 1888.[67]

An outstanding local example of the Neoclassical Revival style in Hannibal, Missouri, is the Rockcliffe Mansion (figure 3.63), built in 1901 with a colossal front portico, a porte-cochere, and a side porch.[68] In Tucson, Arizona, the distinctive Schneider-Healy House

Figure 3.63. *With paired Corinthian columns supporting its colossal front portico, the Neoclassical Revival–style 1901 Rockcliffe Mansion in Hannibal, Missouri, also features a porte-cochere with paired Tuscan columns at the right and a matching side porch at the left. Historic American Buildings Survey photograph, 1966, HABS mo24.*

Figure 3.64. *This Doric colonnade on the front of the Schneider-Healy House in Tucson, Arizona, was designed in the Neoclassical Revival style by architect Henry Trost in 1902.*

(figure 3.64) was designed in 1902 in the Neoclassical Revival style by architect Henry Trost. Its colonnade featuring fluted columns and their exaggerated octagonal capitals are examples of the Paestum variation of the Doric order, based on those found in temple ruins of an ancient Greek colony (circa 530 to 460 BCE) in Paestum, Italy.[69]

Some of the most memorable public and institutional buildings and monuments in North America of the first half of the twentieth century have featured grand porticos and colonnades. Many of these Neoclassical Revival–style designs were based on Roman and Italian Renaissance forms, but some have been based on ancient Greek forms.

The front colonnade of Pennsylvania Station (figure 3.65) in New York City, designed in 1910 by the McKim, Mead, and White architectural firm, provided the main elevation with the timeless dignity of one of the world's most important Neoclassical Revival–style buildings. The public outrage that followed the 1960s demolition of this masterpiece helped to launch the national historic preservation movement in the United States.[70]

With its elevation appearing on the reverse side of U.S. pennies, another well-known Neoclassical Revival-style landmark is the Lincoln Memorial (figure 3.66) in Washington, DC. Instead of using a Roman classical order, architect Henry Bacon based the design on the form of a Greek temple in the Doric order with a peristyle colonnade. Built between 1914 and 1922, the memorial temple measures 204 feet by 134 feet. Its thirty-six peripteral columns of white Colorado marble rise 44 feet high.[71]

Other examples of iconic buildings and monuments with porticos built in the Neoclassical Revival style during this period include the United States Supreme Court

Figure 3.65. *With its grand front colonnade, Pennsylvania Station in New York City, designed in 1910 by McKim, Mead, and White, was one of the world's most important Neoclassical Revival–style buildings. Historic American Buildings Survey photograph, 1962,* HABS NY,31-NEYO,78-2.

Figure 3.66. *Surrounded by a colonnade of thirty-six Doric columns, the Lincoln Memorial, started in 1914, was designed by Henry Bacon in the form of a Greek temple. Historic American Buildings Survey photograph, 1995,* HABS dc206.

Figure 3.67. *The facade of the United States Supreme Court building in Washington, DC, designed by architect Cass Gilbert in 1929, features an octastyle portico in the form of a Roman temple, with two ranks of Italian marble Corinthian columns. Historic American Buildings Survey photograph, 1975, HABS DC,WASH,535-2.*

Figure 3.68. *The Jefferson Memorial in Washington, DC, built between 1939 and 1942, was designed by John Russell Pope in the form of the Roman Pantheon temple, with a circumferential colonnade and portico in the Ionic order. Historic American Buildings Survey photograph, 1991, HABS DC,WASH,453-7.*

Building and the Jefferson Memorial in Washington, DC. Authorized by Congress in 1929, the Supreme Court Building (figure 3.67) was designed by Cass Gilbert, whose fame as an architect had been earned through his designs for the Minnesota State Capitol (1895–1905), Arkansas State Capitol (1900–1917), West Virginia State Capitol (1924–32), and the Woolworth Building in New York City, which was the world's tallest skyscraper when completed in 1913.[72] The most striking feature of the Supreme Court Building's front, west-facing facade is its portico that projects in the form of a Roman temple, with two ranks of Corinthian columns carved of Siena marble from Liguria, Italy.[73]

The Jefferson Memorial (figure 3.68) was built in Washington, DC, between 1939 and 1942, based on a design by John Russell Pope that has the general form of the ancient Roman Pantheon temple (figure 3.17), with a pedimented portico connected to a domed rotunda, surrounded by an Ionic colonnade. The front portico is supported by twelve columns of Vermont Danby white marble. Each measures forty-one feet high. The circumferential colonnade has twenty-six matching columns.[74]

ARCADES

Formed by series of connected arches or vaults, arcades share many liminal qualities with other forms of porches. Although arcades have been commonly used as sheltered linear passageways, protected recessed spaces formed by small arcades also may be considered loggias. Some arcaded loggias may be used as entry porches, and others may be more private quasi-sheltered spaces. When constructed of brick or stone, the exposed surfaces of arcades may be finished and ornamented with lime plaster or cement-based rendering materials known locally as parging, stucco, or plaster. This parging, which is typically applied in several successive layers with trowels and molding tools, also may act as a sacrificial layer that can be patched or replaced as necessary. These innately durable and sustainable aspects of the design have long fostered the use of arcades for high-value public buildings in a broad range of climates.

Some of the earliest examples of arcades date back to the architecture of the ancient Romans, who between the last century BCE and the first century CE, had perfected innovative masonry construction techniques that combined structural arches with the use of mortars and concretes. By using volcanic ash and pumice, some of these Roman mortars had pozzolanic properties that could harden like hydraulic cement, thus facilitating the efficient erection of durable piers, arches, and vaults for arcades by using temporary wooden forms. Voids within these arcade piers and vaults were also filled with concrete made from hydraulic mortars and stone aggregates. By the fifth and sixth centuries CE, however, Roman construction methods generally had shifted toward the use of fired bricks, stone, and mortars instead of concrete for arcades, vaults, and domes.[75]

Arcades were developed further as architectural forms during the Romanesque period by the mid-eleventh century, especially with refinements of "continuous orders" initiated in Southern Europe. These utilized the repetition of rounded arched openings through arcades, as well as moldings and stringcourses, to form repetitive series of vertical and horizontal architectural elements.[76] Whether supported by piers, columns, or both, Romanesque arcades provided continuous openings for light and

Figure 3.69. *The Presbytere features a deep simple arcade supported by load-bearing masonry piers that extend along its entire first story facing Jackson Square in New Orleans. Historic American Buildings Survey photograph, 1934, HABS LA,36-NEWOR,5-1.*

Figure 3.70. *The simple pier arcade at the Mission San Miguel Archangel in San Miguel, California, features twelve arched openings. This is one of the most significant surviving examples of Spanish colonial architecture in the United States. Photochrom view copyrighted by the Detroit Photographic Company in 1898, Library of Congress Prints and Photographs Division, LC-DIG-ppmsca-17980.*

access through load-bearing walls, as well as for sheltering passageways within, between, and along perimeters of buildings. Arcades were also important elements of Gothic architecture, with the openings characterized by pointed arches, instead of the rounded forms of the Romanesque. Long used in public spaces for sheltering small retail shops and stalls in Europe and in other parts of the world, extended arcades may be recessed into the mass of buildings or added as projections along outsides or facing interior courtyards. These traditional forms were brought to the New World and became important features of North American architecture.

Two types of arcades are most common: simple arcades and regular arcades. Simple arcades have arches separated by spandrels that spring from masonry piers. Arcades with piers typically can carry heavier loads than arcades that depend on columns for support. These piers may be constructed of stone, brick, or concrete, and may be surfaced with a stucco plaster finish. Some simple arcades have piers that are finished to look like clusters of small columns or colonnettes. Outstanding examples of simple arcades used as passageways that date from the period of Spanish rule in North America include those on the Presbytere (figure 3.69), built between about 1791 and 1813 in New Orleans and the Mission San Miguel Archangel (figure 3.70) in San Miguel, California, which was constructed of adobe bricks between 1816 and 1818.[77]

Regular arcades have evenly spaced arches that spring from single columns. Each of these columns is typically set on a base and has a capital that supports an impost block at the base of the spandrel of each arch. The columns of regular arcades are commonly made from solid quarried stone; however, they may also be made from bricks or masonry units. Whether supported by piers or columns, the spandrels of arcades are often enriched with decorations, including paterae, which are dishlike ornaments. An example of a regular arcade that serves as a passageway surrounds the inner courtyard of the Boston Public Library (figure 3.71), which opened in 1895. Designed by architect Charles Follen McKim, this arcaded space bears strong similarities to the Palazza della Cancelleria in Rome, constructed during the Italian Renaissance between 1489 and 1513.[78]

During the late 1700s and early 1800s, simple arcades also were being used to support the masonry bases of raised porticos and colonnades, as seen in some Federal and Classical Revival–style works by Charles Bulfinch (figures 3.27, 3.28, and 3.29) and Robert Mills (figure 3.46). For these, the round arch form was most commonly used, but the elliptical arch also gained later popularity for loggias and arcaded piazza openings. Moreover, small arcades of several bays have also been used for entry loggias. An example is the three-bay rusticated stone arcade that forms the raised rear entrance of the James Gibbs–inspired English-American colonial Palladian country house, Mount Airy (figure 3.72), built between 1758 and 1762 in Richmond County, Virginia.[79]

More complex types are coupled arcades and alternating arcades. Coupled arcades are supported by paired columns. Alternating arcades have arches separated by spandrels that spring from two columns that are spaced to resemble the *serliana* or Palladian motif.

Regarded as a classical Roman or Renaissance form and thus rarely used with the Greek Revival style, Asher Benjamin did acknowledge the use of arcades in the 1840s in his pattern book, *The Architect or Practical*

Figure 3.71. *A regular arcade surrounds the inner courtyard of the Boston Public Library, which opened in 1895, as seen in this early 1900s postcard view.*

Figure 3.72. *A three-bay rusticated stone arcade marks the rear entrance loggia at Mount Airy, a Georgian-style country house in Richmond County, Virginia. Historic American Buildings Survey photograph, 1971, HABS VA,80-WAR.V,4-6.*

House Carpenter: "When an aperture in a wall is too wide to be lintelled, it is arched over, and receives the appellation of an arcade, which term, in the plural number, indicates a continued range of such apertures. They are not so magnificent as colonnades, but are stronger, more solid, and less expensive."[80]

Simple arcades became favored features of the picturesque Italianate-style designs that became popular in North America

Classical Order 139

DESIGN VIII.

A VILLA IN THE ITALIAN STYLE.

Fig. 64.

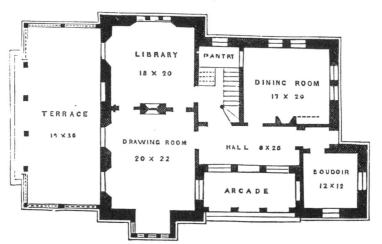

PRINCIPAL FLOOR

Figure 3.73. *A three-bay simple pier arcade with impost moldings at the tops of the piers and paterae in the spandrels serves as the front loggia entrance on this Italianate villa design. A. J. Downing,* Cottage Residences *(1842).*

during the mid-nineteenth century. A. J. Downing included an example of a three-bay front arcade for an Italian villa design in *Cottage Residences*, first published in 1842 (figure 3.73). This simple "arcade or Italian veranda," opened directly to a hall, from which connected all the principal rooms of the first floor.[81]

The English-born American architect Calvert Vaux discussed the visual effects of arcades in his 1857 book, *Villas and Cottages*, and provided a sketch of a two-story arcade design (figure 3.74).

> Recessed arches and arcades will always produce a capital contrast of light and shade if introduced with any judgment, and deserve, I think, more attention than they seem to receive. They differ materially, both in accommodation and artistic effect, from verandas. The arcade being inclosed on three sides, affords much more shelter from weather, throws a deeper shadow, and is more secluded from observation; while the piazza, which is always exposed on two sides, and generally on three, is more open to the cool breezes in hot weather. Arcades should, therefore, be introduced in connection with, and not instead of verandas.[82]

Arcade porches have also been constructed with pointed Gothic arches instead of with the more common round or elliptical arches. An important example of an arcade porch built in the Gothic Revival style lines the rear first story of the "Old Main" building (figure 3.75) at Bethany College in Bethany, West Virginia. Designed by Cincinnati architects Walter and Wilson, this large, brick college building was constructed between 1858 and 1871.[83]

Arcades of the Richardsonian Roman-

Figure 3.74. *Sketch of an Italianate-style simple arcade. The arched openings with keystone enrichments are supported by paneled piers, and the low balustrades have turned, urn-shaped balusters. Calbert Vaux,* Villas and Cottages *(1857); courtesy of Special Collections, University of Vermont.*

esque style that became popular by the 1880s for academic, religious, and institutional buildings in North America were typically supported by squat, stone columns with Romanesque cushion capitals, such as on the regular arcades surrounding the quads at Stanford University (figure 3.76) in Palo Alto, California, built between 1887 and 1891.[84]

Other Richardsonian Romanesque–style passageway arcades and arcaded entry porches used stone piers formed of clustered colonnettes. Built in 1891 in the Richardsonian Romanesque style to designs by local architect Lambert Packard, the Fairbanks Museum (figure 3.77) in Saint

Figure 3.75. *A Gothic Revival–style arcade measuring more than three hundred feet long serves as a passageway recessed into the rear elevation of the "Old Main" building at Bethany College in Bethany, West Virginia. Historic American Buildings Survey photograph, 1979, HABS WVA,5-BETH,3-12.*

Figure 3.76. *The regular arcades supported by squat columns surrounding the Inner Quad at Stanford University in Palo Alto, California, were built between 1887 and 1891 in the Richardsonian Romanesque style. Historic American Buildings Survey photograph, 1975, HABS CAL,43-STANF,10-9.*

Figure 3.77. *The entry porch of the Fairbanks Museum, built in the Richardsonian Romanesque style in 1891 in Saint Johnsbury, Vermont, features a simple arcade with Syrian arches of Longmeadow sandstone and piers carved with colonnettes.*

Figure 3.78. *This alternating arcade added to Trinity Church in Boston in 1897 has paired columns that flank the major arched entrances and solid piers decorated with colonnettes. Historic American Buildings Survey photograph, 1987, HABS MASS,13-BOST,131-11.*

Figure 3.79. *The east arcade at Union Station in Washington, DC, designed by Daniel Burnham, was constructed between 1903 and 1908 with simple arcades supported by massive granite piers and Guastavino tiles covering the vaulted ceiling. Historic American Buildings Survey photograph, 1974,* HABS DC,WASH,536-15.

Figure 3.80. *The 1928 landmark west arcade of the west entrance to Los Angeles City Hall combines Romanesque details and modern forms. Note the vaulted ceiling of Guastavino tiles above and the Romanesque columns of this regular arcade. Historic American Buildings Survey photograph, 1997,* HABS CAL,19-LOSAN,51-37.

Johnsbury, Vermont, features a thirteen-foot-wide arcaded porch. Formed by Syrian arches of Longmeadow sandstone, the three side arches rest on ornamented impost blocks that are supported by piers carved as engaged colonnettes, clustered five wide and two deep. These piers are connected by balustrades with urn-shaped balusters. Paterae ornament the wall spandrels between the arches, bearing carved likenesses of the noted nineteenth-century naturalists, John James Audubon, Louis Agassiz, and Alexander von Humboldt.[85] A front entrance porch with Romanesque Revival–style arches supported by paired and engaged colonnettes was added in 1897 to Trinity Church (figure 3.78) in Boston. It was designed by Hugh Shepley of H. H.

Richardson's successor firm, Shepley, Rutan, and Coolidge.[86]

In addition to the Richardsonian Romanesque style, arcades also were favored features of the Beaux Arts and Neoclassical styles of the late-nineteenth and early-twentieth centuries, especially for institutional and civic buildings. Some outstanding examples of these have vaulted arcades finished in decorative tile. The most striking are the interlocking terra cotta tile vaults that are named for their designer, the Spanish engineer Raphael Guastavino, whose company was based in New York City and whose impressive arcades and domes were featured in many important Beaux Arts and Neoclassical–style structures.[87]

The Beaux Arts style, which was based on

an eclectic array of classical French and Italian Renaissance models, got its name from the École des Beaux-Arts, the French school of arts and architecture at which some of the world's top architects were trained during the nineteenth century. Notable American architects who designed in the Beaux Arts style include Daniel Burnham, who supervised the construction of the 1893 World's Columbian Exposition in Chicago, which helped to launch the City Beautiful movement, and Charles Follen McKim of the architectural firm of McKim, Mead, and White. Outstanding examples of large Beaux Arts–style public buildings with arcades with Guastavino tile vaults include Union Station (figure 3.79) in Washington, DC, designed by Daniel Burnham and constructed between 1903 and 1908, and Los Angeles City Hall (figure 3.80) built in 1928.[88]

4

Various Forms

Although the most common form of entry porch in North America has open sides and a roof supported by posts, there is also a long history of attached porches being enclosed with walls to provide protection for entrances.[1] Indeed such enclosed entry porches were being attached to houses, barns, and other buildings to protect entrances during Elizabethan times in Britain, as well as in New England by the late 1660s and early 1700s.[2] Such enclosed entry porches were also being attached to various types of Georgian-style buildings built by the mid-1700s, especially in New England and in the Canadian Maritimes. Some of these gabled projections featured classical pediments above six-panel doors flanked by pilasters, such as on the circa 1745 Georgian-style Daniel Shute House (figure 4.1) in Hingham, Massachusetts.[3]

Enclosed porches were also appended to meetinghouses built during the second half of the eighteenth century in New England. Single-stairwell porches centered on the front elevations were popular on meetinghouses constructed in coastal communities of New England during this period.[4] The Old Ship Church, started in 1681 in Hingham, Massachusetts, for example, had an enclosed attached porch added in 1755 on the southeast side and another porch (figure 4.2) constructed on the southwest side in 1792.[5] The Rockingham Meetinghouse (figure 4.3), built in the Georgian style between 1787 and 1801 in Rockingham, Vermont, has twin two-story porches with enclosed stairwells, one at each gable end. An important Canadian example of a two-story, enclosed attached porch is on the Commissariat House (figure 4.4) in Saint John's, Newfoundland, built between 1818 and 1820 by British military engineers.[6]

Figure 4.1. *A small, hipped-roof enclosed entry porch with bull's-eye glass transom lights over the front door were features of the Daniel Shute House, built around 1745 in Hingham, Massachusetts. Historic American Buildings Survey photograph, 1935, HABS MASS,12-HING,7-4.*

Figure 4.2. *The enclosed gable-roofed entry porch at the right was added in 1792 to the Old Ship Church in Hingham, Massachusetts. Historic American Buildings Survey, Frank O. Branzetti, photographer, 1941, HABS MASS,12-HING,5-15.*

Figure 4.3. *Two-story, gable-roofed enclosed porches with stairwells within provide access to the upper floor of the Rockingham Meetinghouse in Rockingham, Vermont, built between 1787 and 1801.*

Figure 4.4. *The Commissariat House in Saint John's, Newfoundland, built between 1818 and 1820, and restored to a circa 1830s appearance, features a two-story, enclosed entry porch.*

Figure 4.5. *An enclosed front entry porch with small-paned window sashes and a matching storm door shelters the front entrance of this circa 1915 Colonial Revival–style house in Burlington, Vermont.*

Small, enclosed entry porches also became popular features of Colonial Revival–style homes and other houses built during the twentieth century, especially in northern regions with cold or blustery climates. This shift back to enclosed entry porches reflects the declining popularity of broad front verandas across North America during this period. Often fitted with fixed or operable windows, these small, enclosed entry porches were typically built to provide sheltered transitional spaces with just enough standing room for greeting guests and for dealing with boots, umbrellas, and snow shovels, rather than serving as outdoor living spaces.

OPEN ATTACHED ENTRY PORCHES

Although columned porticos were distinctive features of some noteworthy mansions and institutional buildings in North America during the late colonial period, open attached entry porches of simpler designs have since become very common features of

buildings in the United States and Canada. Indeed these are now the most common type of porches to be found.

As early as 1786, the *Rule Book* of the Carpenters' Company of Philadelphia included prices for such simple entry porches "with posts of pine or oak scantling, the heads turn'd" or with "posts cap'd" or "with red cedar posts."[7] One common form is the gable-fronted attached entry porch supported by boxed pillars that serve as corner posts. This form features a gable roof that is oriented to allow rainwater to flow off the sides, instead of dripping onto the front-facing steps. Designed mainly to shelter entrances without preventing daylight from entering side rooms, some gable-fronted attached entry porches have been just large enough to provide space for some occasional seating, as on the General Samuel Strong House (figure 4.6), built in the late Georgian style in 1796 in Vergennes, Vermont. Unfortunately, this porch, which was documented by the Historic American Buildings Survey in 1936 is no longer standing.[8]

A surviving example, however, of a circa 1814 Federal-style attached entry porch with boxed corner posts and a simple pediment with cornice returns can be found in nearby Ferrisburgh, Vermont, on the front of the Rokeby farmhouse (figure 4.7), a National Historic Landmark once associated with the Underground Railroad. A circa 1890 photograph in the collection of the museum shows the owners' extended family seated on the side benches of this front porch, surrounded by the simple Federal-style railings that are still in place. The scroll-sawn lower skirting was probably added in the late 1800s.[9]

The functionality of this form and size of porch has helped to promote its use with minor variations as architectural styles have evolved. A representative example of a

Figure 4.7. *This circa 1814 gable-fronted attached entry porch with built-in seating and boxed pillars surrounds the formal front doorway at the Rokeby farmhouse in Ferrisburgh, Vermont.*

Figure 4.6. *A small, gable-fronted attached entry porch with boxed pillars, elaborate Doric details on the entablature and pediment, and curved side benches formerly stood on the northeast side of the General Samuel Strong House, built in 1796 in Vergennes, Vermont. Historic American Buildings Survey photograph, 1936, HABS VT,1-VERG,1-5.*

Figure 4.8. *The Greek Revival–style attached entry porch on the Daniel Griffith House in Saint Charles, Missouri, was built in 1836 with boxed pillars and Ionic columns supporting a pedimented gable-front roof. Historic American Buildings Survey photograph, 1937, HABS MO,92-SAICH.V,2-3.*

gable-fronted attached entry porch designed in the Greek Revival style is on the Daniel Griffith House (figure 4.8), built in 1836 in Saint Charles, Missouri. Other common forms of attached entry porches feature flat roofs, shallow hipped roofs, or shed roofs. A typical vernacular Greek Revival–style example of an attached entry porch with a shallow hipped roof was added about 1840 to the older Sheppard-Crump Farmhouse (figure 4.9), which has been preserved at the Meadow Farm Museum in Henrico County, Virginia.

Catherine Beecher, an influential American educator and advocate for women's issues, who wrote about how the designs of houses could be improved to better serve the needs of their inhabitants, offered the following observations about the protective functions of entry porches in 1845: "In the ground-floor plan . . . is the porch, which projects enough to afford an entrance to the two adjacent rooms, and thus avoids the evil of an outside door to a sitting room."[10]

Whether to shelter a front, side, or rear

Figure 4.9. *An attached hipped-roofed entry porch with boxed pillars and railings with square balusters was added about 1840 to the Sheppard-Crump Farmhouse in Henrico County, Virginia.*

entrance, the basic form of the small, attached entry porch continued to evolve through the nineteenth century to serve practical needs for both high-style and vernacular North American houses. Although the broad wraparound veranda became associated with the Queen Anne style, attached entry porches were also often used for sheltering primary or secondary entrances. An example of a Queen Anne–style attached entry porch (figure 4.10) was shown in H. Hudson Holly's influential book, *Modern Dwellings*, published in 1878.[11]

The popularity of the attached entry porch form continued through the twentieth century, especially as a functional substitute for the broad piazzas and verandas of the Victorian era. Examples of such attached entry porches may be seen in the section on Colonial Revival–style porches in chapter 5.

SIDE AND REAR PORCHES

Although the fronts of houses and other buildings were the logical locations for porticos and entrance porches, advantages of practicality and convenience could sometimes gained by placing porches, piazzas, and verandas on side or rear elevations. Indeed for many households, use of the front entrance was traditionally reserved for such formal occasions as greeting special guests, whereas side entrances provided informal routine access for regular inhabitants and those making deliveries or providing services. Many of the service entrances sheltered by such porches open directly into a service hall or kitchen. Slightly out of full public view, some side porches also could provide opportunities for various discreet domestic uses, especially when connected to bedrooms or dining rooms. One of the oldest examples of a house with large side piazzas in New England is the Vassal-Craigie-Longfellow House (figure 4.11), built in the Georgian style in 1759 in Cambridge, Massachusetts. According to Historic American Buildings Survey records, its side piazzas were added in 1793.[12]

In addition to single-story side porches, multitiered side porches also were being built on houses by the early 1800s. An example recorded by the Historic American Buildings Survey is the two-tiered recessed side porch with slender Tuscan columns that lines the rear ell of the circa 1812 General George Hutchinson House (figure 4.12), also known as the General Orrin Hutchinson House, in Onandoga Hill, New York.[13] Multistoried side porches also became favorites for houses built on narrow lots, especially in urban areas. An example is the Federal-style Crawford-Cassin House (figure 4.13), built in 1816, which is one of the few remaining dwellings from the period that retains its side porch in the Georgetown area of Washington, DC.[14]

In some urban areas, multistoried houses have also featured side balcony porches on their upper stories for shade and cooling.

Figure 4.10. *This attached entrance porch is an outstanding example of the Queen Anne style. Character-defining features include the four heavy, turned support posts, the turned spindlework above along the side valances, the elaborate carvings in the tympanum of the pediment, and the crenellated cresting along the ridge of the porch's steeply pitched gable roof. Supporting the posts, the base of this entrance porch features brick half-walls capped with decorative stringcourses that flank a series of shallow stone steps and a landing within. From H. Hudson Holly,* Modern Dwellings *(1878), Rare Books and Special Collections, McGill University Library.*

Figure 4.11. *Two large side piazzas supported by Ionic columns and railed with balustrades were added in 1793 to the Vassal-Craigie-Longfellow House in Cambridge, Massachusetts. Circa 1910s postcard.*

Figure 4.12. *A two-tiered, recessed side porch with slender Tuscan columns lines the rear ell of the circa 1812 General George Hutchinson House in Onandoga Hill, New York. Historic American Buildings Survey photograph, 1963, HABS NY,34-ONDA,2-3.*

Figure 4.13. *One of the last remaining Federal-style houses with a two-tiered attached side porch in the Georgetown area of Washington, DC, is the Crawford-Cassin House, built in 1816. The porch features boxed columns, and an embellished cornice matches the cornice on the brick house. Historic American Buildings Survey photograph, 1969, HABS DC,GEO,107-1.*

An 1847 description of New Orleans, for example, mentioned that "there is scarcely a house of one or more stories, without balconies on one or more sides of the second and sometimes third floors."[15] The 1807 Valery Nichols House (figure 4.14) is an early example of a side balcony porch or "gallery" built of wood in New Orleans that has been documented by the Historic American Buildings Survey.[16]

Often connected to kitchens, rear porches have long provided sheltered workspaces that could be used for a wide variety of domestic tasks, as well as for providing access to rear yards. An 1847 description of a "Cheap Farm-House" published in the *American Agriculturalist* even suggested putting a fireplace in a back porch that "in summer will make a pleasant eating-room, unless indeed the 'gude wife' prefers to move her cooking-stove out there in warm weather." The article also recommended that the space between the columns of this

Figure 4.14. *Curved cantilevered timbers support the ceiling above the side gallery on the service wing of the 1807 Valery Nichols House in New Orleans. Historic American Buildings Survey photograph, 1936, HABS LA,36-NEWOR,15-5.*

Figure 4.15. *Vignette of a rear porch intended for servants' use. H. Hudson Holly,* Modern Dwellings, *(1878), Rare Books and Special Collections, McGill University Library.*

back porch could be "closed up in winter if desired."[17] Another writer in 1847 commented in the same magazine, "The farmer's kitchen, besides being large, should be *light and airy*, with a broad *back* porch, well shaded, where the harvest hands could assemble before their meals, to wash or refresh themselves."[18]

On many larger houses built for families with servants through the nineteenth century and early twentieth century, back porches were typically designed to be used as entrances for the domestic workers and for household chores and deliveries.

H. Hudson Holly, for example, offered a vignette of a "rear porch or servant's entrance" (figure 4.15) in his 1878 book, *Modern Dwellings.*[19]

CHARLESTON PIAZZAS

With a history that dates back to the mid-1700s, a distinctive type of side porch is known as the Charleston piazza. This takes its name from the multitiered porches extending along the sides of houses in Charleston, South Carolina, that were built to take advantage of cooling sea breezes.[20] British traveler Captain Basil Hall offered this

Figure 4.16. *Charleston, South Carolina, is known for its distinctive multitiered side piazzas, such as this example on the Charles Edmonston House. This Charleston piazza is ell-shaped, and its top story was screened at the rear. Historic American Buildings Survey photograph, 1940, HABS SC,10-CHAR,101-7.*

description of Charleston piazzas in the 1820s: "What gives Charleston its peculiar character, however, is the verandah, or piazza, which embraces most of the houses on their southern side, and frequently, also, on those which face the east and west. These are not clumsily put on, but constructed in a light Oriental style, extending from the ground to the very top, so that the rooms on each story enjoy the advantage of a shady, open walk."[21]

A noteworthy representative example of a Charleston piazza is on the Charles Edmonston House (figure 4.16) on East Battery Street in Charleston. According to the Historic American Building Survey, the house was built in the late 1820s, but re-decorated in the Classical Revival style after 1838, when the third story of the side piazza and rooftop balustrade and parapets were added. The first story of the side piazza is supported by Tuscan columns, the second story by fluted Doric columns, and the third with Corinthian columns with Scamozzi capitals.[22]

In her 1853 travelogue, the Finnish-born feminist author Fredrika Bremer shared her impressions of America in this (translated) description of a home with a piazza where she stayed while in Charleston:

I must now tell you something about the home in which I am, and in which I find myself so well off, and so happy, that I would not wish for a better. The house, with its noble garden, stands alone in one of the most rural streets of the city, Lynch Street, and has on one side a free view of the country and the river, so that it enjoys the most delicious air—the freshest breezes. Lovely sprays of white roses, and of the scarlet honeysuckle, fling themselves over the piazza, and form the most exquisite veranda. Here I often walk, especially in the early morning and in the evening, inhaling the delicious air, and looking abroad over the country. My room, my pretty airy room, is in the upper story. The principal apartments, which are on the first story, open upon the piazza, where people assemble or walk about in the evening, when there is generally company.[23]

ARCADED PIAZZAS

As elliptical arches became architecturally fashionable with the Classical Revival style during the 1820s and 1830, especially in New England, some house designs featured arched openings. An early representative example of a vernacular New England house with an arcaded front piazza recessed across the full width of its gable front is shown in figure 4.17. This design represents a combination of three important vernacular forms developed in New England during the early decades of the 1800s.

First, this story-and-a-half wooden

building is an "I-house," a term coined by geographer Fred Kniffen in his studies of North American folk housing types to describe houses built only one room deep. Second, the gable-front form of this house reflects a shift away from the earlier, traditional orientation of eaves at the fronts of houses, an innovative design shift that occurred in New England during this period. Both the gable front and the I-house forms subsequently were diffused by settlers to interior parts of the continent during the Westward Movement.[24] The third and most distinctive aspect of the design of this house, however, is its recessed front piazza, comprising five elliptically arched openings. In the context of the history of porches in North America, this represents a significant example of an arcaded piazza being fully integrated into the body and design concept of the house, rather than being a separate attached amenity. The incorporation of this liminal space into the design of the house builds on the popularity of recessed galleries in the American South, but it also reflects an innovative step that would continue to be refined in the Northeast with the development of recessed side-wing porches and gable loggias, discussed below.

The 1840s and 1850s also saw a growing trend to add arcaded piazzas and pavilions to existing houses. In many cases, the various architectural styles of these additions reflected current trends rather than an attempt to expand the building in its original style. This movement also reflected a shift toward an increased acceptance of eclecticism, the creative and sometimes playful, but perhaps naive mixing of architectural styles. An example is the expansion of Montgomery Place, an 1802 Federal-style mansion located next to the Hudson River in Dutchess County, New York. In 1841,

Figure 4.17. *A five-bay arcaded piazza is recessed across the facade of this neglected circa 1820 gable-front I-house in Essex, Vermont.*

Figure 4.18. *This arched pavilion was designed in 1841 by architect Alexander Jackson Davis as an addition for Montgomery Place in Dutchess County, New York. Historic American Buildings Survey photograph, 1979, HABS NY,14-BARTO.V,3-5.*

architect Alexander Jackson Davis was hired to design portico and pavilion additions, which were constructed in 1844.[25]

Projecting from the north facade of Montgomery Place, the pavilion (figure 4.18) combines both Italian Renaissance forms and Greek Revival motifs, with seven arched openings, engaged Grecian Corinthian columns with "Tower of the Winds" capitals and a frieze decorated with palmettes and tendrils. The roof is crowned with an Italian Renaissance style balustrade with turned balusters supporting the railings that stretch between paneled pedestals. An illustration of this pavilion was included in A. J. Downing's *A Treatise on the Theory and Practice of Landscape Gardening: Adapted to North America*, published in 1850.

The Philadelphia-based architect Samuel Sloan helped to continue popularizing arcades and verandas in the Italianate style in the *Architectural Review and American Builder's Journal*. Of the design of houses built in this style, he wrote in 1869: "Of the comfort and convenience of verandahs, arcades, &c, it would be almost superfluous here to speak, for, although not an absolute essential, yet they have become an almost universal appendage, in our country and climate, to every dwelling with any rural pretensions whatever. Apart from their utility, as affording shelter and protection from the weather, they are capable of so much decoration and graceful effect, that they should be taken advantage of, even more fully than they are, in designs for such residences."[26]

As can be seen in some designs by Sloan and other mid-nineteenth-century American architects, arcaded verandas featuring repetitive round-arches became associated with the Italianate style. These designs were sometimes called "Romanesque" by the 1850s, and thus they may be considered direct precursors to the later Richardsonian Romanesque style.[27] An example of an Italianate-style villa with arcaded verandas designed by Sloan was published in 1860 in *Godey's Lady's Book* (figure 4.19). The description of the illustration reads, "we present a design of an Italian villa, with high

Figure 4.19. *Arcaded verandas flank the tower on this Italianate-style design by architect Samuel Sloan of Philadelphia. From* Godey's Lady's Book *(1860); courtesy of Special Collections, University of Vermont.*

Figure 4.20. *Round arches with lacey cutout spandrels line a mid-nineteenth-century curved-roofed, Italianate-style arcaded veranda on this house in Burlington, Vermont.*

tower, bracketed gables, bay windows, and broad projecting verandas, altogether, a pleasing and agreeable combination of that style."[28] Such published designs served as models for similar arcaded verandas (figure 4.20) to be built on houses during this period.

SIDE-WING PORCHES

Both recessed and attached porches also were constructed on the side wings and ells that were extended from the main block of dwellings initially or as subsequent additions. This incremental pattern of building additions has roots in medieval European vernacular traditions. Early examples emerged in some rural areas of New England and in surrounding regions as the economic prosperity of the "sheep boom" during in the 1820s and 1830s supported a wave of incremental investments in existing farmhouses. This trend continued to be followed with the expanding settlements of the canal era and westward migration of the following decades, especially in western New York, Ohio, Indiana, Michigan, and southern Ontario. Such verandas were also being attached to side wings and ells of rural farmhouses between the 1880s and the 1910s in such areas as Canada's maritime province of Prince Edward Island.[29]

Although some fancy showplaces were built during the 1820s and 1830s with gable-front colonnades and loggias, a more restrained pattern of vernacular innovation was the progressive extension of an existing house with the addition of a side wing with a porch. Inside, the wing provided a series of spaces that made a gradual transition, in stages, from domestic to utilitarian uses—from the kitchen, with its large cast-iron cooking range, to a workspace for seasonal tasks, to a privy, to a storage space

for stove wood, grain, tools, and harnesses, and finally perhaps to a covered workspace or shelter for a carriage or sleigh. Although some side wings and ells were built on houses with doorways that connected the spaces internally, often porches were included to provide direct entrances to the kitchen and as sheltered passageways to the connected unheated utilitarian spaces.

Two forms of side-wing porches were commonly built during this period, especially on farmhouses in New England, the upper Midwest, and Ontario. The first form, the recessed side-wing porch (figure 4.21), is characterized by a recessed arcade or loggia sheltered under the main roof of the wing and supported by a solid foundation. Some other examples featured elliptical arches and trim designs associated with the vernacular forms of the Classical Revival style (figures 4.22, 4.23, and 4.24), while later examples may have classical columns and trim inspired by the Greek Revival style, as shown in figure 4.25.[30]

In addition to recessed side-wing porches, a common second form, the attached side-wing porch is characterized by a porch with a shed roof that projects from the sidewall of a house wing or ell as a separate architectural unit. On some examples, the end of the porch roof is hipped, but more commonly a simple half-gable terminates the roof. For these attached side-wing porches, the porch deck and posts typically are supported by piers set in the ground or by stone footings, rather than by full foundations.

In his book *Homes for the People*, Gervase Wheeler included a design (figure 4.26) for a Gothic cottage "intended for the residence of a clergyman in Massachusetts" with a side-wing porch and a front parlor with a bay window projecting ahead of the main block. Of this plan, Wheeler wrote, "The

Figure 4.21. *The recessed side-wing porch on an early 1800s "Cape Cod"–type farmhouse near Plainfield, Vermont, shelters an entrance to the kitchen while providing space for a simple wooden bench and clotheslines. Note the slanted window on the gable end of the house, another vernacular building trait of the region. Courtesy of Special Collections, University of Vermont.*

Figure 4.22. *This recessed side-wing porch on a circa 1820s Vermont "cape" farmhouse is a simple wooden arcade created by recessing the kitchen wall behind two elliptical arches. The third, open, bay leads to a woodshed, workspace, and possibly a privy. Note the beaten path leading to the side-wing porch entrance instead of the front door. Circa 1910s postcard view; courtesy of Special Collections, University of Vermont.*

Figure 4.23. *An elliptical arch and simple pilasters frame the recessed side-wing porch of the F. D. Carpenter House, built in 1830 in Cuyahoga County, Ohio. Historic American Buildings Survey photograph, 1936,* HABS OHIO,18-OLMN,1-4.

Figure 4.24. *An elliptical brick arch frames the front opening of the recessed rear-wing porch of the Abraham Matson House, built in 1840 in St. Charles County, Missouri. Historic American Buildings Survey photograph, 1939,* HABS MO,92-MAT.V,1-5.

Figure 4.25. *With fluted Greek Doric columns flanking its entrance steps, the recessed side-wing porch reflects the Greek Revival style of a circa 1850 "classic cottage" farmhouse in Plainfield, Vermont. Although the many open windows and doors suggest summer heat, note the lack of chairs on the side porch in this image. Instead, the shallow, recessed side-wing porch is being used to shelter more than a dozen potted plants. Late 1800s stereograph; courtesy of Special Collections, University of Vermont.*

Figure 4.26. *Design for a "Gothic Parsonage" with an attached side veranda. Gervase Wheeler,* Homes for the People *(1867).*

Figure 4.27. *Simple square posts resting on stone slabs support this example of an attached side-wing porch with a vine-draped hipped roof. The raking eaves on the gable-fronted main block reflect faint vernacular Gothic Revival–style influences, while the six-over-six windows and the side ell plan all suggest that this house was probably built between the 1850s and the 1870s. Note the small table in the corner of the porch. Postcard published circa 1907 with an inscription that suggests the photograph was taken in Trumbull County, Ohio.*

Figure 4.28. *The attached side-wing porch on this circa 1870s Gothic Revival–style farmhouse in Holderness, New Hampshire, features a hipped roof, turned posts, and turned balusters. A small hip-roofed hood supported by Italianate-style console brackets shelters a small front stoop entrance.*

front projection affords a convenient abutment for a veranda, which serves as an entrance porch to the hall."[31]

Attached side-wing porches also typically have roofs pitched less steeply than the roofs over the adjoining ells. Owing to the shallow pitches, these porch roofs have often been covered with roofing materials such as metal and composition-roll roofing, instead of the lapped shingles or slates used on steeper roofs. Although some vernacular versions may lack such decorative architectural details (figure 4.27), attached side-wing porches that date from the second half of the nineteenth century are typically trimmed with brackets, turned posts, and other features of the Victorian era styles (figure 4.28).

Another type of porch that became common on small houses in some towns and cities is the attached front side porch. These small porches typically have steps on the front end, but they extend along the side to provide direct access to a side entrance near the middle of the house, leaving space for a full-width parlor at the front. The attached shed roofs that shelter front side porches typically continue over an enclosed side hall, forming a single-story shed-roof projection along the side of the house. In some ways the front side porch house plan can be considered to be a "cousin" of the side-hall plan arrangement that became common for houses by the mid-1800s, but instead of having an interior hallway running along one side within the house, the front side porch serves as both a "outside hall" and a partially sheltered entrance.

One mid-nineteenth-century architect who showed examples of house plans with front side porches was James H. Hammond of Boston. In his 1858 book, *The Farmer's and Mechanic's Practical Architect: And Guide in Rural Economy*, Hammond provided plans and specifications for a small "country residence" and a two-story "village residence" that both featured small "piazzas" on the front sides that provided direct access to small entry halls connected to interior rooms.[32]

Advantages of the front side porch house plan include reduced construction and heating costs, as the volume of the interior is reduced. Also, this plan would allow windows on three sides of the front room, which was typically used as a parlor. Relieved of the need for a front door, fashionable projecting bay windows were installed instead on the front wall of the parlors of many of these small houses. An example, seen in figure 4.29, with a five-foot by seven-foot attached front side porch that serves as the main entrance for the house was constructed in 1888 in Burlington, Vermont, by John W. Roberts, a local builder who put up dozens of similar small story-and-half houses.[33]

This plan also allowed houses to be constructed on very narrow lots, while still offering inhabitants the open-air benefits of a small porch. Hence, the design became popular for low-cost rental and worker housing, especially in growing city and village neighborhoods associated with nearby mills and factories. Many of these front side porch plan houses were built a story-and-a-half high with knee-walls providing headroom

Figure 4.29. *An attached front-side porch serves as the main entrance for this house constructed in 1888 in Burlington, Vermont.*

for upstairs bedrooms. Others were built a full two-stories high.

For a small house or cottage, the front side porch plan could serve needs similar to those filled by the shotgun houses of the South. But with the porch scaled down and with a multistory design with upstairs bedrooms, this was better suited to the needs of inhabitants in cooler climates where heat retention of the house was of greater importance than cooling. Providing an alternative to entering through the formal front door, front side porches also have been constructed on many larger homes to provide entranceways to side rooms.

RECESSED MULTITIERED PORCHES

Multitiered porches recessed into gabled facades became popular for stagecoach inns, general stores (figures 4.30 and 4.32), ferry houses (figure 4.31), and other commercial buildings designed in the Federal and

Figure 4.30. *A two-tiered recessed porch with simple Tuscan columns lines the gabled facade of this early-nineteenth-century Federal-style village store at the Four Corners in North Woodbury, Connecticut. Historic American Buildings Survey photograph, 1940, HABS CONN,3-WOON,1-1.*

Figure 4.31. *A two-tiered balcony porch is recessed beneath the front gable of this vernacular Greek Revival–style brick ferry house built in 1845 on the shore of Lake Champlain on North Hero Island, Vermont. The three colossal, octagonal columns were hewn from logs.*

Figure 4.32. *Built in 1852 in the Greek Revival style, the Marshfield General Store in Marshfield, Vermont, features a two-tiered balcony porch recessed beneath the main gable roof. The ceiling of the upper porch is painted light blue on this otherwise white building.*

Greek Revival styles during the first half of the nineteenth century. These could provide shelter to patrons accessing the building at street level, as well as offering a second-story balcony for quasi-private use by the storekeeper's family, guests, or other inhabitants of the spaces above. By being raised off the ground, the upper story of a multi-tiered porch typically provides users with protection from the outside world and a more expansive view, but like a stage, it may also serve as an elevated place for users to be viewed from below. The form continued to be adapted later in the Italianate Revival and Queen Anne styles.

GABLE LOGGIAS

Multitiered porches with loggias recessed into the tympanums of front gables (also known as recessed balcony porches or Connecticut River valley porches) became curious vernacular variations in a geographical region mainly extending from the Eastern Townships of southern Quebec southward down the Connecticut River valley through Vermont and New Hampshire into Massachusetts.[34] Coinciding with the popularity of other multitiered porches discussed above and with the widespread shift toward orienting buildings with their gables facing front, many of the gable loggias were added to existing stagecoach inns and houses between the 1830s and 1850s, straddling the transition from the Neoclassical to the Greek Revival and Gothic Revival architectural styles.

Perhaps first inspired by the common practice of installing decorative windows and fanlights in attic gables, early examples of gable loggias typically featured elliptically arched openings in the gable tympanums. Some were built with trapezoidal or pointed Gothic Revival style arches, while others have rectangular or round-arched openings. Many of the earlier gable loggias with curved openings have ceilings of plaster, whereas later examples have mechanically planed tongue-and-groove boards covering their ceilings. Access to gable loggias typically was provided through a doorway from an upstairs room, and a simple railing was installed across the front for safety. The earliest railings appear to have simple, square-sectioned spindles, but those installed after the 1850s typically have turned balusters similar those seen on other early Victorian era porches and verandas.

The following examples reflect the range of forms found in this geographical region. Figure 4.33 shows a gable loggia that was added in 1830 to the front of a brick house that was built around 1819 in Windsor, Vermont.[35] Similar patterns of history probably

Figure 4.33. *A gable loggia recessed into the tympanum of the pediment is supported by four slender Tuscan columns of the porch beneath. Records show that although this brick house was built about 1819 in Windsor, Vermont, the extended roof, gable loggia, and porch columns were all added when the house was renovated in 1830.*

account for the gable loggia additions on the front of Rowell's Inn (figure 4.34) in Chester, Vermont, and on the example shown in figure 4.35 in nearby Grafton, Vermont.[36]

The gable loggias found in the Eastern Townships of Quebec and the adjacent Connecticut River valley of New England regions reflect a curious example of how apparent local innovations of a distinctive design spread across a transnational geographical area through the process of diffusion. Indeed, with almost as many examples of these gable loggias documented in Quebec as in New England, one is tempted to speculate about the symbolic feelings associated with the design that inspired so many to be built by English-speaking residents in southern Quebec.[37]

One representative example (figure 4.36), with an elliptically arched gable loggia located in the village of Mystic in the Eastern Townships of Quebec, was probably added

Figure 4.34. *The front porch on Rowell's Inn, built in 1820 in Chester, Vermont, was probably a later addition. It features an elliptically arched loggia with a tongue-and-groove wood-paneled ceiling in the tympanum of the gable. Chamfered porch posts, turned balusters, and milled railings on the lower two tiers appear to be later Victorian-era replacements. Note the abundant growth of the Dutchman's pipe vine. Detail from Historic American Buildings Survey photograph, 1960, HABS VT,14-SIMO,1-1.*

Figure 4.35. *This gable loggia with an elliptical arch, plastered ceiling, and simple spindle railings, as well as the two-tiered balcony porch below were added in 1840 to the front of this circa 1826 Federal-style house and stagecoach hotel in Grafton, Vermont.*

in the 1850s to the house that was originally built in 1833.[38] Other examples in Massachusetts (figures 4.37 and 4.38), New Hampshire (figure 4.39), and Vermont (figure 4.40) reflect the tenacity of this curious regional form, even as the dominant architectural styles changed through the mid-nineteenth century.

Although rare, some examples of houses with loggias recessed into gables were built elsewhere during the 1870s through the 1880s. Two in the central midlands region of South Carolina have been listed on the National Register of Historic Places. One in Leesville, South Carolina, was built in 1878.[39]

Architect H. Hudson Holly included a several designs of Queen Anne–style houses with partially recessed balconies in his book *Modern Dwellings*, published in 1878 (figure 4.41). Recessed balconies, as well as

Figure 4.36. *Located in the village of Mystic in the Eastern Townships of Quebec, this house was originally built in 1833. The elliptically arched gable loggia that was probably added in the 1850s has a railing with cast-iron balusters that may have been made at a local foundry. The first story of the house has a recessed veranda supported by square posts on two sides.*

Figure 4.37. *Greek Revival and Gothic Revival styles merge together gracefully on this mid-nineteenth-century house in Sturbridge, Massachusetts. The gable-front form and tapered Doric columns typical of the Greek Revival are combined with the Gothic-arched shapes of the gable loggia and window trim.*

Figure 4.38. *This 1846 Gothic Revival–style house in Belchertown, Massachusetts, features a recessed gable loggia with a Gothic arch opening and a diagonal lattice railing above a four-bay Gothic front veranda.*

Figure 4.39. *The gable loggia and square columns on the porch of this house in Wentworth, New Hampshire, suggest a vernacular expression of the Greek Revival style, as does the entrance with its projecting entablature and long sidelights surrounding the front door. The thin raking eaves of the roof, however, are typical of the vernacular Gothic Revival style. Combined, these features point to a probable 1850s construction date.*

Figure 4.40. *With a gable loggia on the second story of the front gable and a recessed porch beneath supported by three square columns, this vernacular late Greek Revival–style house was built in 1850 in Hartland, Vermont.*

Figure 4.41. *Design for a partially recessed balcony porch in the Queen Anne style. Note the decorative spandrel panels beneath the railings. H. Hudson Holly,* Modern Dwellings *(1878); Rare Books and Special Collections, McGill University Library.*

projecting balconies, were also incorporated in various Queen Anne–style designs in many areas of North America. Examples of these are shown in the section below devoted to that style.

ATTACHED MULTITIERED PORCHES AND GALLERIES

Attached multitiered porches that project out beyond the general mass of buildings are another form that became popular during the nineteenth century. Supported by posts that define the first-story porch space below,

these combined the features of ground-level porches with those of upper-story balconies. A balcony is a raised open platform that is cantilevered out from a wall without post supports beneath. A balcony porch is cantilevered, but a roof shelters its raised platform.

An important early example of multitiered porches supported by cast-iron columns on an institutional building in the United States is William Strickland's 1827 Greek Revival design for the U.S. Naval Asylum (figure 4.42) in Philadelphia. These shallow porches, also called "piazzas or verandas," served as walkways passing the officer's quarters on the second story and the "apartments for the insane" on the third story. They also provided access from the enclosed stairway of the center section to the flanking wings. In his 1829 report to the hospital fund commissioners, Strickland provided the following description of the center building of the asylum, now known as Biddle Hall: "The wings consist of a granite basement, supporting a marble superstructure, three stories in height with piazzas or verandas on each story of the front and rear, raised on eighty-eight cast iron columns, resting on granite piers."[40]

By the 1850s, production methods for manufactured iron architectural features had advanced to enable the widespread use of cast-iron porch columns, as well as ornate cast- and wrought-iron railings and screens for multitiered porches. At first, the cast-iron columns were used for decay-resistant support at ground level, but soon durable architectural elements of iron were also used for upper tiers, especially for street-front balcony porches along sidewalks in commercial districts.

Multitiered piazzas and balcony porches are typically called *galleries* on buildings

Figure 4.42. *Three-tiered recessed veranda, U.S. Naval Asylum building, William Strickland, architect, 1827–33, Philadelphia. Historic American Buildings Survey photograph, 1964, HABS PA,51-PHILA,577A-4.*

Figure 4.43. *A shallow, two-tiered gallery, probably built in the 1850s, runs along the east-facing front of this two-story brick building that served as slave quarters in Mobile, Alabama. Boxed columns with simple Greek Revival details support the roof along the second story, but iron columns lined the first story when this photo was taken in 1936. Historic American Buildings Survey photograph, HABS ALA,49-MOBI,20C-1.*

Figure 4.44. *Two-tiered commercial galleries from the 1850s with columns, gallery screens, and crestings of cast iron grace facades along Front Street in Natchitoches, Louisiana. Historic American Buildings Survey photograph, HABS No. LA-1319-25.*

with French heritage. Some of the best known are the iron galleries in the Vieux Carré of New Orleans, but outstanding examples are also found in other commercial districts developed during the 1850s and 1860s. Not to be confused with the recessed single-story French galleries discussed above, these attached multitiered galleries are found on buildings in regions with French heritage in North America, including Alabama (figure 4.43), Missouri, and Louisiana (figures 4.44, 4.45, and 4.46), as well as in Quebec (figures 4.49 and 4.50) and other locations in Canada.[41]

With the great development of manu-

facturing industries during the second half of the nineteenth century, housing for workers was often constructed adjacent to the factories and mill sites in town and cities. To make the most efficient use of land, some of these tenement buildings made prominent use of multistory porches to provide both a

Figure 4.45. *Attached iron galleries overlook many streets in the Vieux Carré of New Orleans.*

Figure 4.46. *Elaborate cast-iron screens became notable features of galleries in New Orleans, such as this corner balcony on Le Pretre Mansion in the Vieux Carré (French Quarter). Historic American Buildings Survey photograph, 1936, HABS LA,36-NEWOR,18-9.*

Figure 4.47. *The triple-decker porch on this circa 1870 tenement that provided housing in eighteen units for textile mill workers and families at the Monadnock Mill in Claremont, New Hampshire, measured 127 feet long and 8 feet deep. In addition to providing access to the units, the porches provided space for drying clothes on lines. Historic American Buildings Survey photograph, 1979, HABS NH,10-CLAR,6D-10.*

Figure 4.48. *A projecting balcony porch lines the front of the Danville General Store, built in 1889 in the center of the village of Danville, Vermont. The first story offers a sheltered space for a variety of quasi-public uses, but its second tier, surrounded by a Queen Anne–style scroll-sawn railing, serves as an amenity for the inhabitants of the private upstairs living spaces.*

means of access to the apartment units and as balcony porches to provide quasi-private spaces for drying clothes and for household chores, as well as for sitting. One type of tenement building with multi-story porches that became especially popular in some New England mill towns and elsewhere was a three-story design that became known as a triple-decker. An example built in Claremont, New Hampshire, is shown in figure 4.47.[42]

Shallow balconies, balcony porches, and galleries (figures 4.48, 4.49, and 4.50) continued to be built through the late

Figure 4.49. *Overhanging the sidewalk, a shallow balcony gallery with turned wooden balusters and Italianate-style detailing serves the second-story apartments of this circa 1880s tenement located in the Centre-Sud quarter of Montreal.*

Figure 4.50. *Shallow galleries with exterior stairs providing direct access to upper-story apartments are common in many of the urban mixed-use residential, commercial, and industrial neighborhoods that developed in Montreal during the late nineteenth and early twentieth centuries. This three-tiered example with an open balcony on top has decorative wrought-iron railings extending between boxed pedestals that support wooden Tuscan columns.*

nineteenth and early twentieth century in cities, in mill towns, and in densely built-up urban and village centers across the United States and Canada.

LATTICE PIAZZAS AND PORCHES

Although such English architects as John Papworth and Robert Lugar had employed wooden lattice as a material for trellis-work and for supporting piazza roofs on their early 1800s designs for Picturesque ornamental cottages, it took several decades for this fashion to cross the Atlantic. Architect Ammi Burnham Young, known mainly for his influential Greek Revival designs of the Vermont State House (figure 3.51) and the Boston Customs House (figure 3.52), was one American architect who made prominent use of lattice for porches. His 1840 design for the Rev. John Wheeler House (figure 4.51) built in Burlington, Vermont, in 1842, for example, featured two side piazzas faced with lattice. The use of lattice contrasted with the classical Corinthian entry porticos on this otherwise rather staid Greek Revival–style house, while also reflecting this architect's innovative shift toward the Picturesque eclecticism that would soon become the norm for domestic architectural designs during the Victorian era. Practical advantages of lattice include screening for privacy and the transmission of partially filtered light to the rooms inside.

It was A. J. Downing, however, who helped to popularize lattice more widely by showing several English-based cottage

Figure 4.51. *Patterns of light and shadow cast through diagonal lattice by afternoon sun animate the experience of walking along the rear side piazza of the Rev. John Wheeler House in Burlington, Vermont, designed by architect Ammi Burnham Young in 1840.*

designs with diagonally applied lattice supports on verandas and trellises. In his *Cottage Residences*, first published in 1842, he included a design for an Italianate villa with a lattice veranda.[43] Also in that book, Downing offered a detail of lattice trelliswork for a veranda designed in a chinoiserie motif, shown in figure 4.52.[44] This trelliswork could support the growth of vines for decoration, shade, and privacy. Although sometimes used with earlier styles, trellis verandas became very popular on houses designed in the Gothic Revival and Italianate styles. An example of a small lattice entry porch that dates from the late 1840s or early 1850s is on Steven A. Douglas's birthplace (figure 4.53) in the village of Brandon, Vermont.[45]

In his influential book, *Villas and Cottages*, first published in 1857, Calvert Vaux demonstrated how lattice screening (figure 4.54) could allow light and ventilation into a porch or veranda (figure 4.55), while offering support for plants and limited privacy. All of these designs show the lattice being installed with a diagonal orientation.[46]

Typically produced by re-sawing thin strips from thick planks, wooden lattice became easier for lumber mills to produce with the development of circular saws during the 1840s and 1850s. Milling the lattice surfaces became even less expensive with the refinement of mechanical planers at lumber planning mills in North America during the 1860s and 1870s. Lattice thus became a

Figure 4.52. *The chinoiserie-inspired design of the lattice trelliswork on this veranda drawing provides a light, airy feeling that reflects a British and North American fascination with Chinese motifs for some furnishings and decorative arts during the eighteenth and early nineteenth centuries. A. J. Downing,* Cottage Residences *(1842).*

Figure 4.53. *This small lattice entry porch on the Steven A. Douglas birthplace in the village of Brandon, Vermont, was probably added during the late 1840s or early 1850s. The pointed shape of the main opening formed by the widely spaced, diamond-shaped pattern of the lattice suggests an association with the Gothic Revival style. The two side seats indicate that this east-facing front porch could have served sedentary uses historically associated with the stoops of the Hudson River valley.*

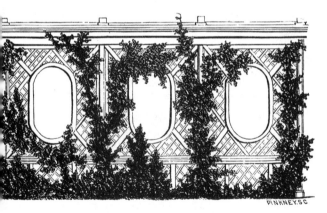

Figure 4.54. *Lattice could be used to support vines, thus forming a screen, as is shown in this illustration of a design for a "partially inclosed veranda." Calvert Vaux,* Villas and Cottages *(1857); courtesy of Special Collections, University of Vermont.*

common material for use on porches and verandas, such as those on the Gothic Revival–style Cornelius Beekman House (figure 4.56) in Jacksonville, Oregon.[47]

By the 1870s, lattice also was being used extensively as skirting to screen spaces between veranda floors and the ground (figure 4.57), especially on Gothic Revival–style houses. This lattice skirting soon became commonly associated with verandas and porches built on Italianate Revival, Queen Anne, and Colonial Revival–style houses. It is discussed in association with these topics below.

Figure 4.55. *Illustration of a latticed veranda along the gabled front of a Gothic Revival–style house. Calvert Vaux,* Villas and Cottages *(1857); courtesy of Special Collections, University of Vermont.*

Figure 4.56. *Set on a corner lot in Jacksonville, Oregon, the circa 1870 Gothic Revival–style Cornelius Beekman House features two latticed entry porches. Note the diagonal orientation of the lattice on the porch posts and balustrades. Historic American Buildings Survey photograph, 1971, HABS ORE,15-JACVI,49-1.*

Figure 4.57. *Diagonal lattice skirting fills the bays beneath the deck of a bracketed side veranda on a mid-nineteenth-century house in Brattleboro, Vermont. Circa 1870 stereograph; courtesy of Special Collections, University of Vermont.*

SHOTGUN PORCHES

Usually less than twelve feet wide, shotgun houses became the most common type of housing built in many urban and rural areas of the American South from the 1860s through the 1920s. On these shotgun houses, porches (also called galleries in the lower Mississippi region) typically were built across their narrow front elevations in two types; either recessed (built-in) beneath the extended main roof, or attached with a separate roof projecting from the front wall. Although not all shotgun houses have front porches, on some an extended front roof without posts overhangs a raised deck (figure 4.58). In some neighborhoods, rows of shotguns were built to provide inexpensive rental housing.

Geographer Fred B. Kniffen's 1936 study on vernacular house types in Louisiana identified *shotgun* as a widely used folk term for

Figure 4.58. *Faint echoes of French heritage may be reflected by the broadly overhanging front roof eaves and the raised* perron *of this circa 1880s Queen Anne–style shotgun house in New Orleans.*

a traditional long, narrow house type with a forward gable of one-room width, compared with *bungalows*, which were a more recent type of small, gable-fronted house that was two rooms wide. The distribution pattern of the shotgun house type in Louisiana closely coincided with river and coastal waterways. More recent research suggests that shotgun houses were being built by 1840 in Lousiana by free Blacks from Haiti where this type of house has been called a *maison basse*.[48]

The historical context in which the proliferation of these very small houses with front porches occurred across the South must recognize that after the end of the American Civil War many former slaves faced challenges of building or obtaining housing in the South. As one report reflected on the situation, "There were no white, green-blinded New England cottages scattered here and there, no middle class dwellings—only the Big House and the slave-pen, and nothing between. The black landholder could not think of building a mansion and he therefore built a slave cabin with some improvements.

He put a porch on the front, perhaps, cut one or two windows, and at last added a lean-to on the back for a kitchen." Although "shotguns" and other very small houses had served the housing needs of many people in the region, this 1908 study showed that in one large area of the South, 40 percent of black families still lived in one-room houses, and 43 percent resided in homes with just two rooms.[49]

"Shotguns" and other small houses with simple front and rear porches were also built in the coal-mining regions of the Appalachian South during the early twentieth century. In the coalfields of Kentucky and Tennessee, for example, a federal Labor Department report from 1920 noted that small, gable-roofed cottages with front and rear porches were most common. "A considerable proportion" of these houses were of two rooms. This report continued, "A type of house more or less peculiar to all small southern towns is the so-called 'shotgun' house, shaped like an oblong box and divided into three rooms in a row and frequently with doors connecting the rooms in alignment."[50]

An example of a 1930s hip-roofed shotgun house with a recessed front porch in rural Lowndes County, Mississippi, recorded by the Historic American Buildings Survey, is shown in figure 4.59.[51] Many shotgun houses also were built with rear porches that could be used for domestic chores and storage. Built in 1912 as one of four closely spaced rental units in Americus, Georgia, an example of a shotgun house with a rear porch recessed into a side corner is shown in figure 4.60.[52] A 1943 study of workers' housing in the Seminole Oil Fields of central Oklahoma observed that although the shotgun house was very common in these oil field camps, most lacked front porches; instead,

Figure 4.59. *This hip-roofed shotgun house with a recessed front porch was constructed in the 1930s in rural Lowndes County, Mississippi. Historic American Buildings Survey photograph, 1978,* HABS MISS,44-CARCH.V,2-1.

Figure 4.60. *Serving various routine domestic needs, a rear porch is recessed into the side corner of this shotgun house, built in 1912 as one of four closely spaced rental units in Americus, Georgia. Historic American Buildings Survey photograph,* HABS GA,131-AMER,2-5.

Figure 4.61. *This row of two-story duplex shotgun rental houses, constructed about 1929 in Columbus, Georgia, was demolished in 1994. Historic American Buildings Survey photograph, 1994,* HABS GA,108 COLM,34-1.

on many, screened porches were attached to the rear.[53]

Although most Southern shotgun houses have just a single story, some were built during the early twentieth century as two-story structures with side halls and with side stairs providing access to the upper-floor units. In some communities, these were built in rows along streets to provide rental housing. A row of two-story duplex shotgun rental houses (figure 4.61), constructed

about 1929 in Columbus, Georgia, were documented by the Historic American Buildings Survey before they were demolished in 1994. Although originally identical, the treatments of the front porches evolved differently to meet the needs of the occupants, with some left open and others screened.[54]

PORTE-COCHERES

The term *porte-cochere* (also spelled *porte cochere* or *porte-cochère*), which literally means a carriage entrance in French, has been used to describe a large, covered porch located adjacent to a building entrance through which carriages or other vehicles may pass to load or discharge passengers. To serve this function, porte-cocheres typically have paving or gravel drives at grade, rather than raised floors or decks.

Perhaps one of the most widely recognized porte-cocheres in the United States serves as the formal front entrance of the

Figure 4.62. *The north portico of the White House was constructed in 1829 to serve as a colossal porte-cochere. This pedimented tetrastyle portico with grand, two-story columns is in the Ionic order. Historic American Buildings Survey photograph, 1985,* HABS DC,WASH,134-18.

Figure 4.63. *The front elevation of a porte-cochere arcade in the Italianate style of rusticated stone with balustrades between the openings at the ground level and along the parapet above. Calvert Vaux,* Villas and Cottages *(1857); courtesy of Special Collections, University of Vermont.*

Figure 4.64. *The prominent Gothic Revival–style porte-cochere sheltering the entrance of Lyndhurst in Tarrytown, New York, was added between 1864 and 1865 when the mansion was enlarged to the designs of Alexander Jackson Davis. Historic American Buildings Survey photograph, 1971,* HABS NY,60-TARY,1A-3.

White House presidential mansion in Washington, DC. Known as the north portico (figure 4.62), this two-story porte-cochere that extends over the driveway was constructed of Seneca sandstone in the Ionic order under the direction of architect James Hoban in 1829.[55]

The forms and functions of porte-cocheres, porticos, and other porches are so closely related that it is sometimes difficult to distinguish one from another. Indeed in his *Villas and Cottages* of 1857, Calvert Vaux offered a design for a porch arcade (shown in figure 4.63) that would project sufficiently far ahead of a villa to permit a carriage to pass beneath and thus could serve as a porte-cochere as well.[56]

A well-known example of a porte-cochere in the Gothic Revival style graces the front entrance of Lyndhurst (figure 4.64), in Tarrytown, New York, a National Historic Landmark owned by the National Trust for Historic Preservation. This stone porte-cochere with crenellated parapets and pointed-arched openings was constructed between 1864 and 1865 to the design of Alexander Jackson Davis. It was attached to the building's smaller, original 1838 porte-cochere, also by Davis, which was then enclosed with leaded-glass sash to become an entrance vestibule.[57] A representative example in the Queen Anne style is the porte-cochere that U.S. President James A. Garfield had constructed of wood in 1880 as an addition to his home, Lawnfield (figure 4.65), in Mentor, Ohio.[58] This modest residential porte-cochere features turned posts and decorative brackets that match those on the adjacent porch.

Porte-cocheres continued to be built on villas and mansions through the nineteenth century and into the early twentieth century, both for prominent architectural displays, as well as for the comfort of those arriving and

Figure 4.65. *Turned posts and scroll-sawn brackets trim the Queen Anne–style porte-cochere and connecting porch on the President James A. Garfield homestead, Lawnfield, a National Historic Landmark in Mentor, Ohio. Historic American Buildings Survey photograph, 1985, HABS OHIO,43-MENT,2-5.*

Figure 4.66. *This porte-cochere attached to the side of Pleasant Home, the John Farson house in Oak Park, Illinois, one of the earliest examples in the Prairie style, was completed in 1898.*

departing by horse-drawn vehicles and later by automobiles and other motor vehicles. A sense of awareness of these two purposes—the practical and the symbolic—is reflected in the following excerpt from a short story published in 1914:

> The only portion of her home visible to Stella Arnold as she sat in her bedroom window was the porte-cochère. And that, even in the twilight, was more than a porte-cochère; it was a symbol of the opulence of the Arnold family. True, two other houses in Paola boasted porte-cochères, but those were mere coverings. The Arnold porte-cochère, upon the contrary, was not merely useful; it was a monument to the idealism of both architect and owner—an idealism which, like cream, thickened at the top. The roof was of blue and yellow slate, of a proud diamond pattern; an ornamental iron fence

reared itself above the apex, also above all vulgar utilitarian considerations. It was a fence of pure adornment.[59]

Befitting the expectations of a mansion built for a wealthy banker and philanthropist during the Gilded Age, a sturdy porte-cochere was attached to one of America's first grand Prairie-style houses, Pleasant Home, in Oak Park, Illinois. Designed by architect George H. Maher, the John Farson house was completed in 1898 and was designated a National Historic Landmark in 1996.[60] Rising from a base of Indiana limestone, the porte-cochere (figure 4.66) has two limestone piers ornamented with carved medallions and moldings. The nearly flat–roofed structure is trimmed with painted wooden cornices. The materials and detailing of the porte-cochere match those of the deep porch that extends across the front of the house.

Porte-cocheres have also long been common features of hotels, whether in urban or country settings, to provide shelter for arriving and departing guests. An especially ornate example from the early twentieth century was built in the Neoclassical style on the Mount Washington Hotel (figure 4.67) in Bretton Woods, New Hampshire.

If the presence of a porte-cochere on a house could symbolically indicate the elevated wealth or social status of an owner, then the existence of such architectural adornments on several nearby houses in a community could similarly color impressions of the social status of the residents of such a neighborhood. Indeed, when we find houses with porte-cocheres clustered together, these may serve as indicators of a time when residents enjoyed periods of relative prosperity. A representative example is the Colonial Revival–style Booth House (figure 4.68), built for a prosperous lumber baron in 1907 adjacent to the University of Vermont campus in the "Hill Section" of Burlington, Vermont.

As might be expected, industrialist Henry Ford had an especially impressive porte-cochere constructed in 1915 as the main drive-up entrance to his Dearborn, Michigan, mansion, Fair Lane (figures 4.69 and 4.70), designed by William H. Van Tine. Supported by piers of rough-faced Ohio limestone ashlar, this porte-cochere has characteristics of a pergola, with its matrix of exposed wooden beams and rafters overhead. More than just a partially shaded entryway, this porte-cochere reflects the design ethic of the era's Arts and Crafts movement by providing a memorable visual and experiential connection between the estate's mansion and its surrounding grounds, designed by the noted landscape architect Jens Jensen.[61]

Figure 4.67. *Neoclassical Doric columns surround the circular porte-cochere of the Mount Washington Hotel, completed in 1902 in Bretton Woods, New Hampshire.*

Figure 4.68. *The prominent porte-cochere that connects to a side porch and the matching front entry porch distinguish the Colonial Revival–style Booth House, built in 1907 in Burlington, Vermont. Although the original porte-cochere had been removed, it was replicated when the building was restored in 2006, using photographic evidence. This porte-cochere and the adjacent porches feature paired Tuscan columns set on paneled pedestals with decorative balustrades that match those on the roof above.*

Figure 4.69. *The pergola-type of porte-cochere on Henry Ford's 1915 Fair Lane estate in Dearborn, Michigan, provides a strong physical and symbolic connection between the mansion and the surrounding landscaped grounds.*

Figure 4.70. *Geometrical patterns of light and shadow animate the experience of walking beneath the pergola-type of porte-cochere at Henry Ford's Fair Lane mansion.*

Figure 4.71. *The boxy marquee of the Tivoli Theater in Chattanooga, Tennessee, built in 1921, originally was illuminated by incandescent light bulbs that consumed more than fifteen thousand watts of electrical power. The steel, wood, and sheet metal marquee is suspended from the building facade by four massive chains. Historic American Buildings Survey photograph, 1983, HABS TENN,33-CHAT,8-2.*

MARQUEES

Marquees serve symbolic functions similar to those of porte-cocheres and porticos. Projecting over quasi-pubic spaces from the facades of buildings, marquees may provide permanent, canopied entrances for commercial buildings, concert halls, opera houses, theaters, cinemas, train and bus stations, airport terminals, and auditoriums. Structural support is typically provided by suspending the marquee from the facade wall or from a parapet above by means of cables, chains, or tension rods, or by cantilevering the projection out from the mass of the

Figure 4.72. *The streamlined marquee of the Pan-Pacific Auditorium was built in 1935 in Los Angeles, California, with a curved, cantilevered slab canopy roof supported by four massive pylons. Historic American Buildings Survey photograph, 1977, HABS CAL,19-LOSAN,41-2.*

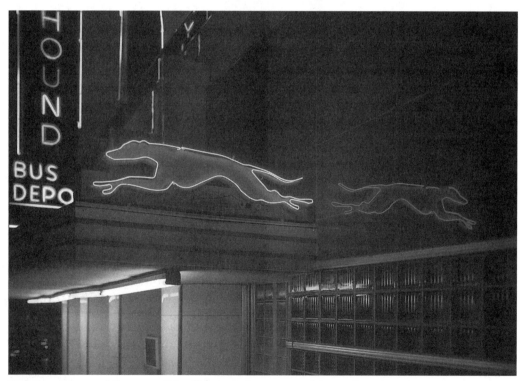

Figure 4.73. *Neon and fluorescent lights illuminate the marquee of the Greyhound Bus Station, built in 1939 in Columbia, South Carolina. White Vitrolite glass panels sheath the supporting piers flanking the doorways, and translucent glass blocks line the walls. Historic American Buildings Survey photograph, 1983, HABS SC13.*

building, rather than by supporting it with posts or piers.

Marquees were often first built as boxy structures, with their exposed sides providing space for signs and decorations, especially when backlit or adorned with electric lights as these became available by the late nineteenth and early twentieth centuries. During the golden age of movie houses, such decorated marquees became prominent features of many downtowns in North America, as was the marquee at the entrance of the Tivoli Theater (figure 4.71) in Chattanooga, Tennessee. Designed by Rapp and Rapp, architects in Chicago, the Tivoli was rehabilitated as a performing arts center in 1989 and for the Chattanooga Symphony and Opera.[62]

In the Streamline Moderne styles of the mid-twentieth century, marquees became more integrated into the designs of the buildings as accent features. The streamlined marquee of the Pan-Pacific Auditorium (figure 4.72), built in 1935 in Los Angles, California to the design of Wurdeman and Becket, architects, combined a curved, cantilevered slab canopy roof with four massive pylon supports. One of the most outstanding examples of the Streamline Moderne style of architecture in the United States, the Pan-Pacific Auditorium was closed in 1972, neglected, and then destroyed by fire in 1989.[63]

The liminal magic of many marquees may beckon most strongly after dusk, as their alluring lights attempt to lure patrons through inviting portals into realms of entertainment and escape. With the advent of colored curves of neon tube signage and fluorescent lighting, as well as structural building materials made from shiny and translucent glass, even bus station marquees could offer intriguing visual experiences for potential patrons. An example is the marquee that was built in 1939 for the Greyhound Bus Station (figure 4.73) in Columbia, South Carolina.[64]

As they provide both public shelter and a structure for signs and decorative lighting, marquees are now subject to regulation as architectural projections in some municipal zoning codes in the United States.[65]

5

Victorian
Porch Styles

A broad range of architectural styles based on Romantic interpretations or "revivals," including the Gothic, Italianate, Venetian, Tuscan, Swiss, French, Oriental, Chinese, and Rustic styles, emerged as the role of the professional architect rose in importance in Europe, North America, and elsewhere in the industrialized world during the nineteenth century. Although the precedents for this remarkable transformation in building design had begun by the early 1800s, the period when these various architectural styles became most popular in North America roughly coincides with the reign of Britain's Queen Victoria (1837–1901), and they are thus informally referred to as "Victorians." This approach to architectural design remained strong, however, for several decades into the 1900s, especially in Canada.

Coinciding with the Industrial Revolution, the Victorian period also brought profound changes to people's lives and standards of living, which was reflected in part by the architectural styles chosen for their buildings. For many of the houses built in the Victorian styles, porches (or verandas as they were commonly called) were important character-defining features. At first, Victorian era architects produced designs that tended to reflect specific, identifiable architectural styles, but after several decades, eclecticism (that is, the mixing of elements of various styles) became more common. A result of his trend was a general loss of stylistic congruency—a porch with features of one style might be built concurrently on a house of a different style, just as a later porch addition might also be built in a style different from that of the original house. An example of how the appearance of an older house could be updated with additions can be seen in figure 5.1, where an 1837 Classical Revival–style house had a pair

Figure 5.1. *Two Gothic Revival–style side verandas were added in 1850 to this house built in 1837 in Brandon, Vermont.*

of Gothic Revival–style side verandas added in 1850.[1]

Existing porches were also often altered during the Victorian era to update their appearances to match more current and fashionable styles. For those researching the history of buildings constructed or altered during this period, such eclecticism can make porch identification challenging, so this chapter focuses mainly on the character-defining features of porches associated with the dominant architectural styles of this era, rather than on their forms or uses.

GOTHIC REVIVAL

The Gothic Revival style was one of the first of the Picturesque architectural styles to sweep North America starting in the late 1830s. Imbued with ecclesiastical references

to features found in thirteenth-century European Gothic cathedrals, the most recognizable identifying features of Gothic Revival porches and verandas include pointed Gothic arches between the bays and pillars with quatrefoil- or cross-shaped sections. As with the orders of classical architecture discussed above, Gothic pillars and other features have generally been based on historical precedents that were documented and then shared through pattern books. Thus, just as ribbed vaults were prominently used to support the lofty ceilings of Gothic cathedrals, ceilings ribbed with decorative rafters may be found on Gothic Revival verandas.

Since the early 1700s a growing movement in England had sought to revive the European Gothic style of ancient landmarks that had employed the pointed arch and

Figure 5.2. *Ribbed ceiling rafters follow the shape of the stone Gothic arch on the west veranda of Lyndhurst (originally known as Knoll), in Tarrytown, New York, designed in 1838 by architect Alexander Jackson Davis.*

Figure 5.3. *Close-up view of a clustered quatrefoil-shaped colonnette and capital, supporting Gothic arched spandrels with trefoil tracery on the Lyndhurst veranda.*

ribbed vaults so prominently displayed on ecclesiastical, palace, and castle buildings built between the late 1100s and the 1500s. By the early 1800s, British architects were applying the Gothic Revival style not just to churches and institutional buildings but also to individual residences ranging from modest ornamented cottages to large picturesque villas, replete with the crenellated ornamentation of medieval castles. A dogged adherence to the ordered principles of Renaissance classicism, however, postponed the popular acceptance of the Gothic Revival style in North America.

One of the first outstanding examples of a Gothic Revival–style residence in North America was Alexander Jackson Davis's 1838 design for Lyndhurst (figures 4.64, 5.2, and 5.3), the home of a former mayor of

New York City, General William Paulding, in Tarrytown, New York, and now a publicly accessible site owned by the National Trust for Historic Preservation.[2] Another well-known early example of a Gothic Revival–style residence with a beautiful Gothic side veranda is Kingscote in Providence, Rhode Island (figure 5.4), originally designed in 1839 by Richard Upjohn. This veranda features a curved roof supported by quatrefoil-sectioned columns. Its four French doors open into double parlors.[3]

As the popular attachment to the Greek Revival and Classical Revival styles started to fade in the United States by the early 1840s, the evocative designs of architect Alexander Jackson Davis and others captured the attention of the landscape gardener, influential author, and self-proclaimed

Figure 5.4. *A four-bay Gothic Revival–style veranda shades the east side of Kingscote, built starting in 1839 in Newport, Rhode Island. Historic American Buildings Survey photograph, 1969,* HABS RI,3-NEWP,61-2.

arbitrator of good taste, A. J. Downing. Indeed, Downing provided American readers with sharp critiques of their stodgy ways—and for many, a first look at Americanized versions of Picturesque English architectural styles that had been fashionable in Great Britain for decades. Downing applauded this new attitude toward house design in *Cottage Residences*, first published in 1842:

> We have pointed out in another work the objections that may fairly be urged against the false taste so lately prevalent among us, in building our country homes in the form of Greek temples, sacrificing thereby the beauty of variety, much convenience, and all the comfort of low and shady verandas, to the ambitious display of the portico of stately columns: and we are happy to see in its place a correct taste, springing up in every part of the country, which shall render cottage homes beautiful, not by borrowing the features or enrichments of a temple or a palace, but by seeking beautiful and appropriate forms, characteristic

of domestic life, and indicative of home comfort.[4]

Concerning the suitability of a portico on a farmhouse, "the cottage of a freeman—the proprietor of the soil he cultivates," Downing wrote in 1846:

> Nothing has been more common for the past ten years, than to see a good substantial farmer building a large plain dwelling—unobjectionable enough as a plain dwelling—but to which he has been persuaded to add a Grecian portico . . ., copied from a great house of the neighboring town or village.
>
> The portico is very well where it belongs—as a part of a handsome villa, every part of which is carefully finished with corresponding elegance. It has nothing whatever to do with a true farmhouse. It is too high to be comfortable by its shade or shelter. It is too costly and handsome to accord with the neat and rustic character of a farm-house. But it has been the fashion of the day, and if the farmer has not reflected for himself, it is ten to one that he has fallen a victim to it, instead of employing the more comfortable and characteristic verandah.[5]

Downing reinforced these points in his 1856 book, *Rural Essays*: "But the Greek temple disease has passed its crisis. The people have survived it. Some few buildings of simple forms, and convenient arrangements, that stood here and there over the country, uttering silent rebukes, perhaps had something to do with bringing us to just notions of fitness and propriety. Many of the perishable wooden porticos have fallen down; many more will soon do so; and many have been pulled down, and replaced by less pretending piazzas or verandas."[6]

By spreading his message in such language, Downing helped to shake Americans free of their parochial obsession with the Greek Revival and Classical Revival styles by rekindling their interests in English and European style trends and by offering imaginative Romantic architectural designs rendered in picturesque suburban settings. At first, some dismissed the efforts of Downing and others to encourage Americans to embrace the Gothic Revival and other Picturesque styles, as the new "gingerbread" features were seen as effete and wastefully expensive embellishments—a "useless profusion of fanciful ornamental carvings" according to one observer.[7]

More than just a new source for building design inspiration, however, Downing's popular introduction of these Romantic styles to North America soon helped to launch a fundamental shift in how domestic architecture was perceived. Instead of seeing buildings as perfected classical forms isolated from their surroundings, this new vision conceived of houses as being part of landscapes, with irregular designs and features like verandas placed to connect with scenic views and to offer comfort to inhabitants. These included elaborately embellished eclectic designs, among them ornamental cottages and cottage villas in the pointed Gothic style, the bracketed Italianate style, and the timbered and balconied Swiss style. Downing also included restrained designs for plainer farmhouses and rustic cottages. Most of these houses featured at least one veranda.

Downing devoted particular attention to verandas in his *Treatise on the Theory and Practice of Landscape Gardening, Adapted to North America*, first published in 1841:

In this country no architectural feature is more plainly expressive of purpose in our dwelling-houses than the veranda, or piazza. The unclouded splendor and fierce heat of our summer sun, render this very general appendage a source of real comfort and enjoyment; and the long veranda round many of our country residences stands instead of the paved terraces of the English mansion as the place for promenade; while during the warmer portions of the season, half of the days or evenings are there passed in the enjoyment of the cool breezes, secure under low roofs supported by the open colonnade, from the solar rays, or the dews of night. The obvious utility of the veranda in this climate (especially in the middle and southern states) will, therefore, excuse its adoption into any style of architecture that may be selected for our domestic uses, although abroad, buildings in the style in question, as the Gothic, for example, are not usually accompanied by such an appendage. An artist of the least taste or invention will easily compose an addition of this kind, that will be in good keeping with the rest of the edifice. These various features, or parts of the building, with many others which convey expression of purpose in domestic architecture, because they recall to the mind the different uses to which they are applied, and the several enjoyments connected with them, also contribute greatly to the interest of the building itself, and heighten its good effect as part of a harmonious whole, in the landscape. The various projections and irregularities, caused by verandas, porticos, etc., serve to connect the otherwise square masses of building, by gradual transition with the ground about it.[8]

The examples of house designs that A. J. Downing included in *Cottage Residences*

Figure 5.5. *Simple drawing of the key details of a Gothic veranda. A. J. Downing,* Cottage Residences *(1842).*

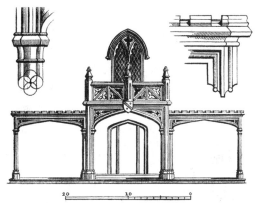

Figure 5.6. *Elaborate Gothic porch and veranda details, showing the design of a clustered colonnette with a quatrefoil section at left, a cornice at right with crenellated cresting, and a three-part veranda in the center, with the extended porch entry surmounted by a balcony and a Gothic window embellished with tracery and diamond-shaped panes. A. J. Downing,* Cottage Residences *(1842).*

Figure 5.7. *"A Cottage in the English or Rural Gothic Style" features a three-part front veranda with shallow Gothic arches, vaulted ceilings, and crenellations along its eaves. A. J. Downing,* Cottage Residences *(1842)*

was included as a prominent feature on all these ornamental cottages. In *Cottage Residences*, Downing even included details of simple (figure 5.5) and elaborately embellished Gothic verandas (figure 5.6).

Of the design of a cottage in the English Gothic style shown in *Cottage Residences* (figure 5.7), Downing commented:

In the English examples, a veranda is rarely seen, as the dampness of their climate renders such appendages scarcely necessary. But its great utility in our hot summers makes it indispensible to every house, and we have introduced it on the entrance front, as affording in this position shelter, prospect, and agreeable promenade. Over the porch is a pleasant balcony for the pointed window in the gable. As the sprit of Gothic architecture lies in vertical lines, a long unbroken horizontal line of veranda would destroy or mar the architectural character of the cottage.[9]

ranged from simple structures suitable for farmhouses to more elaborate Gothic veranda designs that were intended for houses in suburban settings. Some of these were designed and superbly rendered by his collaborator, architect Alexander Jackson Davis. Although the simpler designs offered restrained Gothic ornamentation, the veranda

In *The Architecture of Country Houses*, published in 1850, Downing also remarked on the role of verandas in domestic life:

> The larger expression of domestic enjoyment is conveyed by the veranda, or piazza. In a cool climate, like that of England, the veranda is a feature of little importance; and the same thing is true in a considerable degree in the northern part of New England. But over almost the whole extent of the United States, a veranda is a positive luxury in all the warmer part of the year, since in mid-summer it is the resting-place, lounging-spot, and place of social resort, of the whole family, at certain hours of the day.
>
> It is not, however, an absolute necessity, like a kitchen or a bed-room, and, therefore, the smallest cottages, or those dwellings in which economy and utility are the leading considerations, are constructed without verandas. But the moment the dwelling rises so far in dignity above the merely useful as to employ any considerable feature not entirely intended for use, then the veranda should find its place; or, if not an architectural veranda, then, at least, the arbor-veranda, covered with foliage. . . .
>
> To decorate a cottage highly, which has no veranda-like feature, is, in this climate, as unphilosophical and false in taste, as it would be to paint a loghut, or gild the rafters of a barn: unphilosophical, because all that relative beauty suggested by features which indicate a more refined enjoyment than what grows out of the necessities of life should first have its manifestation, since it is the most significant and noble beauty of which the subject is capable; and false in taste, because it is bestowing embellishment on the inferior

Figure 5.8. *Two Gothic corner porches flank the projecting center back of Roseland Cottage, built in 1846 in Woodstock, Connecticut.*

and minor details, and neglecting the more important and more characteristic features of a dwelling.[10]

Reflecting the principles espoused by A. J. Downing, an outstanding example of a Gothic Revival cottage is the Bowen House, also known as Roseland Cottage, or the Pink House (figure 5.8) in Woodstock, Connecticut. Designed by the English-born architect Joseph Collin Wells in 1846, the fancy cottage was built for Henry C. Bowen, a New York merchant and outspoken abolitionist and supporter of the Congregational religious denomination. The facade of Roseland Cottage features two corner porches supported by Gothic quatrefoil-shaped tracery carved of wood. The nearly flat roofs of these porches have carved cresting boards above the eaves that feature repeating stylized quatrefoils, each embedded with a cruciform.[11]

By the mid-nineteenth century, American life was rapidly changing as new steam-powered technologies brought additional employment opportunities in the burgeoning industrial economy and the expanding railroad network fostered a new mobility for people and their goods and ideas. Soon many of the basic features of A. J. Downing's Gothic Revival–design suggestions, such as verandas, pointed arches, pointed wall dormers, raking eaves with barge boards, and finials, were watered down into the simplified vernacular language of North American house design. The economic and social changes of the mid-1800s also helped to bring new opportunities for women, and their views on home design started to play a more apparent role. Verandas were often part of this vision. In 1848, for example, *Godey's Magazine and Lady's Book* published the design of an ornamental cottage with a veranda (figure 5.9) that reflected the influences of Downing and Davis.

And in 1849, the agricultural journal *The Cultivator*, of Albany, New York, published the following description, along with a design for a "Working Woman's Cottage," that was purportedly contributed anonymously by "A Farmer's Wife."

Thinking it may be of some use to the class to which I belong, I herewith send you a plan of a "Working Woman's Cottage," which is particularly adapted to her use.

In sketching this house, my first and most important object is convenience; the next is pleasantness; the third, is economy in cost of building; the last, is a tasteful and inviting appearance.

The main part of the house is 27 by 30 feet, one story and a-half high, with attic windows, above the veranda; these windows answer every purpose for chambers, and are an ornament to a house.

Figure 5.9. *The "Adelina Cottage" featured a deep front veranda crowned with a striped flared roof and Gothic ornamentation, including carved arched tracery between its open supports and fleurs-de-lis cresting along its lower eaves.* Godey's Magazine and Lady's Book *(1848); courtesy of Special Collections, University of Vermont.*

The veranda will be in front and on one side, with 2 doors and 4 windows opening upon it, the blinds must be alike to all, reaching to the floor.

What a delightful place for the family group to assemble in and spend the fine summer evenings, after they have finished the labors of the day. If any abode on earth ought to be pleasant, it is that of a working family, their social privileges being more limited.[12]

At about the time of A. J. Downing's untimely accidental death by drowning in 1852, two of his English-born associates, Gervase Wheeler and Calvert Vaux, published their own influential volumes. Recognition of the growing importance of verandas in defining the character of mid-nineteenth-century American houses was reflected by Gervase Wheeler's suggestion in *Rural Homes* (1851), that this feature might even be used to name the new style of houses being designed in this period. "Were I asked what should be the feature most prominent in an American villa, I would say 'the veranda,' for to no portion of the house are perfect comfort and effective appearance attributable so much as to its provision for shade. In fact, this may be considered the element of the character of the design, and the 'veranda style' in this age of new nomenclature would be no unfit description of a class of house otherwise difficult to be placed in the list of recognised orders and styles."[13]

Some of Wheeler's suggestions on how Gothic verandas should be built and furnished were quite specific:

In the first place, we will settle the character of the veranda, which we can now do, having grounds to go upon. The building being necessarily regular and of even surface, from the nature of the material, a rough, rustic veranda would be out of keeping, as would also be a classic colonnade, or a light trellis work. The posts supporting its roof may be thus made. Put together studs, two inches by three, in the form of a cross, around a centre stud, four inches square; the outer studs to be furnished with cut brackets at top and bottom, extending say four inches at the bottom and six at the top, so as to form caps and bases, and the edges to be chamfered off until within three or four inches of the top and bottom. The cornice of the roof to be very simple, consisting of a fascia, and above that a heavy roll moulding, and, if means will afford, to be enriched with brackets. The roof to

Figure 5.10. *"Cottage orne" design. Gervase Wheeler,* Homes for the People *(1867).*

be covered with metal or shingles, and the under side to show the rafters, and to be ceiled above them, and not straight across. These posts would be so arranged as not to come in the way of windows in the rooms, and might be placed in pairs, close together, and each pair about nine feet from the next. Where the veranda runs around the bay window in the drawing-room, on the western side, the space above would afford a good opportunity for a balcony entered from the chamber floor, which might again be protected by a light roof, supported on brackets, over the window leading upon it. Simply directing that the floor of the veranda would look best if laid in narrow strips of southern yellow pine, oiled, and that some of the beautiful seats procurable at the Berrians' be scattered here and there, I shall not have occasion to refer to this portion of the building again.[14]

With his "cottage orné" design (figure 5.10) illustrated in *Homes for the People*, first published in 1855, Gervase Wheeler also showed how vine-covered verandas, entry porches, and balconies could contribute to the Picturesque character of a house in the

Gothic Revival–style.[15] In the same volume, he also offered a Gothic Revival–style design for a "Southern Mansion" (figure 5.11) with a large veranda and an ombra. Of this, he wrote:

> The veranda upon one side, and the ombra connected with the library, are intended to be constructed of wood, with supports strengthened by buttresses, and relieved by simple tracery, in the manner that is shown in the illustration. In the ombra a dwarf balustrading of open Gothic panels is placed between each support, and within each division a jalousie or blind could be hung or otherwise attached, if preferred. The coolness of the air within this ombra would be materially increased by constructing a large flue from the corner of its roof where it rises against the walls of the tower and wing building, and discharging into the air above its roof—by which means a constant draft through the out-door apartment would be secured.[16]

The Gothic Revival continued to be a popular style for suburban homes, farmhouses, and summer cottages from the 1840s through the 1870s in many parts of North America. Many were designed and built by contractors whose inventiveness with vernacular designs and "gingerbread" ornamentation has prompted the description, "Carpenter Gothic," to be applied to these creations. Nearly all of these houses featured porches and verandas. Built between 1856 and 1857, the Gothic Revival cottage shown in figure 5.12 is one of the oldest remaining officer's quarters on the grounds of the United States Military Academy at West Point, New York. Its front veranda follows the plan of the building by stepping ahead of the center cross-gabled pavilion.[17] Two

Figure 5.11. *"Southern Mansion" in the Gothic Revival style. The ombra mentioned in the quotation is just behind the woman and child standing in the foreground. Also note the large veranda at the left and the porch sheltering the main entrance. Gervase Wheeler,* Homes for the People *(1867).*

Figure 5.12. *This Gothic Revival cottage was built between 1856 and 1857 at the United States Military Academy at West Point, New York. Historic American Buildings Survey photograph, 1982, HABS ny10.*

Figure 5.13. *With its curved roof extending over the front gallery supported by bracketed posts, this Picturesque mid-1800s French Gothic–style ornamental cottage is located on the north shore of the Saint Lawrence River in Tadoussac, Quebec.*

Figure 5.14. *A shallow veranda surrounds this Picturesque Gothic Revival–style ornamental cottage built as a summer home overlooking the St. Lawrence River in Tadoussac, Quebec. The veranda's clustered colonnettes have quatrefoil cross-sections.*

examples of circa 1850s Gothic Revival–style summer cottages with prominent verandas in Tadoussac, Quebec, are shown in figures 5.13 and 5.14.

A post–Civil War example of an American midwestern vernacular Gothic Revival–style farm cottage built around 1876 in Mason County, Kentucky, is shown in figure 5.15. It features a three-bay, front-attached veranda with large chamfered Stick style brackets ornamented with applied pateras. Gothic finials accent the apexes formed by the brackets. Similar finials are at the apexes of the front wall dormers. The veranda posts are chamfered and trimmed with moldings. The builder is presumed to be the first owner, C. R. Collins, who was identified as a "Carpenter, Contractor, and Builder" in an 1876 county atlas.[18] Vernacular designs of cottages that are sometimes called "Carpenter Gothic" continued to be popular in some regions of North America through the late nineteenth century. An example built in Anderson, South Carolina, with fancy lattice-trimmed verandas is shown in figure 5.16.

RUSTIC

Although less common than the other Picturesque treatments imported by North American architects from England and elsewhere, Rustic verandas and entrance porches enjoyed a popularity that grew through much of the nineteenth century. The use of rustic elements on verandas and porches, combined with the Gothic-style features on other parts of a building, can be traced to such late 1700s and early 1800s English precedents as the Picturesque designs for ornamental cottages produced by English architects John Plaw, Robert Lugar, and others.

Robert Lugar commented in 1805 on the connection between Rustic ornamentation and the Gothic Revival style: "A taste for the Gothic style of architecture having of late become very prevalent, I am induced to make some observations on the true style or character applicable to houses of this description, which may properly be called the ancient English style of building, and commonly called Gothic. I consider this style as

Figure 5.15. *Built around 1876 in Mason County, Kentucky, this vernacular Gothic Revival–style farm cottage features a three-bay, front-attached veranda. Historic American Buildings Survey photograph, 1982,* HABS *ky7.*

Figure 5.16. *Delicate lattice strips ornament the veranda posts on this late Victorian "Carpenter Gothic"–style cottage in Anderson, South Carolina. Detail from Historic American Buildings Survey photograph, 1940,* HABS SC,4-AND,2-1.

Figure 5.17. *Bark-covered cedar poles were recommended for the Rustic veranda and trellises on this Gothic Revival–style "cottage for a country clergyman." A. J. Downing,* Cottage Residences *(1842).*

Figure 5.18. *Built-in side seats made from gnarled branches line the sides of the Rustic Gothic entrance porch shaded by vines as seen in this enlarged detail of an illustration. A. J. Downing,* Cottage Residences *(1842).*

peculiarly suitable to Farm Houses and Parsonages, where a rural or rustic appearance is meant to be produced." In describing the features of one of his designs for a Rustic "fancy cottage," Lugar described its veranda as follows: "A boarded covering shades the lower windows. This may be of thatch, supported by trunks of trees."[19]

In addition to their Gothic and Italianate style designs, A. J. Downing, Gervase Wheeler, and Calvert Vaux also showed interest in bringing the English fascination with the Rustic style to North America with several designs published by the 1840s and 1850s in their pattern books. In *Cottage Residences*, Downing included a Rustic design for "A Cottage for a Country Clergyman" (figure 5.17), which he described as follows: "For the exterior of this cottage we have chosen a simple, rustic style—one that always befits rural scenery, besides affording more room for a given cost than any low roofed style. The rustic veranda and rustic trellises over the windows are intended

for vines—though not merely as supports for vines—but rather as thereby giving an air of rural refinement and poetry to the house without expense." He also offered a design (figure 5.18) for a "small cottage, or gate lodge" in the Gothic style that featured a Rustic front porch with built-in benches flanking the entrance with a Gothic arched opening and a balcony above, all formed by gnarled tree branches.[20]

Architect Gervase Wheeler's designs generally reflect somewhat lighthearted interpretations of the popular mid-nineteenth-century English architectural styles—especially the Gothic Revival. His combination of the Rustic style with the Gothic Revival style brought a well-established English architectural design tradition to North America. In *Rural Homes: or, Sketches of Houses Suited to American Country Life*, first published in New York in 1851, Wheeler showed how rough logs for the posts and braces could give a rustic look to a front veranda. He noted, "The inner side of the building should be sheltered by a rustic veranda, or by the dipping down of the rafters of the house roof; in either case supported by cedar or other timber posts, retaining the bark, and instead of any moulded cornice above, using bark and crooked limbs of trees for tracery and fascia, which may easily be so wrought as to cheaply produce a very pretty effect."[21] Wheeler furthermore suggested, "The veranda may be supported with cedar or cypress posts, upon which the bark has been left, farther preserving its adhesion by small tacks driven in here and there, and the whole varnished with a pitchy varnish to preserve from the weather."[22]

In his *Homes for the People in Suburb and Country*, first published in 1855, Wheeler described the Rustic veranda features for another cottage design: "The veranda posts are such as have been alluded to, and may be either of a single stick of timber from the woods, with the bark adhering, or may be formed of three or more straight stems of smaller diameter grouped together, the latter frequently affording the most pleasant effect when carefully and tastefully done." And describing an additional plan, he wrote: "The verandas are formed by rustic posts, and by a cornice made of slabs, or rounded pieces of the same material, with the bark adhering; or the bark of the whole may be stripped off, and the wood oiled and varnished, as taste, and the species of timber placed at command, may determine."[23]

In a Rustic design for a gate-lodge, Wheeler recommended: "The entrance is under a rustic porch or veranda, of which supporting posts may be of timber from the forests, with the bark remaining thereon, and the floor formed from blocks of hard wood, from five to seven inches diameter, cut about ten inches long, and placed on

Figure 5.19. *This bracketed villa design incorporated a Rustic veranda dressed with bark-covered posts and brackets. Gervase Wheeler,* Homes for the People *(1867).*

Figure 5.20. *House design with a Rustic front porch that would be "suitable for the parsonage of a simple rural church-society." Gervase Wheeler,* Homes for the People *(1867).*

end upon a foundation of earth and broken stones; between these blocks smaller pieces may be driven, and the whole thus wedged together will form a very durable and rustic looking floor."[24]

Gervase Wheeler also offered a design (figure 5.20) "suitable for the parsonage of a simple rural church-society" with a "rustic porch, formed by the overhanging

Figure 5.21. *Rustic cedar logs support the corner porch on this cottage at Raquette Lake in the Adirondack Mountains of New York. Detroit Publishing Company photograph, circa 1906, Library of Congress LC-D4-16811.*

Figure 5.22. *Constructed in 1915, this Craftsman bungalow, located in Canada's Banff National Park, features a veranda with rustic log posts and railings supported by cobblestone piers below the deck. According to a marker at the site, this home in Banff, Alberta, was designed by Harvey Wright, a construction engineer with the Canadian Pacific Railway, and was typical of the housing then being provided to railroad workers in the Canadian Rockies.*

Figure 5.23. *With porch posts, rafters, and walls constructed of peeled logs, the Rustic screened front porch of the Joyce Estate Main Cabin built in 1917 in Itasca County, Minnesota, was used for dining. Historic American Buildings Survey photograph, HABS MINN,31-GDRAP.V,3A-8.*

Figure 5.24. *The Lake Lodge at Yellowstone National Park, built in 1921, features a deep Rustic porch with its gable over the entrance supported by angled posts of rough tree trunks. Historic American Buildings Survey photograph, HABS WYO,20-LAK,2A-2.*

projection, containing a room on the second-floor, surmounted by a gable. . . . This porch is thirteen feet on the front and seven feet deep, making a pleasant and cheerful out-door sitting-place, if desired. Its supports—between which, upon the sides are seats—are simply the rustic stems of trees, of forms chosen for the purpose, the bark being retained thereon by copper nails, and decay prevented by a coat or two of oil and varnish."[25]

The popularity of Rustic designs for cabins, seasonal homes, and resort hotels grew during the second half of the nineteenth century and the early twentieth century. Rustic verandas were popular features of many of the cottages and "great camps" of the Adirondacks of New York (figure 5.21) and for other summer cottages and lodges built by shorelines, and in mountains, forests, and wilderness sites across North America.

The verandas of these seasonal retreats were often finished with porch posts and railings made from the rough trunks of trees or rough timbers, sometimes combined with rough stone. Such rustic materials and motifs were also used in the designs of bungalows, camps, cabins, lodges, ranch houses, and park buildings, including some constructed by the Canadian railroads and by national, state, provincial, and local parks departments. Further reflecting this popular acceptance of the suitability of the Rustic style, many cabins, hunting camps, lodges, and dwellings located in remote locations were constructed with rustic porches made from locally harvested logs and poles during the twentieth century.

BRACKETED MODE AND ITALIANATE STYLE

Coinciding with A. J. Downing's popular introduction of the English Gothic Revival

Figure 5.25. *This log cabin with a recessed front porch decorated with Rustic railings and valances was constructed of local natural materials in 1930 along the Koyukuk River in Wiseman, Alaska. Historic American Buildings Survey photograph, 1984, HABS AK,23-WISMA,1-F-1.*

style to North America in *Cottage Residences* in 1842 was his introduction of the Italianate style or "bracketed mode" of architecture characterized by broadly overhanging eaves supported by ornamental brackets (figure 5.26). As with his other examples included in this book, most of the designs were based on works by English architects that had been published in British pattern books during several previous decades. With regard to the bracketed mode, he explained: "The bracketed mode of building, so simple in construction, and so striking in effect, will be found highly suitable to North America, and especially to the southern states. The coolness and dryness of the upper story, afforded by the almost veranda-like roof, will render this a delightful feature in all parts of our country, where the summers are hot, and the sun is very bright during the long days of that season."[26]

The key features of the bracketed verandas illustrated in Downing's *Cottage*

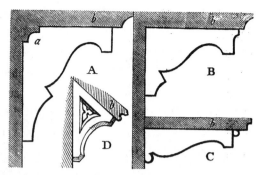

Figure 5.26. *Four basic designs for brackets: bracket A would be suitable for veranda pillars, whereas designs B, C, and D should be used beneath the soffits of roof cornices. A. J. Downing,* Cottage Residences *(1842).*

Figure 5.27. *This detail shows an ornamental cornice (y) that was scroll-sawn from inch-thick boards and trimmed with turned wooden acorns terminating the pendant points. The cross-section of a cottage veranda pillar (z) shows chamfered corners on both the post and the flanking stops. A. J. Downing,* Cottage Residences *(1842).*

Figure 5.28. *Detail of a bracketed veranda with a balustrade. A. J. Downing,* Cottage Residences *(1842).*

Residences and in his *Architecture of Country Houses*, first published in 1850, included the large scroll-sawn brackets that frame the upper openings between the pillars and the plates. The edges of the pillars are chamfered to create an octagonal cross-section. These pillars are set on bases with angled

tops that mimic the chamfering above. The veranda floorboards have rounded outside edges that extend slightly beyond the flat skirt of the simple plinth below. Above, projecting broadly beyond the outside edges of the veranda floor, the flat roof is trimmed with a simple cornice of flat stock, enriched beneath the soffits with slender curved brackets, and surmounted by a balustrade. Downing suggested that roofs should project out from the face of buildings by twenty inches to two feet, with veranda roof projections scaled proportionately.

So important to the Italianate style of architecture, the ornamental bracket was one architectural feature that became much easier to mass-produce with the development of water-powered and steam-driven mill equipment. Although the intricate curving forms of the Italianate style bracket could certainly be produced one-by-one by hand with a scroll saw or with a treadle-powered jig saw, millwork companies in North America began specializing in manufacturing ornamental brackets and other decorative trim elements with steam- or water-powered equipment by the 1850s. Soon building contractors could easily apply these inexpensive, mass-produced trim pieces to provide buildings with fancy dress in the Italianate style.

Houses built in the Italianate style in North America were generally constructed between the late 1840s and the 1870s, although a second wave of popularity was marked by the construction of a subgroup of "high Victorian Italianate"–style residential, commercial, religious, and institutional buildings in the 1880s and later. Small and simple Italianate-style houses were typically referred to as cottages, whereas larger and more elaborate Italianate-style dwellings were considered villas. These villas could contain separate working spaces and living quarters for maids, servants, and other domestic workers, which sometimes were accessed by separate secondary entry porches.

In addition to the high-style architectural designs being offered by leading architects to their wealthier clients and examples of the Italianate style that appeared in the pattern books of A. J. Downing, Calvert Vaux, and Gervase Wheeler, many of these designs were also shared with the public in such popular periodicals as the *American Agriculturalist*, *Godey's Lady's Book*, and others. These, in turn, helped spawn innumerable less sophisticated interpretations by contractors and self-taught designers. Quite suddenly, the North American landscape was being embellished with a broad assortment of architectural curiosities.

The overall effect of the finished veranda as an element of the Picturesque design of one house was well summarized by Gervase Wheeler in 1851:

Figure 5.29. *Design for a small villa overlooking the Hudson River, first published in 1855. This "garden front" features two open stairs leading to small, bracketed verandas that flank the central pavilion and its projecting bay window. Note the simple curved brackets supporting the pillars and the broad eaves of the bay window. Gervase Wheeler,* Homes for the People *(1867).*

Stepping out upon the lawn, we turn and look upon the house. The broad veranda seems like a base to the building, and gives massiveness and apparent firmness to its foothold upon the ground, equally as it imparts lightness and variety to its outline. The overshadowing roof, with its varied light and shade, seems a fitting finish to the building; and the leading parallel lines of the veranda are reproduced in its unbroken horizontal line of cornice, and in the uniform elevation of the windows. There is a peculiar stamp of fitness upon the whole; and the building and the grounds, the natural objects and the result of art, are in perfect congruity, and their union produces a sense of that most charming of all excellencies—home beauty.[27]

But perhaps even more important than the exterior view of the house with its

Figure 5.30. *Designed by Gervase Wheeler, the Patrick Barry House, built between 1855 and 1857 in Rochester, New York, in a picturesque landscape setting was the home of a prominent nurseryman. The polygonal corner veranda at the left complements the Italianate style of the villa. Note the ornamental cornice with scroll-sawn pendants and the fluted columns with stylized Corinthian capitals, features typical of Italianate-style verandas. Also note the brick entry porch at the right, with its round-arched masonry opening and bracketed cornice.*

veranda was the connection of the house to its setting and to the view that could been seen when looking out from its veranda. On this, Wheeler commented: "The other end, towards the veranda and bay-window, should be laid out as a pleasant lawn or flower-garden, and left as open as space will permit; its extremity, where perhaps a neighbor's land joins on, planted in such a manner as to hide the wall or fence, screen from observation, and at the same time appear to connect with the land beyond, (if there be any worth conveying such an idea) so that ownership may seemingly be suggested therewith, and the apparent extent of the grounds increased."[28]

By the late 1840s and 1850s, the open porch evolved in North America from being a practical means of sheltering a building entrance to become the nearly ubiquitous

charming veranda (or piazza as it was still known colloquially in some regions), a fashionable symbol of sophisticated cultural and social values. First embraced by those with aspirations to display refined tastes, the veranda (or piazza, umbrage, or ombra) became a prominent feature of both high style and popular suburban domestic architecture in Canada and the United States as the popularity of the classical Regency and Greek Revival styles was soon eclipsed by a broad array of Picturesque Romantic architectural design themes and styles of the Victorian era.

Coinciding with the social and political upheavals of the mid-nineteenth century was the great industrial transformation that brought profound changes to the methods used to produce building components. By the 1840s and 1850s, waterpower and steam power were harnessed to mechanical saws, planers, and shapers to replace handcrafted production of such architectural components as doors, windows, railings, porch posts, and other types of millwork. Production costs for these components dropped, and with the rapid growth of railroad networks across eastern North America, millwork could be readily shipped great distances from the woodworking mills.

House designers, builders, and carpenters took advantage of the available products and rapidly shifted their work from handcrafting custom designs based on traditional or pattern book forms to simply selecting premanufactured components for assembly. Thus was launched the wide variety of Victorian era architectural embellishment that became popular in North America during the second half of the nineteenth century.

Many designs of mid-1800s bracketed verandas were simple, yet functional, as can been seen in the following description of a

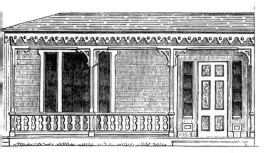

Figure 5.31. (left) *Calvert Vaux suggested that to shelter a front entrance, a veranda could be built instead of a small porch. Illustrated here is a bracketed veranda with chamfered pillars and scroll-sawn fretwork for the cornice trim and the railings. Calvert Vaux,* Villas and Cottages *(1857); courtesy of Special Collections, University of Vermont.*

Figure 5.32. (right) *Calvert Vaux offered various designs for verandas at different levels of ornamentation. The simplest, at left, suggests the influence of the Italianate style, with its chamfered pillars, cutout rounded brackets, and a dentil molding along the entablature. The center design features simple chamfered pillars with impost moldings supporting pointed Gothic arches and simple lower railings with straight balusters. Also on the center design, above the arched openings, Vaux shows a more elaborate entablature and an upper balustrade with turned newels and balusters. The most elaborate Gothic Revival–style design is on the right. It shows pillars with cruciform cross-sections, pointed arches enriched with quatrefoil cut-outs, a fancy lower balustrade with turned balusters, and cresting on the roof. Calvert Vaux,* Villas and Cottages *(1857); courtesy of Special Collections, University of Vermont.*

farmhouse design offered by Lewis Allen in 1852: "The front door opens from a veranda 28 feet long by 10 feet in depth, dropping eight inches from the doorsill. This veranda has a hipped roof, which juts over the columns in due proportion with the roof of the house over its walls. These columns are plain, with brackets, or braces from near their tops, sustaining the plate and finish of the roof above, which may be covered either with tin or zinc, painted, or closely shingled."[29]

In his influential 1857 book, *Villas and Cottages*, the talented English-American architect Calvert Vaux stressed the importance of the veranda through his designs and commentary. From his perspective, "The veranda is perhaps the most specially American feature in a country house and nothing can compensate for its absence." Recognizing that verandas could be dressed for special gatherings, Vaux offered the following

suggestion: "Additional room could easily be gained for a summer entertainment by temporarily inclosing the front veranda outside with calico, or a similar material, lightly affixed; and if the veranda posts are covered with creeping plants, as they should be, the effect of such a leafy gallery as is thus obtained when lighted up at night is very cool and elegant."[30]

After A. J. Downing's death in 1852, the rules of architectural taste that he and Alexander Jackson Davis had so clearly established would continue to dominate American house design for a half-century, as cultured society became increasingly obsessed with displays of fancy ornamentation. Through this period of change, as the column gave way to the pillar, the rules and orders that were fundamental prescripts of classical architecture were reexamined. With a rejection of scholarly authority and traditional order, a new eclectic sensibility evolved that particularly suited the adolescent North American culture, especially through the coming period of great debate and armed sectional conflict in the United States. This shift in attitudes toward architectural design was also seen in parts of the Dominion of Canada, established through confederation in 1867.

The prominent designer George E. Woodward included examples of Italianate-style houses in his book *Woodward's National Architect*, published in 1869. Along with his designs for Italianate, Swiss, and French Second Empire–style ornamental cottages, dwelling houses, and other buildings intended for cities, suburbs, villages, and the country, Woodward also offered a variety of designs (figure 5.34) for ornamenting piazzas, porches, and verandas.[31]

Carpenters' specifications for finishing a piazza on one house design in Woodward's book specified:

> Case up the piazza columns and furnish with caps and bases as shown. Cut in 2¾-inch brackets, form cornice, and mould all as per drawings.
>
> Plane up and chamfer the small columns of veranda and provide with brackets, etc., as per details.
>
> Lay the piazza and veranda floors with narrow, clear 1¼-inch tongued flooring, blind nailed, joints laid in white lead.[32]

The framing specifications for the piazza and veranda on this house show how custom-sawn framing lumber (of chestnut, pine, or spruce) was sized for specific uses:

> Outside Sills and Cross Sills (at each post) 6 x 4 inches
> Floor Joist (2 feet from centres), 6 x 2 do
> Plates (Piazza) cased all around, 7 x 4 do

Figure 5.33. *Paired brackets connecting posts to cornices ornament the front porch and side veranda of this Italianate-style house in Frelighsburg, Quebec.*

> do (Veranda), 8 x 3 do
> Rafters, 4 x 2 do
> The Rafters planed three sides with 1¼-inch half round, nailed to bottom edge, as per details.
> Support the floor upon locust posts set 3 feet in the ground.

For roof planking and covering, these house specifications called for:

> Piazza and Veranda roofs, with 1¼-inch perfectly sound, narrow plank, planed side down (planed smooth)—no beads.
>
> Cover all the roofs and line the gutters with charcoal roof tin I. C. brand, the sheets nailed, clenched and white leaded in the best manner and laid with the standing lock joint.

Woodward included the following specifications for painting a piazza:

> Properly stop with oil putty, all nail holes and other imperfections in the work to be painted, and size all exposed knots, etc.

Figure 5.34. *Veranda and porch details designed by New York architect Samuel F. Eveleth. Note the heavy chamfering details along the corner edges of all the posts and the use of Italianate-style balustrades, brackets, and rosettes. Woodward's National Architect (1869).*

Figure 5.35. *The wraparound veranda on this Italianate-style house built in 1872 in Center Sandwich, New Hampshire, features paired brackets beneath the soffits, a spoolwork valance, vernacular Romanesque columns, a fret-sawn balustrade, and simple lattice skirting beneath.*

Figure 5.36. *This delightful curved-ended side veranda with a bracketed roof cornice and turned posts is a late-nineteenth-century example of a local vernacular design that reflects the transition from the Italianate style to Queen Anne style in Saint Johnsbury, Vermont.*

Paint all the wood work of the building outside and inside, (exclusive of the inside floors, and inclusive of the piazza floors and outside steps, and the cutting in of the stairs) two good coats of the best English white lead and oil paint. . . .

Thoroughly cleanse the tin roofs and gutters, and paint two coats best metallic roof paint.

An example of an Italianate-style house built in 1872 with a highly decorated veranda wrapping around the front and side elevations is shown in figure 5.35.[33] Brackets continued to be featured on veranda designs associated with the Stick style, as well as on some of those built in the Queen Anne style during the late Victorian period (figure 5.36). In his 1881 pattern book, *Modern Architectural Designs and Details*, the architectural publisher William T. Comstock included numerous designs for brackets, many of which were suitable for verandas.

FRENCH SECOND EMPIRE

As with the Italianate style, the French Second Empire style embraced a dramatic tour-de-force of Romantic design motifs that contrasted sharply in feeling with the earlier, more literal emulations of classical forms. Popular in the United States during the aftermath of its Civil War, the French Second Empire style (or Mansard style, as it is also known, owing to its distinct double-pitched, hipped roof shape) was particularly favored for urban institutional buildings and for some houses that seem to have been designed to impress with little regard to subtlety.

Mansard-roofed houses designed in the French Second Empire style during the 1860s and 1870s typically featured attached verandas, entry porticos, and porches ornamented with bracketed posts and other trim features similar to those of the Italianate-style buildings of the same period. Classical Revival orders were also used with the French Second Empire style, especially on large institutional and commercial buildings and on a few high-style houses.

Although some designs offer delightfully romanticized versions of Renaissance Revival classicism, some observers find other French Second Empire–style buildings to be dreadfully ornate. Indeed, the details of the ornamentation on some of these verandas and porches may seem to push embellishment to a level of excess. But it should be remembered that by the 1860s and 1870s, such ornate machine-produced Victorian veranda trim became as important to the garb of a stylish house as were hoopskirts, corsets, and lace to a fashionable Victorian lady's wardrobe. Examples of French Second Empire–style houses with representative porches and verandas include the Captain Edward Penniman House (figure 5.37), built between 1867 and 1868 in Eastham, Massachusetts, and the Mrs. Benjamin Pomeroy House (figure 5.38), built between 1868 and 1869 in Southport, Connecticut.[34]

As with other fashions that have relied on increasing eclectic complexities of fancy details, the French Second Empire style's run was actually rather short-lived. Geographically concentrated in the Northeast and Midwest in the United States, but also found elsewhere in the U.S. and Canada, its reputation for excess soon fueled such strong negative reactions that some such landmarks have even been described as the "ugliest" examples of North American architectural design. Such sentiments, of course, are typically offered as justification for those with no interest in preservation, yet for those who do find fascination in its schemes

of imaginative embellishments, the porticos, verandas, and porches of French Second Empire–style buildings may provide intriguing feasts for observation, while also serving as ongoing opportunities for care and maintenance.

The common use of nearly flat or very shallow pitched roofs on porches and verandas on houses built in the French Second Empire style and Italianate style has contributed to their reputation for requiring high levels of maintenance. As the typical wooden shingles or slates of the era were inappropriate roofing for these shallow-pitched porch roofs, metal roofing (commonly tin-coated iron or "roofing tin") was used extensively instead. George Woodward included the following recommendations for roofing such houses in 1868: "All flat roofs to be trimmed with best quality roofing tin; and all tin work to be thoroughly painted with two coats of paint suitable for the purpose."[35]

The continual routine painting of these "tin roofs" was essential for preventing them from rusting and leaking, but because these low-pitched porch roof surfaces are often hidden, the necessary maintenance regimens were frequently neglected until serious leaks appeared. For flat or nearly flat roofs, this metal sheeting usually would be laid flat with soldered joints. For shallow-pitched veranda roofs, sheet metal also commonly was lapped over vertical battens or installed with standing seams.

Second Empire–style buildings built with mansard roofs were commonly built in Quebec and other parts of Canada from the 1860s and well into the early twentieth century. Many of these feature prominent attached verandas, entry porches, or balconies. One important representative example, recognized as a heritage building in

Figure 5.37. *Paired Corinthian columns and engaged pilasters dress the attached front portico of the Captain Edward Penniman House in Eastham, Massachusetts, built between 1867 and 1868 in the French Second Empire style. A balustrade with urn-shaped balusters lines the edge of the balcony tier above the denticulated cornice of the portico. Historic American Buildings Survey photograph, 1962,* HABS MASS,1-EAST,12-2.

Figure 5.39. *The attached front and side verandas on this Second Empire–style house in Saratoga Springs, New York, feature bracketed cornices, chamfered posts, very low balustrades with turned balusters, and diagonal lattice skirting beneath.*

Figure 5.38. *Built between 1868 and 1869 in the French Second Empire style, the Mrs. Benjamin Pomeroy House in Southport, Connecticut, features a three-part front veranda. The central bay serves as an entry porch projecting ahead of the shallower flanking veranda sections to reinforce the dominance of the central pavilion of the front facade. This projecting bay has large, square-sectioned, paired posts set on low, paired pedestals that are each trimmed with lozenge-shaped bolection moldings. The caps of these pedestals align with the railings that are masked in this photograph by shrubbery. The faces of the central bay porch posts are trimmed with applied Italianate-style bolection moldings. The soffits of the veranda entablatures are lifted upward with half-round ends. The trim on the flanking bays of the front veranda is slightly less ornate. The entire veranda cornice is trimmed with bracketed modillions along the edge of its nearly flat roof. This design matches the cornice trim where the sidewalls meet the mansard roof of the house. Historic American Buildings Survey photograph, 1969, HABS CONN,1-SOUPO,11-2.*

Figure 5.40. *Corner steps lead to the attached front veranda and side porch on this Second Empire–style house in Brandon, Vermont. Single scrolled brackets trim the veranda and porch cornices, while paired brackets trim the cornice above on the double-pitched mansard roof of the house. Square-sectioned veranda posts with chamfered edges are set on low, paneled pedestals, connected by very low balustrades with top rails that align with the windowsills behind.*

Figure 5.41. *An attached veranda with curved corners wraps around the Second Empire–style Superintendent's House, built in 1867 in Chambly, Quebec.*

Figure 5.42. *This circa 1865 view of the French Second Empire–style Boston City Hall shows its shallow entrance portico and tiered balconies dressed with paired Corinthians columns. Copy of a lithograph attributed to Bryant and Gilman. Historic American Buildings Survey photograph, HABS MASS,13-BOST,70-19.*

Canada, is the Chambly Canal Superintendent's House (figure 5.41), built in 1867 at the northern terminus of the Chambly Canal in Chambly, Quebec. Beneath its mansard roof is a veranda, supported by Tuscan columns, that wraps around three sides of the building that originally housed offices for the toll-collector and superintendent of the canal.[36] This building was restored by Parks Canada to resemble its appearance of 1929, when shingled roofing on the mansard was changed to match the sheet metal roofing on its veranda.[37]

Two of the most important monumental examples of French Second Empire–style government buildings in the United States are the Old City Hall in Boston (figure 5.42), built starting in 1865, and the massive State, War, and Navy Building (now called the Old Executive Office Building or Eisenhower Executive Office Building) in Washington, DC. Of the design of its new city hall, an 1866 report to the Boston City Council observed:

"The style of the new city hall is that of the Italian Renaissance as modified by the French architects of the last thirty years. This manner is the only style in which it will doubtless ere long be fully recognized by sound architectural critics as the true vernacular style of our age and country."[38]

Filling an entire city block, the immense Old Executive Office Building (figure 5.43) in Washington, DC, was designed in the French Second Empire style by Alfred B. Mullett, the Supervising Architect of the U.S. Treasury Department, and built in four stages between 1871 and 1888.[39] The tiered porticos and balconies on both of these buildings are finished with elaborate Renaissance Revival enrichments. Its granite porticos and tiered balconies are embellished with paired Doric columns on raised pedestals, and urn-shaped balusters line the low balustrades between.[40]

The French Second Empire style also became very popular for North American

Figure 5.43. *Filling an entire city block, the immense Old Executive Office Building in Washington, DC, was built in the French Second Empire style between 1871 and 1888. Historic American Buildings Survey photograph, 1969,* HABS DC,WASH,521-5.

Figure 5.44. *The Hotel Mitchell, which opened as the "Sea Cottage" in 1871 in York, Maine, and its adjacent annex featured broad attached verandas for summer guests.*

Figure 5.45. *A veranda measuring several hundred feet long wraps around three sides of the Grand Isle Lake House, built in 1903 as the Island Villa Hotel, overlooking Lake Champlain in Grand Isle, Vermont.*

resort hotels—including some built into the early twentieth century—with top stories partially masked by the mansard roofs providing additional useable floor space and with long, attached verandas offering plentiful space for sitting and promenading of guests. With its prominent mansard roof that was typical of some of the largest North American resort hotels built in the early 1870s, the Crossmon House in Alexandria Bay, New York, for example, provided its guests with generous opportunities to enjoy promenades while viewing the St. Lawrence River's Thousand Islands from its grand, two-story, wraparound veranda. According to one promotional account for this hotel, "There are spacious and elegantly furnished drawing rooms, wide corridors and broad verandas, and, from the latter, one of the most delightful views to be found in this entire region may be had."[41] Other examples include the Hotel Mitchell (figure 5.44), which opened as the "Sea Cottage" in 1871

in York, Maine; the Grand Isle Lake House (figure 5.45), built in 1903 as the Island Villa Hotel in Grand Isle, Vermont; and the Hotel Tadoussac, built in the 1940s in Tadoussac, Quebec (figure 5.46).[42]

OCTAGONS

Piazzas were a prominent feature of the octagon style of houses that was first popularized by the American phrenologist and amateur architect, Orson Squire Fowler. In

Figure 5.46. *With a view of the St. Lawrence River, an enclosed front veranda with a painted metal roof lines one side of the mansard-roofed Hotel Tadoussac, built in the 1940s in Tadoussac, Quebec, to replace an earlier grand resort hotel that had been destroyed by fire.*

Figure 5.47. *Surrounded on all eight sides by a veranda and balconies above, Orson Fowler's residence in Fishkill, New York, is shown in this engraving. Orson Squire Fowler,* A Home for All *(1854).*

his book *A Home for All*, Fowler published in 1850: "Only one other thing remains to complete the most perfect dwelling ever created—A PIAZZA ALL AROUND, AT EVERY STORY. Those who have ever enjoyed these luxuries, are loth to do without them, while those who have not, know not how duly to prize them. For one, I dearly love sunrise and sunset. They diffuse through my whole being so sweet and holy a calm, as literally to ravish my soul with earth's sweetest pleasures."[43] Fowler's expanded 1854 edition of *A Home for All* featured illustrations (figures 5.47 and 5.48) of two octagon houses with piazzas wrapping around all sides, including his own three-storied octagonal mansion that he completed that year in Fishkill, New York.[44]

Few other octagonal houses were built with piazzas or verandas surrounding on all eight sides, however. Of the octagonal houses built during their period of greatest popularity between the 1850s through the 1870s, only a few thousand may survive in the United States and probably less than

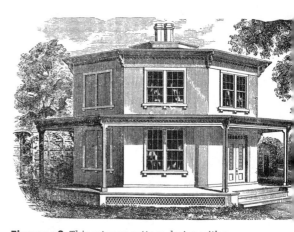

Figure 5.48. *This octagon cottage design with a veranda on three sides employs simple bracketed details. Orson Squire Fowler,* A Home for All *(1854).*

a hundred in Canada. The trim features on these piazzas typically reflected the popular architectural style of the period, the Italianate Revival, with bracketed embellishments; however, some, like Fowler's own residence, had piazza posts trimmed with simple classical moldings and others were trimmed with Gothic Revival details. Examples of octagonal houses with verandas include the Alonzo Benedict House (figure 5.49), built of stone in 1853 in Prairie du Chien, Wisconsin, and

Figure 5.49. *A curved-roofed veranda with bracketed posts extends around this stone octagonal house, built in 1853 in Prairie du Chien, Wisconsin. Historic American Buildings Survey photograph, circa 1961, HABS WIS,12-PRACH,3-1.*

Figure 5.50. *This brick octagon house with a front veranda on three sides with Tuscan columns was built about 1854 in Saint Johnsbury, Vermont.*

another (figure 5.50) built in Saint Johnsbury, Vermont, about 1854.[45]

One of the most eclectic historic octagonal houses (and among the few in the United States with domed roofs) is the Armour-Stiner House (figures 5.51 and 5.52) in Irvington, New York. Although the house was built between 1859 and 1860, the elaborate veranda that surrounds the entire house was added about 1872, reportedly at a cost of $26,000. This Italianate-style veranda features paired Corinthianesque colonnettes, paired cornice brackets, and a fancy balustrade with foliated cast-iron panels inset with roundels with carved dog heads.[46]

RICHARDSONIAN ROMANESQUE

Mainly an architectural style reserved for institutional buildings, the Richardsonian Romanesque is named for the influential Boston-based American architect Henry Hobson Richardson, whose architectural works of the 1880s evolved with some iconic porch designs featuring bold arches that combined medieval inspirations with simple modern forms. Also known as the Romanesque Revival, the style is based on architectural forms used in Europe from the seventh century through the twelfth century, characterized by heavy masonry, picturesque massing, and the semicircular arch supported by squat columns or clusters of colonnettes. Series of semicircular arches are used to form arcades and arcade porches. On these, Romanesque Revival columns typically feature cushion capitals with square tops that are reduced to cylindrical forms by curved corners, semicircular lunettes, scallops, or other shapes with embellished surfaces. On some Richardsonian Romanesque buildings, however, a single, large semicircular Syrian arch springs from the floor without supporting columns to form a porch opening.

Examples include the main porch entrance of Henry Hobson Richardson's 1885 design for the Frederick Billings Library (figure 5.53) at the University of Vermont in

Figure 5.51. *An elaborate veranda added in 1872 surrounds the octagonal Armour-Stiner House in Irvington, New York. Historic American Buildings Survey photograph, 1974, HABS NY,60-IRV,3-11.*

Figure 5.52. *View inside the 1872 veranda showing the paired Corinthianesque colonnettes and exposed ceiling framing with molded edges at the octagonal Armour-Stiner House, Irvington, New York. Historic American Buildings Survey photograph, 1974, HABS NY,60-IRV,3-12.*

Figure 5.53. *A single, large Syrian arch of Longmeadow sandstone marks the recessed front entry porch of the 1885 Frederick Billings Library at the University of Vermont in Burlington, designed by Henry Hobson Richardson.*

Figure 5.54. *Henry Hobson Richardson combined medieval and modern forms into one of his last and most iconic porch designs, the arched, recessed side entrance of the John J. Glessner House, built in 1886 in Chicago.*

Figure 5.55. *The Pequot Library in Southport, Connecticut, erected in 1893, features squat columns with square cushion capitals supporting the center stone arch. Piers of quarry-faced stones support the ends of the arcaded entrance porch. Historic American Buildings Survey photograph, 1966,* HABS CONN,1-SOUPO,23-4.

Burlington, and Richardson's renowned design for the recessed side entrance of the John J. Glessner House (figure 5.54) in Chicago, built in 1886 of rusticated granite ashlar. This porch design is remarkable for its symbolic balance of convenient urban access with fortress-like protection.[47]

A series of three arches forms an arcaded porch entrance of the Pequot Library (figure 5.55) in Southport, Connecticut, which was designed between 1885 and 1887 in the Richardsonian Romanesque style by Robert H. Robertson and erected in 1893. Squat columns with square cushion capitals support the stone arches.[48]

STICK STYLE

With their faux half-timbered exterior walls and Elizabethan references, Stick-style buildings reflect a transition between the Gothic Revival and the Queen Anne styles.[49] Origins can be traced back to the Picturesque designs published by A. J.

Downing and Gervase Wheeler in the 1840s and 1850s, but the main period of popularity of the Stick style of architecture extended through the 1860s and mid-1870s, with notable works designed by architects Richard Morris Hunt and Henry Hobson Richardson. As its name implies, the Stick style was characterized by the prominent use of exposed timbers for veranda posts and braces and for decorative gable trusses and screens, as well as by the use of boards applied as decoration to exterior walls in patterns simulating half-timbering. This applied trim was typically painted to match the color of the timbers and other stickwork in polychrome decoration schemes.

Stick-style veranda posts and exposed timbers typically had square cross-sections with chamfered edges. The decorative chamfering of exposed timbers has a long tradition. For practical reasons, the removal of the wood along an edge of a timber at forty-five degrees makes the timber edge less likely splinter off from weathering or wear. Although one could find some other practical advantages of beveling the corners of posts and trim elements, from the 1860s through the 1880s, chamfering also became an important design element that was often accentuated by contrasting colors of paint.[50] In addition to chamfering, exposed timbers and their faux counterparts on Stick-style and Queen Anne–style buildings were sometimes ornamented with incised decorative designs based on simple Gothic motifs, such as those that were popularized by the English designer Charles Eastlake, whose influential book *Hints on Household Taste in Furniture, Upholstery, and Other Details*, was first published in London in the late 1860s.[51]

Representative examples of Stick-style houses with verandas that have been recorded by the Historic American Buildings

Figure 5.56. *Veranda brackets with chamfered edges are character-defining features of the Stick-style Isaac P. White House, built between 1871 and 1874 in Newport, Rhode Island. Historic American Buildings Survey photograph, 1969,* HABS RI,3-NEWP,58-2.

Figure 5.57. *The Stick-style Frances M. Mackay House, built in 1875 in Cambridge, Massachusetts, has a front entry porch ornamented by chamfered posts and brackets. Detail from Historic American Buildings Survey photograph, 1967,* HABS MASS,9-CAMB,27-1.

Figure 5.58. *Bold, sawn brackets accent the wraparound veranda on the Emlen Physick House, built in 1879 in Cape May, New Jersey. Detail from Historic American Buildings Survey photograph, 1961,* HABS NJ,5-CAPMA,68-1.

Survey include the Isaac P. White House (figure 5.56), built between 1871 and 1874 in Newport, Rhode Island; the 1875 Frances M. Mackay House (figure 5.57), in Cambridge, Massachusetts, designed by Boston architects Peabody and Stearns; and the Emlen Physick House (figure 5.58), built in 1879 in Cape May, New Jersey.[52]

QUEEN ANNE

A sharp break from the Gothic Revival, Italianate, and French Second Empire styles that had dominated North American architectural design during the mid-nineteenth century was inaugurated by the widespread adoption of the Queen Anne style. Closely related to the Stick, Shingle, and Colonial Revival styles, the Queen Anne style was well suited to the times, especially as the United States celebrated the one hundredth anniversary of the nation's founding with the Centennial International Exposition of 1876 held in Philadelphia. At that grand exposition, the inclusion of a model structure built by the British government for display of the new Queen Anne–style of architectural design prompted great interest.

Although the name suggests that the Queen Anne style was a revival of English architectural designs common during the reign of Queen Anne from 1702 to 1714, in fact, most of the initial motifs of the Queen Anne style in Britain and North America were based on details of English vernacular buildings constructed at least a century or two earlier, during the late medieval and Elizabethan eras. Eclectic from the start, the Queen Anne style's loose historicism contrasted with the more scholarly perfectionism of the Greek Revival and Gothic Revival styles.

Largely inspired by the imaginative creations of architect Richard Norman Shaw in England that were published in the *American Architect and Buildings News* magazine starting in 1876, the Queen Anne style was quickly popularized through pattern books produced by Palliser, Palliser & Company, publisher William T. Comstock, and others. Many of these designs combined design motifs from medieval England with those from colonial America. In his influential 1878 book, *Modern Dwellings in Town and Country Adapted to American Wants and Climate*, architect H. Hudson Holly even found ways to justify the incorporation of verandas into American Queen Anne–style designs:

Architecture is a comparatively new art in this country, and has had but little earnest and intelligent study; so we cannot be said to have any styles and systems peculiarly our own. In the absence of such, we have been too apt to use, inappropriately, the orders of foreign nations, which express the especial needs of those countries, and those idiosyncrasies of building which point toward an American style. Doubtless we may introduce from abroad methods of design which meet our requirements, but we must not hesitate to eliminate those portions for which we have no use, or to make such additions as our circumstances demand. . . .

So, too, it would be the merest folly, in building an English cottage, not to have a veranda, simply because its prototypes in England have none. We evidently have need of this appliance in our dry and sunny climate. From such requirements a distinctive feature of American architecture must arise.[53]

Holly continued with a criticism of the "slavish conformity" to the Gothic Revival style that had so gripped architectural design since the days of Augustus Welby Pugin in England and A. J. Downing in America, noting:

In fact, Gothic architecture was not originally intended to meet domestic wants.

There are some who are so carried away with the architecture that happens to be in vogue, that they consider it indispensable, regardless of its adaptability, like the quack doctor, who, finding that a certain medicine is efficacious in one disease, advertises its infallible power to cure "all the ills that flesh is heir to." . . . So, too, in this country. An expensive villa near our city, built after a Gothic design, is so wedded to the style, that, notwithstanding the absence of natural shade, it has neither porch nor veranda to serve as a protection from the rays of our almost tropical sun. Common-sense should be at the base of all true art, as well as of all true living and thinking.[54]

Holly then advocated moving away from the Gothic Revival style in America, offering instead examples of "most beautiful and suitable specimens of modern cottage architecture in England," designed by Norman Shaw and those erected at the Philadelphia Centennial by the British government. He summed up by claiming:

> . . . [I]n what is loosely called the "Queen Anne" style we find the most simple mode of honest English building, worked out in an artistic and natural form, fitting with the sash-windows and ordinary doorways which express real domestic needs (of which it is the outcome); and so, in our house-building, conserving truth far more effectively than can be done with the Gothic. One great advantage in adopting this and other styles of the "free classic" school is, that they are in their construction, and in the forms of the mouldings employed, the same as the common vernacular styles with which our workmen are familiar.[55]

Holly's *Modern Dwellings in Town and Country* includes numerous illustrations of Queen Anne–style houses with prominent verandas. Some wrapped around three sides of cottages (figure 5.59), and of another Picturesque design feature (figure 5.60) he noted, "The veranda, being exposed to the morning sun, is protected by an awning, which, while affording ample shade, is at such an elevation as not to cut off the view. This awing can, of course, be raised when the sun has retreated so as to leave the piazza in the shade."[56]

Another prominent promoter of the Queen Anne style was the publisher William T. Comstock of New York. Many of his pattern books of architectural plans included renderings and scaled drawings of piazza and porch designs and construction details. The Queen Anne style was further developed by such notable North American architects as William Appleton Potter, Robert Henderson Robertson, Charles Follen McKim, William Mead, Stanford White, W. Ralph Emerson, Henry Hobson Richardson, John Calvin Stevens, Peabody & Stearns, Rossiter & Wright, and Bruce Price. Other architects, contractors, and builders also soon transposed the Queen Anne and related styles into a potpourri of vernacular forms that were so eclectic and improvised that it is sometimes difficult to differentiate between these variations. Indeed, the term "folk Victorian" may used to describe such designs produced from the 1880s through the early 1900s in the United States and Canada.

Most Queen Anne–style verandas were built by contractors using simple tools and basic materials. Here, for example, is a description of a "cheap verandah" published in the *Canadian Architect and Builder* in 1899:

> The whole work is plain and within the range of most workmen. The posts are turned from 5 x 5 inch stuff, and the plate, which forms part of the finish may be formed of a 5 x 5 inch timber, or it may be built up of dressed one inch stuff. The brackets are sawn out of two inch plank with a jig or band saw. The roof may be covered with shingles or with tin or galvanized iron. The cresting, where such is required, may be cut from one inch pine or cedar and the rails and balusters may be wrought by hand or machine, out of pine,

Figure 5.59. *This early Queen Anne–style design for a "simple frame cottage of small cost" featured a wide veranda surrounding the living room on three sides. Note the straight-timbered posts and braces on the wraparound veranda and the decorative gable truss at the left, which reflect the transition from the Stick style. H. Hudson Holly,* Modern Dwellings *(1878); Rare Books and Special Collections, McGill University Library.*

Figure 5.60. *The wrap-around veranda and attached to a porte-cochere are distinctive features of this Picturesque Queen Anne–style cottage. Also note the balconies on second story and an attic. H. Hudson Holly,* Modern Dwellings *(1878); Rare Books and Special Collections, McGill University Library.*

Figure 5.61. *Eastlake-inspired millwork, with lathe-turned brackets and scroll-sawn balustrades, accents the Queen Anne–style wraparound veranda on the 1885 headquarters of the New Hampshire Veterans Association in Weirs Beach, New Hampshire.*

Figure 5.62. *Turned posts and valances and balustrades with fancy spindlework and scroll-sawn details dress the curved corner veranda on this Queen Anne–style house in Pasadena, California. A small balcony porch is recessed above the main entrance.*

as may be thought best. The top rail may be 2½ inches thick, and the middle and lower rails may be made from two inch stuff. The frieze should be not less than an inch wider than the joists and project down low enough to receive lattice strips. The base may be any width to suit the position. The lattice strips should be ⅜ inch thick and about 1¼ inches wide. The gutter or trough forms the finish for the cornice, and is made of tin or galvanized iron. The design is very simple, low priced, and withal attractive.[57]

The Queen Anne style's relaxed approach and flexibility fit well with the trend toward more suburban development patterns and with the construction of seasonal resort homes on attractive sites, all made possible by North America's rapidly expanding rail-based transportation systems and the accumulation of great wealth among some families who profited directly and hugely from the industrial revolution and global trade.

Key design elements of Queen Anne–style houses in North America are the deep verandas that often were built to extend across entire front elevations and to wrap around at least one corner. Closely tied to the earlier Stick style, decorative half-timbered wooden trim and lattice-screened aprons beneath porch decks were common. Although some early Queen Anne–style verandas were ornamented by chamfered stickwork, soon lathe-turned posts, baluastrades, and spindlework valances became common (figures 5.61, 5.62, and 5.63). According to one study, about half of Queen Anne–style houses have turned porch posts and spindlework, about 35 percent have classical columns, about 5 percent have decorative half-timbering, and about 5 percent have patterned brickwork or masonry with little wooden trim detailing.[58]

Balcony porches projecting beyond building walls or roofs also became decorative features of houses built in the Queen Anne style across North America between the 1880s and 1890s. Some were set in front gables with full-width verandas below. The

Figure 5.63. *Delicate fretwork ornaments the Queen Anne–style veranda of this circa 1892 former rectory in Saint-Pierre-de-Véronne-à-Pike-River, Quebec. The simple, thin, wooden railings are recent additions. These extend higher up from the floor than do most original veranda railings.*

Figure 5.64. *Three attached balcony porches with turned posts grace this Queen Anne–style house built in 1880–81 in Jackson, Tennessee. Historic American Buildings Survey photograph, circa 1974, HABS tn18.*

John L. Wisdom House (figure 5.64) in Jackson, Tennessee, for example, was built in 1880–81 with three attached balcony porches with turned posts.[59] Figure 5.65 shows another typical example of a Queen Anne-style house with a balcony porch sheltered by a shed roof.

In addition to these porches and verandas, other character-defining features of the Queen Anne style are complex shapes, irregular massing, steeply pitched hipped and gable roofs with cresting on the ridges, asymmetrical facades, decorative detailing, and a variety of rich contrasting colors and textures. Mixed shingles and clapboards are common wall sheathings on Queen Anne–style houses when constructed in wood, as are combinations of decorative tile, patterned brick, and stone when constructed of masonry. Some examples even combined rusticated stone or brick on the first story and clapboards or shingle sheathing on the walls above. Other Queen Anne–style

Figure 5.65. *An attached balcony porch projects above the wraparound front veranda of this circa 1880s Queen Anne–style house in Danville, Vermont.*

houses made prominent use of lattice. A large apron of diagonal lattice screen surrounds the base of the wraparound veranda of the Ninth and Eleventh Regiment building of the New Hampshire Veterans Association (figure 5.66), for example, built in the Queen Anne style in 1888 at Weirs Beach, New Hampshire.[60]

Figure 5.66. *A prominent apron of diagonal lattice surrounds the base of the wraparound veranda of the Ninth and Eleventh Regiment building of the New Hampshire Veterans Association, built in the Queen Anne style in 1888 at Weirs Beach, New Hampshire. On the first story, square posts with decorative scroll-sawn brackets support the overhanging tentlike roof. The projecting second-story balcony porch is trimmed with broadly arched valances.*

Figure 5.67. *A vernacular Queen Anne–style porch with simple turned posts shelters the front of this hearse house built next to the village cemetery in 1890 in Bakersfield, Vermont.*

Figure 5.68. *This small, circa 1900 Queen Anne–style cottage at the Chautauqua retreat in Boulder, Colorado, features a recessed front porch with turned posts and thin decorative brackets. Its ceiling is painted very light blue, a color that has long been popular for porch ceilings in many parts of North America.*

Although during the second half of the nineteenth century, trained architects designed many higher-quality houses as individual artistic creations, many other dwellings, cottages, and utilitarian buildings were built across North America by builders and contractors without the involvement of architects. A hearse house (figure 5.67), for example, was built next to the village cemetery in 1890 in Bakersfield, Vermont, with simple turned posts supporting its front porch.[61] Queen Anne–style turned posts were also used to support the front porch of a small cottage (figure 5.68) at the Chautauqua retreat in Boulder, Colorado.

Many of these Queen Anne–style buildings were vernacular interpretations of pattern book designs that reflected both popular tastes and the availability of mass-produced millwork products. This trend away from individually designed houses

accelerated with the rise of companies that provided stock plans by mail order. Houses designed in the Queen Anne style were among the first to be marketed directly to consumers through architect-designed plans offered in pattern book catalogues. These designs were especially popular as model

Figure 5.69. *An octagonal porch wraps around the projecting front bay of this Shoppell-designed Queen Anne–style catalogue house in Prince George's County, Maryland, built in 1888. Historic American Building Survey photograph, 1989,* HABS MD,17-BERHTS,1-4.

Figure 5.70. *An octagonal gazebo with arched bays supported by paired Tuscan columns on paneled pedestals accents the L-shaped front porch of the Jeremiah Nunan House, built in 1892 in Jacksonville, Oregon. Connected to the porch is a gable-roofed portico sheltering the front entrance. Above this portico is a corner balcony on the second floor. This Queen Anne–style design was offered in* The Cottage Souvenir *catalogue. Historic American Buildings Survey photograph, 1971,* HABS ORE,15-JACVI,58-2.

homes built at modest prices by developers of commuter suburbs.

Among the first who found success offering mail-order house designs were George and Charles Palliser, who published their *Model Homes for the People* in 1876, followed by *Palliser's American Cottage Homes* in 1878, and the Cooperative Building Plan Association of New York City, led by architect Robert W. Shoppell. An example of a Shoppell-designed Queen Anne–style house with a prominent front porch built in 1888 in Prince George's County, Maryland (figure 5.69) has been documented by the Historic American Buildings Survey.[62] Another example is the Jeremiah Nunan House (figure 5.70) in Jacksonville, Oregon, erected in 1892 from plans offered by George Franklin Barber of Knoxville, Tennessee, in his book *The Cottage Souvenir*.[63]

SHINGLE STYLE

Shingle-style houses are readily identifiable by the prolific use of wooden shingles that act as a scalelike covering for the walls and other exterior building surfaces. The style was most popular during the 1880s and 1890s, especially in New England and other locations where it became fashionable for grand summer "cottages" built in picturesque locations near the seacoast, by lakes, and in the mountains. Vernacular variations often include some architectural features of the contemporaneous Richardsonian Romanesque style, as well as on concurrent Queen Anne and Colonial Revival–style buildings. Although certainly not as common as the Queen Anne or Colonial Revival, examples of Shingle-style houses may still be found in towns, suburbs, and scenic locations across North America.[64]

Figure 5.71. *The William G. Low House in Bristol, Rhode Island, designed in 1887 by McKim, Mead, and White, architects, was one of the most memorable examples of the Shingle style built in the United States. Detail from Historic American Buildings Survey photograph, 1962,* HABS RI,1-BRIST,18-3.

Figure 5.72. *With shingles covering the porch posts, parapets, and walls, this suburban Shingle-style house displays a playful eclecticism of details and asymmetry. Note how a bay window merges into the recessed front porch on the left. Also note the arched porch spandrel railings with decorative fretwork on the bays beneath the American flag and under the furled awning.*

Figure 5.73. *As with many vernacular examples of the Shingle style, the flowing curve of this corner veranda is skinned with wooden shingles. Also note the application of shingles to the veranda posts on this house in Rutland, Vermont.*

One of the most beautiful examples of a summer residence done in the Shingle style was the William G. Low House (figure 5.71) in Bristol, Rhode Island, designed by McKim, Mead, and White, architects. Built in 1887, but demolished in 1962, this long, narrow house featured a large, room-size veranda recessed beneath the south eaves of its broad gable roof.[65]

Verandas and porches on Shingle-style houses are typically very prominent features, often wrapping around two or more sides or placed to take advantage of a scenic view. They may have shingles covering

Figure 5.74. *Built in 1902, this late example of a Shingle-style house in Burlington, Vermont, features shingles flowing down from the gable wall to form a flared roof over the partially recessed entrance porch. Stained wooden shingles also cover the porch posts and its low parapet walls.*

their posts, but there are also examples with boxed or turned posts, or simple classical columns. Either balustrades with simple balusters or solid half-walls covered with shingles commonly extend between these porch posts (figures 5.72, 5.73, and 5.74).

COLONIAL REVIVAL

Drawing on a variety of neoclassical forms and motifs that were popular with the earlier Georgian and Federal architectural styles, the Colonial Revival style (and its Georgian Revival and Neoclassical variations) grew in popularity during the late nineteenth and on through the twentieth century, especially in the United States. In a move way from the fancy frills, encumbering verandas, and the rusticated sternness of preceding Victorian styles, Colonial Revival–style houses of the 1880s and 1890s instead commonly featured crisp, white-painted front porticos and side porches trimmed with classical detailing including single or

paired Tuscan, Doric, Ionic, or Corinthian columns, and ornate balustrades and parapets with turned balusters. The Colonial Revival style has such strong symbolic connections to patriotism and tradition in the United States that it might even be considered *the* traditional American style.

An early representative example of a Colonial Revival–style house, the Annie Longfellow Thorpe House, built in 1887 in Cambridge, Massachusetts, was designed by Alexander Wadsworth Longfellow Jr., an architect who had worked in the office of noted architect Henry Hobson Richardson before establishing his own practice.[66] Drawing freely on forms, motifs, and designs of architectural elements found on Georgian and Federal-style houses, the Annie Longfellow Thorpe House (figures 5.75 and 5.76) features a semicircular front portico that is similar to those on some distinguished Federal-style buildings in the Massachusetts Bay area. A deep side porch was balanced with a porte-cochere on the opposite side, creating a symmetrical massing that was somewhat similar to that of the nearby Vassal-Craigie-Longfellow House (figure 4.11). The fancy balustrades above the portico, porch, and porte-cochere, combined with the building's high gambrel roof, massive chimneys, dormers, and large tripartite windows on the first story, all provide clues that this Colonial Revival–design is of the late Victorian era.

A wide variety of porch designs inspired by the Colonial Revival style continued to evolve through the 1890s and into the post-Victorian era of the early twentieth century, especially on vernacular and contractor-built houses. Many of these combined older conservative house forms with the various contemporary manufactured moldings, railings, and columns for porches being stocked by local millworks.

Figure 5.75. *The Annie Longfellow Thorpe House, a Colonial Revival–house built in 1887 in Cambridge, Massachusetts, features a semicircular front portico with a shallow loggia balcony above, a deep side porch on the left, and a porte-cochere hidden behind the foliage at the right. Historic American Buildings Survey photograph, 1964, HABS MASS,9-CAMB,63-1.*

Figure 5.76. *The front portico on the Annie Longfellow Thorpe House, 1887, features columns and entablature in the Corinthian order, enriched with urns and swags along the frieze. The roof of the portico is ringed by an open balustrade with turned balusters that defines a second-story balcony. Two Ionic columns trim a shallow loggia that extends the depth of the balcony space. Historic American Buildings Survey photograph, 1964, HABS MASS,9-CAMB,63-3.*

Figure 5.77. *Slender boxed columns frame the view from the west portico at Hill-Stead, the Colonial Revival–style Pope-Riddle House in Farmington, Connecticut. Historic American Buildings Survey photograph, 2006, HABS ct81.*

Figure 5.78. *Slender Ionic columns support the deep corner porch of this Colonial Revival–style house in Pasadena, California. Simple, square balusters line the railings on the first story and along the parapet railings on the edge of the porch roof.*

Figure 5.79. *The small front porch on this Colonial Revival–style house, built in 1900 in Burlington, Vermont, features Tuscan columns and low balustrades with square balusters. A matching low balustrade surrounds its nearly flat roof. Square newel posts support bannisters that flank the front steps.*

An important example of a turn-of-the-century Colonial Revival–style house is Hill-Stead (figure 5.77), the Pope-Riddle House in Farmington, Connecticut, built between 1898 and 1901 to the designs of the noted female architect Theodate Pope Riddle, who worked in collaboration with the architectural firm of McKim, Mead, and White. The west portico of this house features slender, boxed columns trimmed with delicate recessed panels.[67]

Although the use of colossal columns continued to be popular for hotels, institutions, and mansions built in the Colonial Revival style during this period, there was a general trend for town and country houses to have smaller front entrance porches or porticos, especially as shallow side porches became popular for service access and deep side or rear "living porches" were designed and furnished for comfort and leisure use.

Many porches on Colonial Revival–style houses were built by contractors using stock components available through North American millwork suppliers. One of the largest of these was the Morgan Woodwork Organization, based in Oshkosh, Wisconsin, which manufactured stock designs of windows, doors, moldings, trim, columns, and even complete porch kits that were distributed by the 1920s from warehouses in Chicago, Detroit, Baltimore, and Jersey City, and with sales offices in Cleveland, New York City, and Atlanta. In the 1921 Morgan Woodwork Organization's catalogue, *Building with Assurance*, four types of full-height

MORGAN STANDARDIZED PORCH COLUMNS

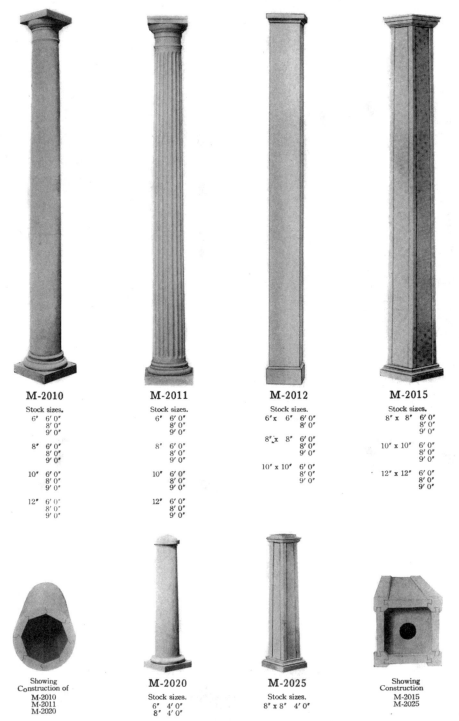

M-2010

Stock sizes.

6″	6′ 0″	
	8′ 0″	
	9′ 0″	
8″	6′ 0″	
	8′ 0″	
	9′ 0″	
10″	6′ 0″	
	8′ 0″	
	9′ 0″	
12″	6′ 0″	
	8′ 0″	
	9′ 0″	

M-2011

Stock sizes.

6″	6′ 0″	
	8′ 0″	
	9′ 0″	
8″	6′ 0″	
	8′ 0″	
	9′ 0″	
10″	6′ 0″	
	8′ 0″	
	9′ 0″	
12″	6′ 0″	
	8′ 0″	
	9′ 0″	

M-2012

Stock sizes.

6′ x	6′	6′ 0″	
		8′ 0″	
8′ x	8′	6′ 0″	
		8′ 0″	
		9′ 0″	
10′ x	10′	6′ 0″	
		8′ 0″	
		9′ 0″	

M-2015

Stock sizes.

8″ x	8″	6′ 0″	
		8′ 0″	
		9′ 0″	
10″ x	10″	6′ 0″	
		8′ 0″	
		9′ 0″	
12″ x	12″	6′ 0″	
		8′ 0″	
		9′ 0″	

Showing
Construction of
M-2010
M-2011
M-2020

M-2020

Stock sizes.

6″	4′ 0″
8″	4′ 0″

M-2025

Stock sizes.

8″ x 8″	4′ 0″

Showing
Construction
M-2015
M-2025

These Morgan Designs can be built in other sizes

Figure 5.80. *Four types of full-height columns and two half-height versions in various stock sizes. 1921 Morgan Woodwork Organization catalogue.*

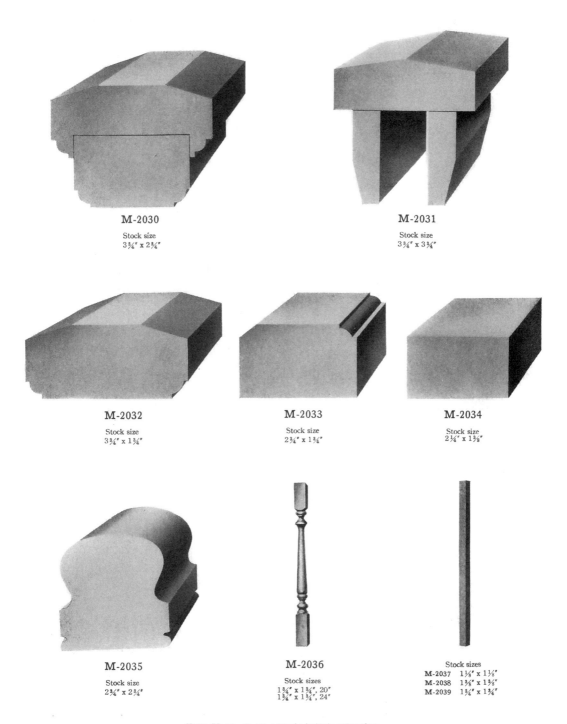

M-2030
Stock size
3¾" x 2¾"

M-2031
Stock size
3¾" x 3¾"

M-2032
Stock size
3¾" x 1¾"

M-2033
Stock size
2¾" x 1¾"

M-2034
Stock size
2¼" x 1⅜"

M-2035
Stock size
2¾" x 2¾"

M-2036
Stock sizes
1¾" x 1¾", 20"
1¾" x 1¾", 24"

Stock sizes
M-2037   1⅛" x 1⅛"
M-2038   1⅜" x 1⅜"
M-2039   1¾" x 1¾"

These Morgan Designs can be built in other sizes.

Figure 5.81. *Standardized designs for stock porch railings and balusters were offered by millwork suppliers. 1921 Morgan Woodwork Organization catalogue.*

columns (figure 5.80) and two half-height versions in various stock sizes were offered, as well as stock porch railings and balusters (figure 5.81).[68]

As a result of the widespread availability of these components, hundreds of thousands of homes were built in a "mix-and-match" array of stock forms and standardized millwork features in the growing North American suburbs during the first three decades of the twentieth century. Although some types of these forms and features may be concentrated in local neighborhoods that were developed during this period, other examples of these "catalogue porches" are widespread from coast to coast.

6

Post-Victorian Styles

The post-Victorian Progressive era of the early twentieth century brought such innovation and prodigious eclecticism to domestic architectural design in North America that it can be challenging to make precise classifications among the many architectural styles of houses with porches built during this period. Indeed, evidence of specific architectural styles of twentieth-century houses is based not so much on the symbolic use of architectural embellishments, as had been the norm during the preceding Victorian era, but rather more on the loosely coordinated application of manufactured building parts and the use of stock plans that were marketed to builders and designers by catalogues and millwork companies. Typical shapes and forms of houses and their exterior features may help with the identification of the various popular styles of this period, however.

An example of the houses being built during the first decade of the twentieth century in an upscale neighborhood in Dallas, Texas, can be seen in a circa 1910 postcard view of Munger Place (figure 6.1). This planned development, started in 1905, was one of the first deed-restricted neighborhoods in Texas. Most of its houses were built in the Prairie style with broad porches.[1]

PRAIRIE

Houses designed in the Prairie style, which was freely fashioned on some of the early works by George W. Maher, Frank Lloyd Wright, and other Chicago school architects, were widely propagated by contractors and builders using pattern books and house plan catalogues during the late 1890s and early 1900s. These Prairie-style houses may be identified by their broadly overhanging eaves with boxed cornices extending from shallow-pitched, hipped roofs. With a

Figure 6.1. *With broadly overhanging eaves and deep front porches supported by massive piers, the two-story houses that lined Munger Place in Dallas are typical of those being built in planned suburbs across the North America between 1905 and 1915. Circa 1910 postcard view.*

deep, full-width front porch supported by massive piers, a curved corner sun porch, and a shallow side porch, the John Farson House (Pleasant Home) (figure 6.2) in Oak Park, Illinois, is one of the earliest examples of a Prairie-style house. It was designed by Maher in 1897.[2] Another representative example of the style, featuring a front porch supported by massive piers, is the J. B. Butler House (figure 6.3) in Fort Dodge, Iowa, built in 1903.[3]

Especially common in the central regions of the United States, but also built elsewhere, Prairie-style houses typically have deep porches that are supported by massive piers of brick, dressed stone, or stucco. These vertical piers may extend all the way to the ground or may be supported by solid half-walls. On many Prairie-style porches, these knee-walls extend between the support piers. The straight lines and cubist forms of these structures were precursors of

Figure 6.2. *The Prairie-style John Farson House (Pleasant Home) in Oak Park, Illinois, features a deep, full-width front porch supported by massive piers, a curved corner sun porch, and a shallow side porch.*

Figure 6.3. *With its front porch and side porte-cochere supported by massive piers faced with long Roman bricks, the J. B. Butler House in Fort Dodge, Iowa, was built in 1903 in the Prairie style. Historic American Buildings Survey photograph, 1977, HABS IOWA,94-FTDO,1-1.*

Figure 6.4. *Massive brick piers support a hip-roofed side porch on this Prairie-style residence in Buffalo, New York, the Darwin D. Martin House, designed in 1904 by Frank Lloyd Wright. The stone-topped brick half-walls of the porch project ahead of the piers and are articulated with vertical and horizontal details to emphasize the cubist geometry of the design. Historic American Buildings Survey photograph, 1965, HABS NY,15-BUF,5-5.*

Figure 6.5. *A full-width front porch supported by massive stucco-covered piers was added in 1906 when this older house in Oak Park, Illinois, was renovated in the Prairie style. The solid, uninterrupted half-wall between the two corner piers is slightly recessed to emphasize the verticality of these supports.*

Figure 6.6. *Massive brick piers on the corners support a full-width opening of the east front porch of the Ernest J. Magerstadt House in Chicago, built in 1908 to the design of George W. Maher. The stone-capped brick half-wall that extends across the front of the porch projects slightly ahead of the corner piers, instead of being recessed slightly behind, as is also common on Prairie-style porches. Historic American Buildings Survey photograph, 1963, HABS ILL,16-CHIG,26-1.*

the cubical Modern movement designs developed soon after by Frank Lloyd Wright and other architects.

AMERICAN FOURSQUARE

The American Foursquare house (also known as the Prairie Box) is something of a vernacular bridge between the Colonial Revival style and the Prairie style of houses that were also being built during the early twentieth century. American Foursquare houses typically have a square footprint, a steep pyramidal hipped roof, symmetrical two-story facades, and a full-length porch across the front. These porches are generally supported by wooden "colonial" columns, arranged singly or in pairs, rising full height from the porch deck or as half-columns standing on piers or on solid half-

walls. Although some Foursquare porches may have massive corner piers instead of columns, porches supported by piers that extend all the way to the ground are more common on Craftsman or Prairie-style house porches.

The general massing of American Foursquares may be similar to Prairie-style houses, but the hipped roofs on Foursquares are typically more steeply pitched and embellished with large dormers, thus providing more space and headroom in attics. The roof eaves on the porches and main blocks of Foursquare houses typically have boxed cornices, but these eaves do not project as far out from the walls as do those on Prairie-style houses.

Offering a conservative, traditional appearance that was less frilly than the earlier

Figure 6.7. *Paired and single Tuscan columns standing on boxed piers support the broad front porch of this American Foursquare house built in 1905 in Burlington, Vermont. Note the symmetrical facade and the mimicking of millwork elements along the cornices of the porch and beneath the eaves of the pyramidal roof of the house. Also note that the stout newel posts that support the railings flanking the front steps match the boxed piers that support the porch columns and railings.*

Figure 6.8. *A screened porch extends across the entire front of the Bert W. Leavitt House in Lincoln, Nebraska, constructed in 1910 of rusticated concrete block walls, and with clay tiles covering the hipped roof. Historic American Buildings Survey photograph, 1984. HABS NEB,55-LINC,8-1.*

Victorian styles, Foursquares were featured as a "square type of house" in mail-order house catalogues of the period and were promoted as being especially suitable for farmhouses. Catalogue descriptions of some of these boasted about the full-width "large front porch." As an alternative to the smaller, single-story bungalows, American Foursquares were often also built in urban small-lot subdivisions and in streetcar suburbs.[4] Their main period of popularity was between 1900 and the late 1910s, although some examples date from before 1900, and a few others were still being built into the 1920s.

MISSION REVIVAL

Recognizable by their characteristic stucco walls with ornamental parapets and red tile roofs, Mission Revival–style houses typically have deep front porches supported by stucco piers or arches. Coinciding with the Craftsman movement, the Mission Revival style was popular from about 1900 to the 1930s, especially in California, Florida, and the American Southwest; however, examples are scattered throughout most regions of the United States, as well as in central and western Canada.

The first design included in Gustav Stickley's *Craftsman Homes* was a "craftsman house founded on the California Mission style." Planned to be built with cement stucco on the walls and a red tile roof, the two-story house featured a recessed front porch with shallow round arches to provide "light and air."[5]

Published in 1912, another description of a proposed porch for a red tile–roofed Spanish Mission house suggested: "The porch ceiling could be a very pale blue with good effect, and the porch floor red tile or red

Figure 6.9. *This restored 1905 Mission Revival–style house in Tucson, Arizona, features a recessed corner porch with arched openings that connects to an open terrace surrounded by low parapet walls.*

Figure 6.10. *Built in 1907 in the Mission Revival style, the Corbett House in Tucson, Arizona, features an arcaded front porch with a curved upper parapet.*

Figure 6.11. *This example of a stucco-walled Mission Revival–style house with a prominent arcaded front porch was built in 1907 in Dalton, Georgia. Note the curved upper parapets trimmed with decorative capstones and the lower railings with scupper openings to provide drainage from the tile floor of the porch. Historic American Buildings Survey photograph, 1989, HABS GA,157-DALT,1-1.*

Figure 6.12. *The Mission Revival–style design of the front porch of this stucco-covered bungalow in Tucson, Arizona, is accentuated by Moorish curved copings on its parapet, shallow arched openings, and flaring side buttresses.*

brick with gray joints, though of course cement will answer where it is advisable to economize."[6] The Mission Revival style was applied to both two-story houses and single-story bungalows built during the early 1900s.

CRAFTSMAN MOVEMENT

An influential trend in North American house design of the early twentieth century has been characterized as the Craftsman movement, which was rooted in the inspired writings of English art historian and preservationist John Ruskin and the works of William Morris, the architect, designer, writer, preservationist, and socialist who led the English Arts and Crafts movement. In reaction to the negative effects of industrialization on workers' lives, this discipline celebrated handcrafted works and the skills of the individuals who made them.

The leading proponent of the Craftsman movement in the United States was Gustav Stickley, architect, furniture maker, and editor of *The Craftsman* magazine, which he published from 1901 to 1916. Porches were considered an important part of these houses, as Stickley observed in his highly influential book, *Craftsman Homes*, in 1909: "In a front porch which must serve for a sitting room as well as for an entrance, the coping, surmounted by flower boxes, acts as a screen and, with the aid of a generous growth of vines, serves as a very satisfactory shelter from the street. Where there is also a garden veranda it can be made into a charming outdoor living or dining room both for summer and for the mild days in winter by being so recessed and protected that it is like a summer house or an outdoor room always open to the sun and air."[7]

Indeed, many Craftsman designs sought to merge the functions of verandas and

Figure 6.13. *Typical of Craftsman-style houses, this 1906 example in Burlington, Vermont, features a deep front porch with boxed wooden posts that are arranged in a pair beside the entry steps and tripled on the corners. These boxed posts stand on piers of quarry-faced sandstone ashlar that also forms the foundations and walls of the house. Between these piers are simple porch railings with closely spaced square balusters that mimic the form of the posts above.*

living rooms into what were called "outdoor rooms," as Stickley also noted:

In these days when the question of light and air is of so much importance in planning of the home, the tendency is more and more toward the provision of ample room for as much open-air life as possible. In all the Craftsman houses, as well as in the best modern dwellings of other styles, the veranda, whether open in summer or enclosed for a sun room in winter, is one of the prominent features. . . .

Outdoor living and dining rooms, to be homelike and comfortable, should be equipped with all that is necessary for daily use so as to avoid the carrying back and forth of tables, chairs and the like, as when the veranda is used only occasionally.[8]

Figure 6.14. *A simple, gable-roofed entry porch with overhanging eaves shelters the entrance of this circa 1906 Craftsman-style house in Pasadena, California, designed by architects Greene and Greene.*

Figure 6.15. *With a prominent second-story sleeping porch on the front right corner, the David B. Gamble House of 1908 in Pasadena, California, is one of the most famous works by Greene and Greene.*

Inspired in part by Stickley's writings, Craftsman movement houses and bungalows were among the last popular house types built to fully embrace the porch as an essential element of their style.

Heavy timbers support the porch roofs on many Craftsman houses. These are sometimes boldly expressed, with purlins and rafters that extend out beyond the edges of the roof planes. These exposed timbers are typically planed to dimensions, but they are often left unfinished or protected with just an oil finish or stain so as to reveal the natural texture of the wood. Wood stains were also sometimes applied to shingled walls; dark brown, dark green, and reddish brown were popular colors.

Craftsman porches and outdoor living rooms were often designed to use handcrafted materials that would to help connect the building to the landscape. Decorative stone, for example, might be used for both porch piers and garden retaining walls, or unfinished logs that match the trunks of the surrounding trees might serve as porch posts. Similarly, open pergolas that could support flowing vines were sometimes attached to Craftsman homes to provide both shade and a connection to surrounding gardens. By using such natural materials as prominent features, the Craftsman design is closely linked to the Rustic designs discussed above.

The architectural works of Charles and Henry Greene are perhaps some of the best-known examples of the Craftsman movement with these features. Many of these houses, which were mainly built in Southern California, feature prominent porches (figures 6.14 and 6.15).

Commonly engaged beneath the main roof of the house but sometimes added as extensions on the front, side, or rear, Craftsman porches were typically built in a very solid fashion with piers and parapets (also known as half-walls or knee-walls) of shingled wood, stone, logs, stucco, or concrete, and with floors of wood, tile, or patterned concrete. These porches were often deeper and darker than the lighter and frillier Queen Anne porches of an earlier generation.

Figure 6.16. *The eclectic design of this house built in 1910 in Burlington, Vermont, combines Arts and Crafts movement elements with those of the Shingle and Colonial Revival styles. Note that the shingles covering the prominent battered piers supporting the front porch match those on the upper sidewalls and pedimented gable.*

Figure 6.17. *Rough sandstone ashlar piers and parapet walls frame the porch openings of this 1915 Craftsman–style house in Santa Clara County, California. Historic American Buildings Survey photograph, 1980, HABS CAL,43-SARA,4-5.*

BUNGALOWS

Although bungalows were often built in the Craftsman style, they warrant separate mention here, owing to their distinctive single-story forms and characteristic porch designs. With a period of popularity that extended from the 1910s through the 1930s, bungalows were widely built across North America, especially when smaller, more efficient housing solutions were sought. Porches remained very important features of bungalows in this last era before home air conditioning became common, however. As with the other early-twentieth-century house types, these bungalow porches were usually scaled to serve as outdoor living rooms rather than as simple entry shelters. Moreover, they were often physically and stylistically integrated into the house designs, rather than just being attached amenities.

Architect C. E. Schermerhorn, in his influential 1915 book, *Bungalows, Camps and Mountain Homes*, included the following recommendations for planning bungalow porches to accommodate the broad range of uses that these spaces could provide:

The bungalow porch should be readily accessible from the main hall or artery of the house and should have proper exposure and protection from sun, drafts or the elements. The width of the porch should be generous, so as to provide ample space for passage about chairs and other furniture. The porch may adjoin or connect with a floored terrace that may be covered with a pergola or left uncovered. Removable sash provided to enclose the porch in winter make it useful as a sun parlor and in colder climates radiator connections are also recommended. The radiators may be removed for the summer season and the glazed sash replaced with wire screens. Open fireplaces are often provided on large porches which

Figure 6.18. *Stained wooden shingles cover the full-height battered porch posts and walls on this well-preserved Craftsman bungalow in West Lebanon, New Hampshire. Simple open railings without balusters extend along the edges of the porch deck beside the front steps.*

Figure 6.19. *Built in 1928, this bungalow in West Tampa, Florida, is typical of the hundreds of thousands of similar small houses. Characteristic features of the porch include the raised brick piers that serve as bases for the battered cast concrete posts and open railings without balusters. Historic American Buildings Survey photograph, circa 2005, HABS FL-484-8.*

are almost used as living rooms. The need for supports for swinging seats and hammocks should be anticipated. The service porch should be enclosed with wood lattice or insect wire for summer use and it is frequently provided with moveable sash for winter use in cold climates. . . . Dining or breakfast porches are often an adjunct of the bungalow. Opening from the living room in a secluded location, they may be enclosed with French windows.[9]

Several types of porch supports on bungalows are common. As with larger Craftsman houses, many bungalow porches have "battered" posts that taper in toward the top. These may be full-height battered posts (figure 6.18) or short battered posts that rest on raised piers of brick, stone, or masonry (figure 6.19). Another type that became very common had heavy stucco-covered piers sculpted into flowing shapes (figure 6.20).

Columns and simple railings in the Neoclassical and the Colonial Revival styles

were also used on bungalow porches during the first three decades of the twentieth century in both Canada and the United States (figures 6.21 and 6.22).

Just as a wide range of colors were popular for houses built during the early decades of the twentieth century, so too, were the various color schemes applied to porches. Although white and pale blue have long been popular color choices for porch ceilings, one homebuilder's guide from 1904 offered painting suggestions for a house with a "low toned green" on the walls and trim to have the "porch floor and steps to be dull green, and the porch ceiling a tawny yellow."[10] For another, an architect called for the body of the house to be "a dark wine color or maroon," the roof shingles to be black, white paint on the trim, including porch pillars and balustrade, the porch floor and steps to be gray, and the porch ceiling to be "old gold."

For a suburban cottage painted with white walls and trim, an architect called for the house and porch roofs to be stained

Figure 6.20. *Finished in painted stucco, the front porch on this bungalow in Jacksonville, Florida, features a broad elliptical arch supported by squat corner piers. The exposed wooden rafter tails beneath the flared eaves and the ornamental dormer above the porch are also common bungalow features. Circa 1915 postcard view.*

Figure 6.21. *A deep Neoclassical front porch with Tuscan columns is recessed beneath the gable roof of this early-twentieth-century brick bungalow in St. Lambert, Quebec.*

Figure 6.22. *A Colonial Revival–style front porch with stock Tuscan columns and a balustrade with straight spindles graces a bungalow in Danville, Vermont, painted in a typical early-twentieth-century color scheme of ivory trim contrasting with dark green shingled walls, green lattice skirting, and a brown porch floor.*

"a rich green" with gray on the porch floor and steps and a "bright apple green" on the porch ceiling. And for a red brick cottage with brown stained trim, it was suggested that the porch ceiling of "Georgia pine" be finished to show "the natural yellow of the wood slightly with an orange stain." In another proposal, the "cold bare effect" of a square house with white walls could be relieved with a "vivid red" stain on the roofs and the "ceiling of the porch may be painted a very light red, thus reflecting a pleasing rosy light below." And for a summer cottage, a recommended color scheme included light gray walls; moss green stained roofs; gray on the trim, porch pillars, and porch floor; and for the porch ceiling, a "canary yellow."

More restrained color schemes were suggested for porches in a 1913 guide for home decorators published by the Sherwin Williams Company; for a Colonial Revival–style house in a shady location, light yellow or cream was suggested for the body, with the porch ceiling to be painted gloss white, matching the trim and shutters.[11]

CATALOGUE PORCHES

Sometimes the styles of porch elements on houses from the early twentieth century seem to have been chosen through arbitrary efforts to mix and match components, especially as a way for developers to create a variety of diverse designs in suburban neighborhood developments. Also, individual homeowners might have worked with developers and builders to select from catalogues available designs of elements that would best suit their tastes and needs. In addition to the widespread use of stock porch parts, kits for bungalows and other house types were being marketed across North America by the early 1900s.

Continuing the trend of producing standardized house plans for American consumers distributed by mail order at a low cost, the Radford Architectural Company in Chicago was producing catalogues of house plans designed by their team of architects by the turn of the century. Published by William A. Radford, some of the most popular of these volumes were *Radford's Artistic Bungalows* of 1908, with more than two hundred designs, and *Radford's Portfolio of Plans* of 1909, with more than three hundred designs for houses, bungalows, stores, apartment houses, banks, churches, schools, and barns. Nearly all of the house and bungalow designs had porches, but none of these were called by the older terms, *verandas* or *piazzas*, in the text.[12]

Even the popular women's magazine, *Ladies' Home Journal*, provided assistance by offering articles and mail-order house plans, including some designed by Frank Lloyd Wright. The April 1907 issue, for example, included Wright's design for "A Fireproof House for $5000" with the suggestion that "should a covered porch be a necessity," a concrete slab could be installed over the terrace shown in the plans.[13]

The mail-order catalogue retail giant, Sears, Roebuck and Company, by 1908 was offering both plans and ready-cut packages of materials for a range of houses that could be shipped by rail to sites all over the United States and Canada to be built by local contractors. Sears was not alone in selling

Figure 6.23. *Battered posts rise from brick piers and half-walls on a "very serviceable" Craftsman porch. 1921 Morgan Woodwork Organization catalogue.*

this product. Competition came from catalogue mail-order rival Montgomery Ward, as well as from such firms as the E. F. Hodgson Company of Dover, Massachusetts; the Gordon-Van Tine Company of Davenport, Iowa; and the Aladdin Company of Bay City, Michigan. During their heyday in the 1920s, these and other similar mail-order house companies produced illustrated catalogues with a hundred or more designs that ranged from substantial two-story suburban houses to single-story five-room homes, workers' cottages, and seasonal camps.

The 1923 Gordon-Van Tine catalogue, for example, included thirty examples of bungalows, more than twenty two-story Prairie-style houses with broadly overhanging eaves, eighteen single-story cottages, and nearly a dozen "colonials," as well as several two-story, hip-roofed, "square" houses (often known as American Foursquares), various farmhouses, and a half dozen garages. Nearly every house in this catalogue had a porch. Most front porches were eight feet deep, but some cottage porches were as shallow as six feet. Room-size side porches graced many of the two-story "colonials." One stucco-finished Prairie-style home featured both a sun porch off the living room and a second-story sleeping porch adjacent to the upstairs bedrooms. Even if the stock design did not offer a side or rear porch, these could be ordered for an additional charge. Two designs were available—one with a simple railing with square balusters and another screened with wooden lattice.[14]

Whether through the use of mail-order plans or precut packages, the designs offered in these catalogues reflect the range of affordable houses that were built by the hundreds of thousands annually during the first three decades of the twentieth century.

TUDOR REVIVAL

Inspired by the quaint folk architecture of medieval England, the Tudor Revival style that became popular in North America between about 1900 and the early 1930s was another eclectic post-Victorian outgrowth of the earlier Queen Anne and Craftsman architectural styles. The scale of Tudor Revival–style houses (and the closely associated Jacobethan Revival style), ranged from small cottages to substantial suburban homes to large manors. Asymmetrical plans with prominent porches, stone or brick walls, and false half-timbering on stucco gable walls are typical features of this style.

As with the Craftsman, Prairie, and Bungalow styles, Tudor Revival–style porches were often integrated into the body of the building or located on a side elevation rather than being prominently attached as projecting elements on the front.

Figure 6.24. *The asymmetrical facade of this Tudor Revival–style house in Pasadena, California, features a single-bay porch on the left and a two-bay porch in the center. These two porches function mainly to protect entrances and are ornamented by balustrades and bracketed soffits. The wooden porch posts are set on masonry half-walls.*

Figure 6.25. *The Tudor Revival–style Rockwell Building, built in 1908 in Tucson, Arizona, features a recessed corner porch supported by wooden timber posts trimmed with small brackets and base moldings. A shallow porch with a projecting Tudor gable also shelters the front door.*

Figure 6.26. *Beneath the soft curves of a faux thatched roof, a side porch with segmentally arched bays is recessed into the fieldstone mass of the Richard Sommers House, built in the Tudor Revival style in 1924 in Indianapolis. The main entrance is sheltered by a projecting porte-cochere. Historic American Buildings Survey photograph, 1970, HABS IND,49-IND,28-1.*

Figure 6.27. *The recessed front porch on this circa 1920s Tudor Revival–style house in Globe, Arizona, is supported by corner posts made of the same tufa stone used on the walls and chimney. Iron trellises and crestings ornament the porch. The rolled eaves that mimic the look of a thatched, cross-gable roof reflect the Tudor style's association with medieval English folk cottage designs.*

Figure 6.28. *With the pointed Tudor arch above the front door echoed by the porch ceiling, the eclectic English Canadian design of this early-twentieth-century suburban home in Ottawa combines Tudor Revival–style ornamentation with such Bungaloid features as battered wooden porch posts set on brick and stone-capped parapets and a late-Victorian front bay window with heavily rusticated corners.*

Generally, porches were less important parts of the design of Tudor Revival–style houses, however. On some, a small front porch may protect the front entrance, while a larger, living room–size porch may be located on the side or oriented to the sun and equipped with glazing to serve as a solarium.

MODERN MOVEMENT AND INTERNATIONAL STYLE

The preceding pages have traced the complex history of how porches have been shaped by intended functions and stylistic influences. The dramatic changes to the context of architectural design wrought by the Modern movement of the early twentieth century, however, so affected all forms of building features that new solutions were sought to fulfill functions that traditionally had been served by porches. These products of the Modern movement and the International style consciously rejected classical

Figure 6.29. *Broadly cantilevered roofs create porch spaces that are dramatically free from supporting posts on Frank Lloyd Wright's 1908 Robie House in Chicago. Historic American Buildings Survey photograph, 1963, HABS ILL,16-CHIG,33-3.*

Figure 6.30. *Frank Lloyd Wright used a projecting slab roof to shelter the cantilevered upper balcony, which in turn shelters the ground-floor porch space on the Mrs. Thomas H. Gale House in Oak Park, Illinois, which he designed in 1909.*

orders and Romantic design motifs in favor of simple geometric forms.[15] Arising in part from the cubist forms developed by the Dutch de Stijl artistic movement and by the Bauhaus school designers of the German Weimar era, houses, factories, and commercial buildings designed in the International style thus often featured simple porches with projecting slab roofs, either cantilevered or supported by cylindrical columns.

An intent and effect of these modern porch features was to transcend traditionally defined architectural boundaries with inside and outside spaces that could flow seamlessly together. Frank Lloyd Wright, who described this concept as "change from the box to free plan and the new reality that is space instead of matter," created such transitional spaces with the extended rooflines and cantilevered overhangs that can be seen on such familiar landmarks as the Robie House of 1908, the Mrs. Thomas H. Gale House of 1909, and on his most famous work, Fallingwater, built in 1937 (figures 6.29, 6.30, and 6.31).[16]

Figure 6.31. *A cantilevered upper-story porch balcony with smooth parapets is protected by an overhanging slab roof on Frank Lloyd Wright's Fallingwater, built in 1937 in Fayette County, Pennsylvania. Historic American Buildings Survey photograph, 1985, HABS PA,26-OHPY.V,1-16.*

Figure 6.32. *Modern geometric forms produced from concrete characterize this porch entrance of the International-style Horatio West Court Apartments in Santa Monica, California. Historic American Buildings Survey photograph, 1968, HABS CAL,19-SANMO,1-5.*

Another hallmark of the International style was its use of poured concrete. An early example of this style used for social housing in the United States was the Horatio West Court Apartments project (figure 6.32) in Santa Monica, California, designed by Irving John Gill and built between 1919 and 1922. Constructed of concrete, the apartment units featured simple entry porches with arched openings.[17]

In 1929, Walter Gropius demonstrated how simple horizontal planes projecting from exterior walls could serve as balconies and porchlike roofs on the Bauhaus Studio Apartments in Dessau, Germany. After moving to the United States, the house that Gropius built for his family in 1938 in Lincoln, Massachusetts (figure 6.33), features a

variety of Modern-style porch forms. A narrow, partially cantilevered porch with a thin slab roof, simple steel pipe supports, and a glass block wall shelters the walkway to the front entrance. A small service porch is recessed into a corner of the cubic house. On the west elevation, an elevated deck porch is sheltered with a series of spaced vertical planks and a partial roof. But the most functional porch on the Gropius House is the screened porch that projects deeply into the rear garden at right angles to the building. This porch has a thin slab roof supported by steel pipe columns set on a concrete slab base with framed floor-to-ceiling screens on three sides. By locating this porch next to a pantry, it barely shades the abundant natural light cast into the adjacent rooms of the house. According to Historic New England, the current owner of this National Historic Landmark, the screened porch was "a favorite gathering place" that supported year-round activities for the Walter and Ise Gropius family.[18]

Less famous versions of Modern movement and International-style houses also were built with simple porches, entry shelters, and balconies. Common features include floor-to-ceiling screens, posts and railings of steel pipe, large glass doors opening inside, thin slab roofs, and on-grade concrete slab floors. An example documented by the Historic American Buildings Survey before it was demolished in 1983, was the Charles Collier house (figure 6.34). Designed by architect George Locke Howe in 1938–39, it balanced Art Moderne details with traditional features, including a large, screened, two-story sleeping porch on the rear.[19]

One of the best-known examples of an International-style residence in the United States is the Edith Farnsworth House (figure

Figure 6.33. *The screened porch projecting from the rear, south side of the Gropius House, built in 1938 in Lincoln, Massachusetts, was "a favorite gathering place" that supported year-round activities for the Walter and Ise Gropius family. A recessed service porch is screened at the right. Historic American Buildings Survey photograph, 1986,* HABS MASS,9-LIN,16-22.

Figure 6.34. *Designed in 1938–39 by architect George Locke Howe, and with grounds designed by landscape architect Dan Kiley, the Charles Collier house (demolished in 1983) in Falls Church, Virginia, balanced Art Moderne details with traditional features, including a screened two-story porch on the rear, southeast elevation. The sleeping porch was accessed by single and double steel-and-glass doors from an upstairs hall accessible from bedrooms. Two sets of four steel-and-glass doors opened to the ground-floor porch from the dining room and living room. Historic American Buildings Survey photograph, 1983, HABS VA,30-FALCH.V,3-7.*

Figure 6.35. *The Edith Farnsworth House in Plano, Illinois, designed by Ludwig Mies van der Rohe, is shown here with its original screens on the porch at the right. Historic American Buildings Survey photograph, circa 1970, HABS ILL,47-PLAN.V,1-8.*

6.35), a small, riverfront weekend home in Plano, Illinois, designed between 1946 and 1951 by Ludwig Mies van der Rohe, the noted Bauhaus architect who emigrated from Germany to the United States in 1937. In 1929, Mies van der Rohe had achieved international recognition by using cantilevered horizontal slab roof planes and simple cylindrical pipe columns to provide sheltered spaces for the German Pavilion at the Barcelona International Exposition in Spain.

Known best for its simple rectangular plan with glass walls, flat roof, and raised slab floor, what is less well recognized is that the Edith Farnsworth House also initially featured screens on its large engaged porch. Carefully designed by the architect and custom fabricated to provide protection from insects at this riverside site, these screens

contributed to the original visual character of the structure by subtly defining the planes of the screened porch with partial transparency, much as do the glass walls of the house. But beyond their effect on the building's appearance, perhaps the most significant contribution that these porch screens made to the character of the Edith Farnsworth House was their role in creating an intermediary space—an outdoor room—that provided protection from mosquitoes and other unwelcome visitors while offering open views and fresh air at this private riverfront site. Truly one of the most significant examples of a Modern movement screened porch, it is unfortunate that the screens were removed in the 1970s.[20]

In addition to these well-recognized examples of Modernist architecture, hundreds

Figure 6.36. *Vestigial porches without posts shelter the front and side entries of this midcentury Modern-style house in Asbestos, Quebec.*

Figure 6.37. *The projecting roof plane of the Borrego Appliance Store, built in 1961 in Borrego Springs, California, serves as a both a commercial porch and a marquee with minimalist midcentury Modern lines.*

Figure 6.38. *The sharply angled canopy on this gasoline station, built in 1960 in Burlington, Vermont, provided both porchlike protection for drive-through service and an easily identifiable roadside presence that was reinforced by a petroleum firm's use of this same bold design nationally.*

of thousands of mundane residential, institutional, commercial, and industrial buildings were constructed during the mid-twentieth century. Many of these featured porches. But to create such spaces free from vertical obstructions, even posts were eliminated on some minimalist midcentury porches (figure 6.36).

In keeping with the philosophy of the movement, the designs of many midcentury Modern porches were typically confined to simple, but sometimes bold, geometric forms. The planes of a roof might be cantilevered out to shelter spaces that could project over sidewalks without intruding elements, such as on the Borrego Appliance Store (figure 6.37), built in 1961 in Borrego Springs, California.[21] On commercial buildings such as gasoline stations, some Modern movement canopies (figure 6.38) were designed to serve porchlike functions for drive-through service, while also permitting strong corporate brand messages to stand out amid the roadside clutter of the automobile age.

Epilogue

As times and attitudes have changed with passing generations, so too have the designs of their buildings. The symbolic social messages of openness, leisure, and welcome that porches convey stand in sharp contrast with the defensive, protective, and exclusionary warnings implied by the strongbox-like house designs more popular before *and after* the Porch Age. And so, after the final fling of popularity extending through the 1920s, and even to the 1940s in some regions, public attitudes toward porches generally soured through the remaining years of the twentieth century, and some rituals of North American porch life slowly began to fade from fashion. Indeed by the mid-twentieth century, the popularity of the open public porch had faded, as feelings about the home had shifted toward security and fortification during the Depression and wartime, when anxieties, fears, and also prejudices gripped an increasingly fragmented North American culture. For those with sufficient means, air conditioning provided a comforting indoor refuge, automatic clothes dryers replaced back-porch clotheslines, and outdoor domestic activities moved to the discreet privacy of rear yards, patios, and decks. Routine front porch use in some areas of North America even quietly became associated with class and racial stereotypes.

With this shift in attitudes toward porches, one common mid-twentieth-century response, discussed above, was to change both form and symbolism by enclosing an existing porch with rows of windows. Although a frequently cited reason was that this alteration would extend the usability of the porch into colder-weather months, many found that the glazing in fact extended the use of the porch for only a few weeks in the spring and fall, and with the loss of openness and ventilation, many of these porches became much less desirable places for occupancy during the summer months. This physical change of enclosure also brought a much more profound change of use, as the old porch, now more protected from the weather, became a convenient, though often unsightly, refuge for such items as bicycles, boots, old sofas, automobile tires, kids' toys, yard equipment, cook-out grills, trash barrels, recycling bins, brooms, shovels, firewood, et cetera, et cetera!

The many ways in which such changes occur incrementally over decades can sometimes be best seen when comparing analogous buildings in the same neighborhood. A fine case study is presented by three similar duplex houses constructed in 1899 for workers by the nearby Queen City Cotton Company in Burlington, Vermont. It is apparent that they have evolved in three different ways. In the first example (figure 7.1), the open summer porches with turned posts and opening railings have been maintained. In the second example (figure 7.2), however, the pair of porches were enclosed with double-hung windows sometime in the 1930s after the textile factory closed, but they remained unheated to provide sheltered winter storage and summer porch use. In the third example (figure 7.3), the porches were enclosed and heated for year-round indoor living, and the recessed area between them is now used as a summer porch space.

To many who reached adulthood by the mid-twentieth century, porches were often seen as the frilly, cluttered refuges of aged grandparents, of the sick, of the poor, and sometimes of "others not like us." Indeed, tearing off the old screened porch "to let in more light" became a symbolic rite of mid-twentieth-century social modernism, much as the demolishing of the laundry-draped,

Figure 7.1. *This duplex has matching open summer porches with turned posts and spindled railings.*

Figure 7.2. *These porches were enclosed with double-hung windows, probably during the 1930s.*

Figure 7.3. *On this duplex, the porches were enclosed and heated, and the recessed area between them is now used as a summer porch space.*

triple-decker porches of "blighted slums" became paternalistic political acts of "urban renewal" planning.

Yet another wave of assault on porches came with the backyard patio fad of the 1950s and the private deck fad of the 1960s, especially as suburban homeowners caught up in the do-it-yourself craze of home renovations stripped off the cluttered and neglected enclosed rear porches of the previous generation's "home improvement" efforts. Even some architectural historians and "restorationists" looked down on porch additions, arguing as a justification for their removal that such alterations compromised the "integrity" of the "original" architecture.

The tide of attitudes began to shift back in favor of porches by the 1970s. A swell of interest in the American past sparked by the United States Bicentennial celebrations revived a renewed appreciation for the porch as a potential stage for public expressions of patriotism, typically symbolized by decorations of American flags and bunting of red-white-blue, swinging baskets of flowers, and a few pieces of nicely painted, but rarely used antique or faux-antique porch furniture. But also with the growth of the counterculture movement among the young, students, and various "antiestablishment" folks, porches provided a convenient liminal space for their music, parties, gatherings, escapes, recreational drug use, and the other social activities that in turn became symbols of alternative directions for North American culture.

In response, to discourage such discordant activities and vehicles of expression, but with stated goals of maintaining property values and discouraging fire risks, some communities passed ordinances prohibiting the placement old sofas on porches.[1] Ordinances, planning covenants, and

condominium association rules even have been imposed to prohibit the drying of clothes or the storage of bicycles on porches and balconies.[2]

With the growing public interest in Victorian architecture and historic preservation over the past several decades, and perhaps with the maturing of the baby boom generation, interest has grown, however, in working to save porches as functional features of both houses and neighborhoods. Indeed many homeowners have learned that because of their openness and exposure to the weather, porches require routine maintenance, which if done incrementally on a timely basis will help preserve them in perpetuity.

Even "New Urbanism" resort developments, such as Seaside on the Florida Gulf Coast, developed codes mandating that new houses be built with eight-foot-deep front porches in the hope that these will foster a closer sense of a friendly, neighborhood community.[3] Moreover, at the time of writing, fresh waves of interest in the many benefits of porches have emerged with public concerns over future impacts of global climate change. Indeed, Vermont, Colorado, and Utah have just passed laws to outlaw covenants and regulations that restrict clothes drying on porches, while several other states have debated this "right to dry" issue in their legislatures.[4]

For those concerned with the preservation of porches, it is encouraging to see maintenance and repairs being carried out on older buildings in ways that maintain the historic character-defining features. Often this work involves replacing trim boards, stair treads, risers, and flooring. Ideally, if these are of wood, naturally decay-resistant species should continue to be used, rather than trying pressure-treated lumber or

Figure 7.4. *With columns and deck temporarily removed for repairs, angled planks support the upper part of this Colonial Revival–style entrance porch.*

Figure 7.5. *Temporary supports hold up the corner of a veranda under repairs.*

manufactured substitute materials. For re-placing hidden sills, floor joists, stringers, plates, and support posts that may suffer from chronic dampness or pest infestations or ground contact, preservative treatments and pressure-treated lumber may be best, however. Roofing and roof sheathing boards are also vulnerable porch features that require regular inspection and maintenance to avoid costly repairs. Of course, such work should comply with applicable regulations and code requirements.

A common issue now facing many who maintain older porches is the challenge of complying with current minimum railing height standards imposed by insurance companies, life safety regulations, and building code requirements. In the United States and Canada, building code requirements vary regionally and by state, province, and municipality, but many of these codes now require guardrails or balustrades at least thirty-six inches above floor height along edges of residential porches where there is a drop of thirty inches or more. For other building uses, such guardrails or balustrades may need to be a minimum of forty-two inches or more above the floor. These barriers must be strong and solid enough to prevent adults, children, babies, pets, and objects from falling through.

Even though a low railing height may be considered an important historic character-defining feature of a porch, it is important to find solutions that meet both heritage standards and safety requirements. Rather than replacing historic railings to meet new height requirements, a better conservation solution may be to keep and repair the existing features, replacing any missing elements to match originals (if actual designs are known) and to add unobtrusive railings on top and other subtle materials to satisfy the

Figure 7.6. *To satisfy safety concerns, new steel pipe railings were installed above the existing historic balustrades on the veranda of this century-old summer resort hotel.*

safety needs. Given the variability and complexity of the codes and regulations, appropriate officials or qualified architects should be consulted when planning such projects.

Another porch maintenance issue that warrants careful consideration is the selection of appropriate replacement roofing materials for porches. While compatibility with existing roofing materials may be important, performance and durability should be considered along with appearance. For porches with such shallow roof slopes that their roofing materials are not visible from the ground, the main goal should typically be durability.

Even the choice of the color of replacement roofing materials, whether visible or not, should be considered carefully, as the results of such decisions may have long-term implications on the usability of a porch, as well as on household summer cooling costs and other environmental impacts. Black, dark gray and dark green roofing surfaces absorb much more heat from the sun's infrared radiation than do white, red, and other light-colored surfaces, which reflect more of the infrared light. Indeed, one study for this project found that the application of a white-pigmented paint coating on an existing dark green asphalt-covered porch roof could reduce surface temperatures of the roofing by as much as thirty-five degrees Fahrenheit (twenty degrees Celsius) in summer. This reduced the temperature of the exposed roof boards beneath by twenty-five degrees, resulting in a five-degree reduction in the air temperature on the porch at seating levels. This change in roofing color allowed the porch to be used comfortably on many more summer days, thus reducing the amount of electricity consumed for air conditioning.[5]

Both the United States National Park Service and Parks Canada have developed standards and treatment guidelines for conserving porches on heritage buildings that are accessible on the Internet. For the rehabilitation of porches on historic buildings in the United States, the National Park Service offers both standards and guidelines. The *Secretary of the Interior's Standards for Rehabilitation* are used by federal and state regulators and agencies, as well as some local governments, when reviewing projects subject to their jurisdiction on historic buildings eligible for listing on the National Register of Historic Places. The U.S. National Park Service's *Guidelines for Rehabilitating Historic Buildings* offer more detailed information on recommended treatments and approaches for porches and other building features that are consistent with the *Secretary of the Interior's Standards for Rehabilitation*. Parks Canada also offers guidelines for the conservation of building entrances and porches on heritage buildings. These are included in the *Standards and Guidelines for the Conservation of Historic Places in Canada*.

In closing, it is perhaps worth noting that major portions of this book, including these very words, were written on a porch.

Notes

CHAPTER 1. HISTORY

Epigraph from A. J. Downing, *Cottage Residences: or, A Series of Designs for Rural Cottages and Cottage Villas, and Their Gardens and Grounds. Adapted to North America* (New York: Wiley and Putman, 1842), 21.

1. W. David Driver, "An Early Classic Colonnaded Building at the Maya Site of Blue Creek, Belize," *Latin American Antiquity* 13, no. 1 (March 2002): 63–84; accessed at http://www.jstor.org/stable/971741.

2. *Indian Tepes [sic], Mescalero Agency, N.M.*, Denver Public Library, DPL Western History Photos; accessed at http://photoswest.org.

3. William A. (Andy) Cloud, Steve Black, and Jennifer Piehl, "La Junta de los Rios," Texas beyond History, University of Texas at Austin, 2007; accessed at http://www.texasbeyond history.net/junta/sites.html.

4. *Indian House with Veranda, Sacaton Vicinity, Pinal County, AZ*, F. D. Nichols, photographer, January 1938, Historic American Buildings Survey, American Memory from the Library of Congress; accessed at http://hdl.loc.gov/loc.pnp/hhh.az0123.

5. Father Gabriel Sagard, *Long Journey to the Country of the Hurons* (Toronto: Champlain Society, 1939), 94, 95. Edited by George M. Wrong and translated from French into English by H. H. Langton from the original edition, Paris, 1632; accessed at http://www.library.utoronto.ca/champlain/9_96836/0149.pdf and http://www.library.utoronto.ca/champlain/9_96836/0150.pdf.

6. William Bartram, *Travels through North & South Carolina, Georgia, East & West Florida, the Cherokee Country, the Extensive Territories of the Muscogulges, or Creek Confederacy, and the Country of the Chactaws; Containing an Account of the Soil and Natural Productions of Those Regions, Together with Observations on the Manners of the Indians* (Philadelphia: James & Johnson, 1791), 455. Electronic version published by the University of North Carolina at Chapel Hill, 2001; accessed at http://docsouth.unc.edu/nc/bartram/bartram.html.

7. Charles D. Arnold and Elisa J. Hart, "The Mackenzie Inuit Winter House," *Arctic Profiles* 45, no. 2 (June 1992): 199–200; accessed at http://pubs.aina.ucalgary.ca/arctic/Arctic45-2-199.pdf.

8. Alexander Badawy, "Architectural Provision against Heat in the Orient," *Journal of Near Eastern Studies* 17, no. 2 (April 1958): 122–28.

9. "4,000-Year-Old Timber Circle Found in Tyrone," BBC News; accessed at http://news.bbc.co.uk/2/hi/uk_news/northern_ireland/8202364.stm.

10. Badawy, "Architectural Provision," 123.

11. 1 Kings 7:6–7 (King James Version).

12. Richard J. Klonoski, "The Portico of the Archon Basileus: On the Significance of the Setting of Plato's 'Euthyphro,'" *Classical Journal* 81, no. 2 (December 1985–January 1986): 130–37; accessed at http://www.jstor.org/stable/3296742.

13. "Stoic" in *The Merriam-Webster New Book of Word Histories* (Springfield, MA: Merriam-Webster, 1991), 444.

14. Leland M. Roth, *Understanding Architecture: Its Elements, History, and Meaning* (Boulder, CO: Westview Press, 2007), 233.

15. John Henry Parker, *A Glossary of Terms Used in Grecian, Roman, Italian and Gothic Architecture*, 5th ed. (London, 1850), 366–369.

16. James F. White, "The Spatial Setting," in Geoffrey Wainwright and Karen Beth Westerfield Tucker, eds., *The Oxford History of Christian Worship* (New York: Oxford University

Press US, 2006), 795, 812. John Henry Parker, *A Glossary of Terms used in Grecian, Roman, Italian and Gothic Architecture* (London, 1838), 100–101; available online at http://books.google.com.

17. *Oxford English Dictionary*, 2nd ed., s.v. "Galilee, n."; accessed at http://dictionary.oed.com.

18. *Oxford English Dictionary*, 3rd ed., s.v. "porch," "portico," "porticus." Richard Brown, "Dissertation XX. On the Character of Porches," *Domestic Architecture* (London: George Virtue, 1841), 166; available online at http://books.google.com.

19. Clement Clarke Moore, "A Visit from St. Nicholas," in *The New-York Book of Poetry* (New York: George Dearborn, 1837), 218; available online at http://books.google.com.

20. A. J. Downing, *A Treatise on the Theory and Practice of Landscape Gardening, Adapted to North America* (New York: Wiley & Putnam, 1841), 303; available online at http://openlibrary.org.

21. J. J. Thomas, *Rural Affairs: A Practical and Copiously Illustrated Register of Rural Economy and Rural Taste, Including Country Dwellings, Improving and Planting Grounds, Fruits and Flowers* . . . (Albany, NY: L. Tucker, 1858), 255.

22. Jocelyn Hazelwood Donlon, *Swinging in Place: Porch Life in Southern Culture* (Chapel Hill: University of North Carolina Press, 2001), 61–62. Jay D. Edwards, "The Origins of Creole Architecture," *Winterthur Portfolio* 29 No. 2/3 (Summer–Autumn 1994): 157; accessed at http://www.jstor.org/stable/1181485.

23. Mark L. Brack, "Domestic Architecture in Hispanic California: The Monterey Style Reconsidered," *Perspectives in Vernacular Architecture* 4 (1991): 166; accessed at http://www.jstor.org/stable/3514232.

24. *El Palacio Real de Santa Fe*, Historic American Building Survey, American Memory from the Library of Congress; accessed at http://hdl.loc.gov/loc.pnp/hhh.nm0109.

25. Charles Nordhoff, *California: For Health, Pleasure, and Residence* (New York: Harper, 1873), 242.

26. Helen Jackson, *Ramona* (Boston: Roberts Brothers, 1886), 19–20; available online at http://books.google.com.

27. David Gebhard, "Some Additional Observations on California's Monterey Tradition," *Journal of the Society of Architectural Historians* 46, no. 2 (June 1987): 161–62; accessed at http://www.jstor.org/stable/990184.

28. Brack, "Domestic Architecture in Hispanic California," 166.

29. *Vallejo Adobe, Adobe Road at Casa Grande, Petaluma Vicinity, Sonoma County, CA*, Roger Sturtevant, photographer, 1934, Historic American Building Survey, American Memory from the Library of Congress; accessed at http://hdl.loc.gov/loc.pnp/hhh.ca1106.

30. *Pacific House, Historic Monterey*; accessed at http://www.historicmonterey.org/?p=pacific_house.

31. *Casa de Geronimo Lopez, 1102 Pico Street, San Fernando, Los Angeles County, CA*, Historic American Building Survey, American Memory from the Library of Congress; accessed at http://hdl.loc.gov/loc.pnp/hhh.ca0285.

32. Rosalys Coope, "The 'Long Gallery': Its Origins, Development, Use and Decoration," *Architectural History: Journal of the Society of Architectural Historians of Great Britain* 28 (1986): 44; accessed at http://www.jstor.org/stable/1568501.

33. Jean Morrison, review of *L'Evolution de la maison rurale laurentienne*, by Georges Gauthier-Larouche, *Technology and Culture* 10, no. 3 (July 1969): 446–47.

34. Eugène Viollet-le-Duc, "coyau," *Dictionnaire raisonné de l'architecture française du XIe au XVIe siècle* (1856).

35. Michel Bergeron, Claude Bergeron, Luc Noppen, and Lucie K. Morisset, "Glossaire," *De pierre, de bois, de brique, Histoire de la maison au Québec*. Société rimouskoise du patrimoine, Rimouski, Quebec; accessed at http://www.maisonlamontagne.com/glossaire.asp?.

36. Charles Lanman, *Adventures in the Wilds of the United States and British American Provinces* (Philadelphia: J. W. Moore, 1856), 82; accessed at http://name.umdl.umich.edu/acp1978.0002.001.

37. *Planter's Cabin, 7815 Highland Road, Baton Rouge, East Baton Rouge Parish, LA*, Historic American Buildings Survey, American Memory from the Library of Congress, 1978; accessed at http://www.loc.gov/pictures/item/LA0080/.

38. Mark L. Evans, *The Commandant's Last Ride* (Cape Girardeau, MO: Ten-Digit Press, 2001), 5–8.

39. Joseph Holt Ingraham, *The South-west* (New York: Harper & Brothers, 1835), 2:81; available online at http://books.google.com.

40. *Cooper-Beasley House, County Road 96 (Old Saint Stephens Road), Mount Vernon, Mobile, AL*, Historic American Buildings Survey, American Memory from the Library of Congress; accessed at http://hdl.loc.gov/loc.pnp/hhh.a10385.

41. *Caldwell-Hutchison Farm, County Road 93, Lowndesville Vicinity, Abbeville, SC*, Historic American Buildings Survey, American Memory from the Library of Congress; accessed at http://hdl.loc.gov/loc.pnp/hhh.sc0075.

42. Joseph Manca, "On the Origins of the American Porch," *Winterthur Portfolio* 40, no. 2/3 (2005): 91–132.

43. Patricia Heintzelman, "Dyckman House," National Register of Historic Places Inventory—Nomination Form (Washington, DC: National Park Service, 1975); accessed at http://pdfhost.focus.nps.gov/docs/NHLS/Text/67000014.pdf.

44. *Johannes Van Nuyse House, 150 Amersfort Place, Brooklyn, Kings, NY*, Historic American Buildings Survey, American Memory from the Library of Congress; accessed at http://hdl.loc.gov/loc.pnp/hhh.ny0251. Van Nuyse-Magaw House, landmark designation findings memo LP-0175, New York Landmarks Preservation Commission, February 11, 1969; accessed at http://neighborhoodpreservationcenter.org/db/bb_files/VAN-NUYSE-MAGAW.pdf.

45. John E. Crowley, *The Invention of Comfort* (Baltimore: Johns Hopkins University Press, 2001), 243–44.

46. "The Stadt Huys," *Harper's New Monthly Magazine* (September 1854): 449.

47. This painting by Ferdinand Bol now hangs in the Louvre Museum. An image of the painting and information from the French Ministry of Culture is available online at http://www.culture.gouv.fr.

48. *Oxford English Dictionary*, 3rd ed. (Oxford: Oxford University Press, 2010), s.v. "perron, n."; OED Online version.

49. Peter Kalm, *The America of 1750: Peter Kalm's Travels in North America*, trans. and ed. Adolph B. Benson (first publ. in English in 1770; New Haven, CT: Yale University Press 1937; reprinted 1966 by Dover Publications), 341–42; accessed at http://www.nysm.nysed.gov/albany/art/kalm.html#source. Peter Kalm, *Travels into North America; Containing Its Natural History, and a Circumstantial Account of Its Plantations and Agriculture in General, with the Civil, Ecclesiastical and Commercial State of the Country, the Manners of the Inhabitants, and Several Curious and Important Remarks on Various Subjects*, trans. John Reinhold Forster, 2nd ed. (London, T. Lowndes, 1772.)

50. Jacques-Pierre Brissot de Warville, *New Travels in the United States of America*, vol. 1 (London, 1794), 267.

51. *Crounse Homestead, Altamont Vicinity, Albany County, NY*, Historic American Buildings Survey, American Memory from the Library of Congress; accessed at http://hdl.loc.gov/loc.pnp/hhh.ny0448.

52. Diedrich Knickerbocker [Washington Irving], *A History of New-York from the Beginning of the World to the End of the Dutch Dynasty* (London: Robert Thurston, 1828), 260; available online at http://books.google.com.

53. Diedrich Knickerbocker [Washington Irving], *A History of New-York from the Beginning of*

the World to the End of the Dutch Dynasty, rev. ed. (London: Henry G. Bohn, 1850) 169; available online at http://books.google.com.

54. Washington Irving, "Communipaw," *Spanish Papers and Other Miscellanies, Hitherto Unpublished or Uncollected*, ed. Pierre Irving (New York: G. P. Putnam, 1867), 2:455; available online at http://books.google.com.

55. Noah Webster, *An American Dictionary of the English Language, 4th ed.* (New York: N. &. J. White, 1830), 795, s.v. "Stoop"; available online at http://books.google.com.

56. "A Modern Pilgrimage." *The New-England Magazine* (Boston) 9, no. 7 (July 1835): 36.

57. James Gallier, *The American Builder's General Price Book and Estimator* (New York: Lafever and Gallier, 1836), 111; available online at http://books.google.com.

58. Ibid.

59. Catharine Parr Traill, *The Backwoods of Canada: Being Letters from the Wife of an Emigrant Officer, Illustrative of the Domestic Economy of British America* (London: Charles Knight, 1836); available online at http://www.gutenberg.org.

60. Ibid.

61. John Romeyn Brodhead, *History of the State of New York* (New York: Harper & Brothers, 1853), 533.

62. George E. Woodward, *Woodward's Architecture and Rural Art, no. II* (New York: Geo. E. Woodward, 1868), 19.

63. "Diary of Annie L. Youmans Van Ness," September 1864, 35; April 1865, 84; August 1865, 114; June 1866, 204; accessed from North American Women's Letters and Diaries database published online by Alexander Street Press at http://www.alexanderstreet.com.

64. Danielle Pigeon, e-mail correspondence with author, December 23, 2010.

65. Frank D. Graham and Thomas J. Emory, *Audels Carpenters and Builders Guide #3* (New York: Theo. Audel, 1923), 1005–06, 1008.

66. Hans Kurath, *A Word Geography of the Eastern United States* (Ann Arbor: University of Michigan Press, 1966), 22, 29. Hans Kurath, *Handbook of the Linguistic Geography of New England* (Providence, RI: Brown University, 1939), 24, 31.

67. James A. Drake, "The Effect of Urbanization on Regional Vocabulary," *American Speech* 36, no. 1 (February 1961): 17–33; accessed at http://www.jstor.org/stable/3090551.

68. Henry Glassie, *Vernacular Architecture* (Bloomington: Indiana University Press, 2000), 118.

69. John E. Crowley, "Inventing Comfort," in Ann Smart Martin and J. Ritchie Garrison, eds., *American Material Culture: The Shape of the Field* (Winterthur, DE: Winterthur Museum, 1997), 277–78.

70. "Whitehall," written historical and descriptive data addendum, Historic American Buildings Survey, American Memory from the Library of Congress, p. 3; accessed at http://hdl.loc.gov/loc.pnp/hhh.md0210.

71. Fiske Kimball, *Domestic Architecture of the American Colonies and of the New Republic* (New York: Charles Scribner, 1922; reprint Mineola, NY: Dover, 2001) 276. Jedidiah Morse, *American Universal Geography* (Charlestown: Lincoln and Edmunds, 1819) 479; accessed at http://books.google.com.

72. *George Washington's Mount Vernon—Porch*, Mount Vernon Ladies' Association; accessed at http://www.mountvernon.org/visit/plan/index.cfm/pid/223.

73. Nathalie Clerk, *Palladian Style in Canadian Architecture* (Ottawa: Ministry of the Environment, 1984), 128.

74. Michelle Guitard, "Charles de Salaberry: A Biography," The War of 1812 Website (University of Toronto/Université Laval, 2000); accessed at http://www.warof1812.ca/salaberry.htm.

75. Government House, Office of the Lieutenant Governor, Prince Edward Island; accessed at http://www.gov.pe.ca/olg/index.php?number=1022336&lang=e.

76. C. W. J. Eliot and Reginald Porter, "The Changing Face of Fanning Bank," *Island*

Magazine 29, no. 3 (1991): 29–33; available online at http://www.islandarchives.ca/node/76.

77. "Copy of an Account Furnished 19th October, 1843, for Repairs at Government House," *Journal of the House of Assembly of Prince Edward Island: Anno Octavo Victoriae Reginae, Third Session of the Sixteenth General Assembly* (Charlottetown: "The Islander" Office, 1845); available online at http://www.canadiana.org/ECO.

78. *Plattsburgh Air Force Base, U.S. Route 9, Plattsburgh, Clinton County, NY*, Historic American Buildings Survey, American Memory from the Library of Congress; accessed at http://hdl.loc.gov/loc.pnp/hhh.ny1864.

79. Margaret Bayard Smith, letter from Margaret Bayard Smith to Maria Kirkpatrick, June 1812, in Gaillard Hunt, ed., *The First Forty Years of Washington Society in the Family Letters of Margaret Bayard Smith* (New York: Frederick Ungar Publishing, 1906), 88; accessed from North American Women's Letters and Diaries database published online by Alexander Street Press at http://www.alexanderstreet.com.

80. Margaret Bayard Smith, letter from Margaret Bayard Smith to Maria Boyd, August 17, 1828, in ibid., 236.

81. "The Beauties of Architecture," *Parley's Magazine: With Fifty Engravings* 9, no. 4 (1841): 381; available at American Antiquarian Society (AAS) Historical Periodicals Collection, Series 2 online database at http://www.americanantiquarian.org/.

82. Miles Lewis, "The Piazza," *Australian Building: A Cultural Investigation*; accessed at http://www.mileslewis.net/australian-building.

83. Carl R. Lounsbury, "Beaux-Arts Ideals and Colonial Reality: The Reconstruction of Williamsburg's Capitol, 1928–1934," *Journal of the Society of Architectural Historians* 49, no. 4 (December 1990): 377–78.

84. *Itinerant Observations in America, Reprinted from The London Magazine 1745–46* (Savannah: Estill, 1878) 16; accessed at http://books.google.com/. "To Be Lett," *Pennsylvania Gazette*, March 14, 1749. "To be Sold," *Pennsylvania Gazette*, April 26, 1750. "To be Sold," *New-York Mercury*, March 1, 1756. "To be Sold," *New-York Gazette*, March 23, 1761. "To be Sold by the Subscriber," *Georgia Gazette*, December 27, 1764. Retrieved from ReadEx *Archive of Americana America's Historic Newspapers* database at http://infoweb.newsbank.com.

85. Quoted in Kimball, 98–99.

86. Isaac Weld Jr., *Travels through the States of North America and the Provinces of Upper & Lower Canada during the years 1795, 1796 & 1797* (London, 1807; reprint ed., New York: Augustus M. Kelley, 1970), 156.

87. Ibid., 246.

88. John Plaw, *Ferme Ornée* (London, 1795, 1813), 7.

89. Washington Irving, "The Legend of Sleepy Hollow," *The Complete Works, with a Memoir of the Author* (Paris: Casimir, 1834), 336; available online at http://books.google.com.

90. *John Jay House, State Route 22, Katonah, Westchester County, NY*, Jack Boucher, photographer, Historic American Buildings Survey, American Memory from the Library of Congress; accessed at http://hdl.loc.gov/loc.pnp/hhh.ny0859.

91. James Fenimore Cooper, *The Traveling Bachelor* (New York: 1852), 1:85; available online at http://books.google.com.

92. Capt. Basil Hall, "Village of Riceborough in the State of Georgia," *Forty Etchings from Sketches Made with the Camera Lucida in North America in 1827 & 1828* (Edinburgh, 1829), plate 21.

93. *Snee Farm, 1240 Long Point Road, Mount Pleasant Vicinity, Charleston County, SC*, John McWilliams, photographer, 1990, Historic American Buildings Survey, American Memory from the Library of Congress; accessed at http://hdl.loc.gov/loc.pnp/hhh.sc0291.

94. Mary Anna Fox, "A Visit to Bangor," *The Discontented Robins, and Other Stories, for the*

Young (Boston: Charles Fox, 1849), 99; available online at http://books.google.com.

95. Caroline Howard Gilman, *Recollections of a Southern Matron* (New York: Harper & Brothers, 1838), 101; available online at http://books.google.com.

96. Ingraham, *The South-west*, 97–98.

97. Ibid., 98–100.

98. "Historical and Social Sketch of Craven County," *Southern Quarterly Review* (Columbia, SC: E. H. Britton) 9, no. 18 (1854): 405–6; accessed at http://quod.lib.umich.edu/m/moajrnl/acp1141.2-09.018/429.

99. *Oxford English Dictionary*, 2nd ed., 1989., s.v. "veranda, verandah, n.," OED Online, Oxford University Press; accessed at http://dictionary.oed.com/cgi/entry/50276181.

100. Jessie Poesch, "A British Officer and His 'New York' Cottage: An American Vernacular Brought to England,"*American Art Journal* 20, no. 4 (1988): 91–97; accessed at http://www.jstor.org/stable/1594528. Janet Wright, *Architecture of the Picturesque in Canada* (Hull, Quebec: Minister of Supply and Services Canada, 1984), 25–27.

101. Wright, *Architecture of the Picturesque*, 34.

102. John B. Papworth, *Rural Residences: Consisting of a Series of Designs for Cottages, Decorated Cottages, Small Villas and Other Ornamental Buildings; Accompanied by Hints on Situation, Construction, Arrangement and Decoration in the Theory & Practice of Rural Architecture; Interspersed with Some Observations on Landscape Gardening* (London: R. Ackermann, 1832), 103.

103. Ibid., 57.

104. Lt. Francis Hall, *Travels in Canada and the United States in 1816 and 1817* (Boston: Wells and Lilly, 1818), 20; available online at http://books.google.com.

105. E. A. Talbot, "Five Years' Residence in the Canadas; including a Tour through part of the United States in 1823," *Somerset House Gazette and Literary Museum* (London: W. Wetton, 1824), 2:372; available online at http://books.google.com.

106. "Erindale, the Magrath Residence," Erindale Gallery, Mississauga Library, Mississauga, Ontario; available online at http://www.mississauga.ca/portal/residents/erindalegallery.

107. Mrs. Ana Jameson, *Winter Studies and Summer Rambles in Canada* (London: Saunders and Otley, 1838), 308–9; accessed at Early Canada Online at http://www.canadiana.org/view/35745/0324.

108. Capt. Basil Hall, *Travels in North America* (Edinburgh, 1828), 3:316.

109. Lewis F. Allen, *Rural Architecture: Being a Complete Description of Farm Houses, Cottages, and Out Buildings* (New York: C. M. Saxton, 1852), 163–64; available online at http://books.google.com.

110. A. J. Downing, "Remarks on the Fitness of Different Styles of Architecture for the Construction of Country Residences, and the Employment of Vases in Garden Scenery," *American Gardener's Magazine* (August 1836): 283; available online at http://books.google.com.

111. Ibid.

112. Papworth, *Rural Residences*, 103.

113. Asher Benjamin, *The Builder's Guide* (Boston: Perkins & Marvin, 1839), 47.

114. *Grove Farm, G. N. Wilcox House, Nawiliwili Road (State Route 58), Lihue, Kauai County, HI*, David Franzen, photographer, Historic American Buildings Survey, American Memory from the Library of Congress; accessed at http://hdl.loc.gov/loc.pnp/hhh.hi0066.

115. Harriet Beecher Stowe, *Uncle Tom's Cabin; or, Life among the Lowly* (Boston: J. P. Jewett, 1852), 89, 134, 140–41.

116. J. J. Thomas, *Illustrated Annual Register of Rural Affairs* (Albany, NY: Luther Tucker & Son, 1863), 3:254, 256.

117. Harriet Beecher Stowe, *Palmetto-Leaves* (Boston: Osgood, 1873), 228.

118. John William De Forest, *Overland: A Novel* (New York: Seldon, 1872), 173.

119. Mark Pencil, Esq., *The White Sulphur Papers*

(New York: Samuel Colman, 1839), 49; available online at http://books.google.com.

120. *White Sulphur Springs, Paradise Row, U.S. Route 60, White Sulphur Springs, Greenbrier County, WV*, Historic American Buildings Survey, American Memory from the Library of Congress; accessed at http://hdl.loc.gov/loc.pnp/hhh.wv0224.

121. Harriet Otis, "Diary of Harriet Otis, July, 1819," in Caroline G. Curtis, ed., *The Cary Letters* (Cambridge, MA: Riverside Press, 1891), 270–71; accessed from North American Women's Letters and Diaries database published online at Alexander Street Press at http://www.alexanderstreet.com.

122. Talbot, "Five Years' Residence in the Canadas," 372.

123. Capt. Basil Hall, *Travels in North America*, 24.

124. N. P. Willis, Esq., *American Scenery* (London, 1840; reprint, Portland, ME: Antheosen Press), 28–30.

125. James Ewell Heath, "A Visit to the Virginia Springs, no. II," *Southern Literary Messenger, Devoted to Every Department of Literature and the Fine Arts* (Richmond, VA) (1835): 546; accessed at Making of America, http://name.umdl.umich.edu/acf2679.0001.010.

126. Ibid., 547.

127. *Old Beersheba Inn, Armfield Avenue, Beersheba Springs, Grundy County, TN*, Historic American Buildings Survey, American Memory from the Library of Congress; accessed at http://hdl.loc.gov/loc.pnp/hhh.tn0069. Henry M. Burt, *Burt's Illustrated Guide of the Connecticut Valley* (Northampton, MA: New England Publishing Co., 1867), 284; accessed at Making of America, http://quod.lib.umich.edu/m/moa/AAB2140.0001.001.

128. Nathaniel Hawthorne, *Passages from the American Notebooks of Nathaniel Hawthorne* (Boston: Osgood, 1876), 200–201; available online at http://books.google.com.

129. Charles Richard Weld, *A Vacation Tour in the United States and Canada* (London: Longman, Brown, Green, and Longmans, 1855), 76.

130. Fanny Fern, *Ginger-Snaps* (New York: Carleton, 1870), 206; available online at http://books.google.com.

131. Mary Elizabeth Wilson Sherwood, *Etiquette: The American Code of Manners* (New York: George Routledge & Sons, 1884), 161–62; available online at http://books.google.com.

132. Ibid., 166–67.

133. William Alexander MacCorkle, *The White Sulphur Springs* (New York: Neale Publishing Co., 1916), 313; available online at http://books.google.com.

134. *Leland House, Schroon Lake*, New York State Archives website; accessed at http://iarchives.nysed.gov/dmsBlue/viewImageData.jsp?id=130413. Edwin R. Wallace, *Descriptive Guide to the Adirondacks* (Syracuse, NY: Bible Publishing House, 1889), 289; available online at http://books.google.com. "Hotels of the Adirondacks," Chapman Museum; accessed at http://chapmanmuseum.org/Adirondack_hotels.htm.

135. Cleveland Amory, *The Last Resorts* (New York: Harper & Brothers, 1952), 21, 25.

136. George E. Woodward, *Woodward's Country Homes* (New York: Orange Judd & Co., 1865), 23.

137. *Laws of the State of New York* (New York: Thomas Greenleaf, 1792), 2:276; available online at http://books.google.com.

138. Grace H. Peirce, "Aesthetic Children," *Lippincott's Magazine* (February 1885): 204; available online at http://books.google.com.

139. Dona Brown, *Inventing New England: Regional Tourism in the Nineteenth Century* (Washington, DC: Smithsonian Institution Press, 1995), 90.

140. Sally Dagnal et al., "A Brief History of The Martha's Vineyard Campmeeting Association," Martha's Vineyard Campmeeting Association; accessed at http://www.mvcma.org/brief.htm.

141. Dr. George Clarkson, "The Old Cottage Porch," *Songs and Specialties* (Paterson, NJ: J. W. McKee, 1871), American Memory from

the Library of Congress, Music Division; accessed at http://hdl.loc.gov/loc.music/sm1871.07085.

142. "The Residence of President Rutherford B. Hayes," Rutherford B. Hayes Presidential Center; accessed at http://www.rbhayes.org/hayes/hayeshouse.

143. Eugene Clarence Gardner, *Homes, and How to Make Them* (Boston: J. R. Osgood, 1875), 167; available online at http://quod.lib.umich.edu/m/moa.

144. Isabella Maud Rittenhouse Mayne, "Diary of Isabella Maud Mayne," July 1881, in Richard Lee Strout, ed., *Maud* (New York: Macmillan, 1939), 593; accessed from North American Women's Letters and Diaries, Alexander Street Press at http://www.alexanderstreet.com.

145. William D. Howells, *The Rise of Silas Lapham* (Boston: Houghton Mifflin, 1884; reprint, Cambridge, MA: Riverside Press, 1922), 187; available online at http://books.google.com.

146. Horace Smith, "Under the Porch," *Littell's Living Age*, 5th ser., 86, no. 2366 (November 2, 1889): 258; available online at http://books.google.com.

147. Sherwood Anderson, *Winesburg, Ohio: A Group of Tales of Ohio Small-Town Life* (New York: Modern Library, 1919), 7–8.

148. Dorothy Scarborough, *From a Southern Porch* (New York: G. P. Putnam's Sons, 1919), v–vi; available online at http://books.google.com.

149. Ibid., 1. Sylvia Ann Grider, "Dorothy Scarborough," *Texas Women Writers: A Tradition of Their Own* (College Station, TX: Texas A&M University Press, 1997), 137; available online at http://books.google.com.

150. Scarborough, *From a Southern Porch*, 1–3.

151. Ibid., 28.

152. Sue Bridwell Beckham, "The American Front Porch: Women's Liminal Space," in Marilyn Ferris Motz and Pat Browne, eds., *Making the American Home: Middle Class Women & Domestic Material Culture 1840–1940* (Bowling Green, OH: Bowling Green State University Popular Press, 1988), 88.

153. Donlon, *Swinging in Place*, 13.

154. "The History of Postcards," Emotions Greeting Cards; accessed at www.emotionscards.com/museum/historyofpostcards.htm.

155. "Historic American Buildings Survey/Historic American Engineering Record/Historic American Landscapes Survey (HABS/HAER) — About This Collection," American Memory from the Library of Congress; accessed at http://memory.loc.gov/ammem/collections/habs_haer/hhintro.html.

156. "About the FSA/OWI Black-and-White Negatives," Farm Security Administration/Office of War Information Black-and-White Negatives, Library of Congress; accessed at http://www.loc.gov/pictures/collection/fsa.

157. Brent Colley, "History of Gilbert & Bennett Mfg. Co. in Georgetown, Connecticut," History of Redding; accessed at http://www.historyofredding.com/HGgilbertbennett.htm.

158. United States Patent Office, *Subject-Matter Index of Patents for Inventions Issued by the United States Patent Office from 1790 to 1873 . . .* (Washington, DC: Government Printing Office, 1874), 942–43; available online at http://quod.lib.umich.edu/m/moa.

159. Eben E. Rexford, "Around the Country Home," *Outing Magazine* 51, no. 4 (January 1908): 501; available online at http://books.google.com.

160. United States Department of Agriculture, *Farmer's Bulletins*, no. 607 (Washington, DC: Government Printing Office, 1915), 9–10; available online at http://books.google.com.

161. "History of New York Wire"; accessed at http://www.newyorkwire.com/company/history.html.

162. Mary Hotaling, "Trudeau Sanatorium," National Register of Historic Places Registration Form (Washington, DC: National Park Service, 1995); accessed at http://www.oprhp.state.ny.us/hpimaging/hp_view.asp?groupView=3639.

163. "2004 Cure Chair Raffle Winner," Historic

Saranac Lake; accessed at http://www
.historicsaranaclake.org/curech.htm.

164. Leonard T. Davidson, "The Winter Cure
at Trudeau," *American Journal of Nursing*
18, no. 1 (October 1917): 14–15; accessed at
http://www.jstor.org/stable/340604915.

165. Thomas Spees Carrington, *Tuberculosis Hospital and Sanatorium Construction* (New
York: National Association for the Study and
Prevention of Tuberculosis, 1911), 119; available online at http://archive.org.

166. Ibid., 135–36.

167. Ibid., 121–23.

168. *Twenty-Second Annual Report of the Department of Agriculture* (Albany: State of New
York Department of Agriculture, 1915), 2076;
available online at http://books.google.com.

169. Anne M. Niquette and R. Brooks Jeffery, *A
Guide to Tucson Architecture* (Tucson: University of Arizona Press, 2002), 24, 28.

170. "For Sleeping and Comfort in Camp," *Boy's
Life* (June 1917): 45; available online at
http://books.google.com.

171. Robert C. Spencer Jr., "Planning the Home,
A Chapter on Porches," *House Beautiful* 17
(1905): 27.

172. Gustav Stickley, "Porches, Pergolas and Ter-
races: The Charm of Living Out of Doors,"
Craftsman Homes (1909; reprint, Guilford,
CT: Lyons Press, 2002), 26.

173. "Sun Room," White House Museum; accessed at http://www.whitehousemuseum
.org/floor3/sun-room.htm. Donald Lang-
mead, *Icons of American Architecture* (West-
port, CT: Greenwood Press, 2009), 533.

174. Thomas Spees Carrington, M.d., *Fresh Air
and How to Use It* (New York: National Association for the Study and Prevention of
Tuberculosis, 1912), 83; available online at
http://books.google.com.

175. C. E. Schermerhorn, "Planning the Bungalow," *Bungalows, Camps and Mountain
Homes* (New York: William T. Comstock Co.,
1915; reprint, Washington, DC: American Institute of Architects Press, 1990), 18.

176. *James A. Allison Mansion, 3200 Coldspring*
Road, Indianapolis, Marion County, IN, Historic American Buildings Survey, American
Memory from the Library of Congress; accessed at http://hdl.loc.gov/loc.pnp/hhh
.in0045.

177. "Alpha Iota—Iowa State," *Phi Gamma Delta*
(October 1916): 562; available online at
http://books.google.com.

178. Andrew H. Palmer, "Climatic Influences on
American Architecture," *Scientific Monthly*
(September 1917): 278; accessed at http://
www.jstor.org/stable/22574.

179. Phil M. Riley, "The Sleeping-Porch Problem," *House Beautiful* (February 1917): 136.

180. Ibid., 138, 182, 183.

181. Greta Gray, *House and Home, A Manual and
Textbook of Practical House Planning* (Philadelphia: Lippincott, 1923).

182. Aeroshade Company, *Catalogue*, no. 60
(Waukesha, Wisconsin: 1920), 14.

183. "Canvas Curtains for the Sleeping-Porch,"
Popular Science (September 1920): 98-99;
available online at http://books.google.com.

184. Alison Bent, "The Outdoor Living Room,"
Good Housekeeping (June 1907): 586; available online at http://books.google.com.

185. Henry H. Saylor, *Distinctive Homes of Mod-
erate Cost; Being a Collection of Country and
Suburban Homes in Good Taste, with Some
Value in Suggestion for the Home-Builder*
(New York: McBride, Winston & Co., 1910),
39.

186. Ibid., 39, 40.

187. Lillie Hamilton French, *Homes and Their Decoration* (New York: Dodd, Mead and Co.,
1903), 345.

188. R. O. Buck, "An Enclosed Porch Adds to
Your Home," *Popular Mechanics* (July 1935):
121-25; available online at http://books
.google.com.

189. "Alexander Graham Bell National Historic
Site and the Bras d'Or Lakes," Parks Canada;
accessed at http://www.pc.gc.ca/nature/
eaudouce_freshwater/itm4-/index_e.asp.

190. *Porch of "Beinn Bhreagh," A. G. Bell's residence, Cape Breton, NS, 1915*, McCord

Museum; available online at http://www
.mccord-museum.qc.ca/en.

191. Sears, Roebuck and Company, *Honor Bilt Modern Homes* (Chicago: Sears, Roebuck and Co., 1926), 108; reprinted as *Small Houses of the Twenties* (New York: Dover Publications, 1991).

192. "America's Most Popular Plan," *Popular Mechanics* (February 1929): 351; available online at http://books.google.com.

193. Stewart Brand, *How Buildings Learn* (New York: Penguin, 1994), vi.

194. "Porch Furniture," *House Beautiful* (April 1904): 292; available online at http://books.google.com.

195. "The Garden Front," *Canadian Architect and Builder* (June 1905): 83; accessed at http://digital.library.mcgill.ca.

196. Ruby Ross Goodnow and Rayne Adams, "The Pleasure of Porches," *The Honest House* (New York: Century, 1914), 121.

197. Esther Johnson, "Back Yard versus Front Porch," *House Beautiful* (June 1922): 602, 604.

198. "Placing Our Houses on the Small Lot," *House Beautiful* (June 1922): 540.

199. Helen Kline and Anna M. Cooley, *Shelter and Clothing, a Textbook of the Household Arts* (New York: Macmillan, 1913), 22–23.

200. Mary J. Quinn, *Planning and Furnishing the Home* (New York: Harper & Brothers, 1914), 19.

CHAPTER 2. CHARACTER, FUNCTIONS, AND FURNISHINGS

1. Gervase Wheeler, *Homes for the People in Suburb and Country; the Villa, the Mansion, and the Cottage, Adapted to American Climate and Wants* (New York: American News Co., 1867), 175.

2. Herman Melville, "The Piazza," *The Piazza Tales* (1856; reprint, New York: Hendricks House, Farrar Straus, 1948). "Arrowhead," National Register of Historic Places, National Park Service, 1975; accessed at http://pdfhost.focus.nps.gov/docs/NHLS/

Text/66000126.pdf. "Herman Melville's Arrowhead—Berkshire Historical Society"; accessed at http://www.mobydick.org. *Arrowhead, 780 Holmes Road, Pittsfield, Berkshire County, MA*, Historic American Buildings Survey, American Memory from the Library of Congress; accessed at http://hdl.loc.gov/loc.pnp/hhh.ma0507.

3. A. J. Downing, *The Architecture of Country Houses; Including Designs for Cottages, Farm-Houses, and Villas, with Remarks on Interiors, Furniture, and the Best Modes of Warming and Ventilating* (New York: D. Appleton, 1850; reprint, New York: Dover, 1969), 308.

4. Eugene C. Gardner, *Illustrated Homes: A Series of Papers Describing Real Houses for Real People* (Boston: J. R. Osgood, 1875), 98–101.

5. Eben E. Rexford, "Around the Country Home," *Outing Magazine* 51, no. 4 (January 1908): 501; available online at http://books.google.com.

6. Gustav Stickley, *Craftsman Homes* (1909; reprint, Guilford, CT: Lyons Press, 2002), 77.

7. Winnifred Fales and Mary Northend, "The Outdoor Living Room," *The Independent* (May 4, 1918): 22; available online at http://books.google.com.

8. Dorothy Scarborough, *From a Southern Porch* (New York: G. P. Putnam's Sons, 1919), 17.

9. The Design Review Committee of the city of Ventura, California, for example, published design guidelines in 2008, recommending an eight-foot minimum width for new construction of porches. City of Ventura, "Porches," 2008 Design Guidelines; available online at http://www.cityofventura.net/cd/planning/citydesign.

10. Downing, *Architecture of Country Houses*, 117–18.

11. Wheeler, *Homes for the People*, 297.

12. General Egbert L. Viele, "A Glimpse of Nature from My Veranda," *Harper's New Monthly Magazine* 57, no. 339 (August 1878): 405.

13. Thomas Meehan, *Meehan's Monthly. A Magazine of Horticulture, Botany and Kindred*

Subjects (Germantown/Philadelphia, PA: Thomas Meehan & Sons) 9 (1899): 24; available online at http://books.google.com.

14. All quotations are from Grace Tabor, "Vines and Harmonizers," *The Landscape Gardening Book: Wherein Are Set Down the Simple Laws of Beauty* (New York: McBride, Winston & Co., 1911), 55; available online at http://books.google.com.

15. Sinclair Lewis, *Babbitt* (New York: Harcourt, Brace, 1922), 2–3.

16. J. Stogdell Stokes, "The American Windsor Chair," *Bulletin of the Pennsylvania Museum* 21, no. 98 (December 1925): 47.

17. A. J. Downing, *Cottage Residences: or, A Series of Designs for Rural Cottages and Cottage Villas, and Their Gardens and Grounds. Adapted to North America* (New York: Wiley and Putman, 1842), fig. 55.

18. Ibid., figs. 53, 123.

19. Gervase Wheeler, *Rural Homes: or, Sketches of Houses Suited to American Country Life, with Original Plans, Designs, &c.* (New York: C. Scribner, 1851), 87–88.

20. Wheeler, *Homes for the People*, 142–43.

21. "Our History," Old Hickory Furniture Co.; accessed at http://www.oldhickory.com/history.phtml.

22. "Old Hickory Porch Set," *Good Housekeeping* 36, no. 6 (June 1903): 617; available online at http://books.google.com.

23. Fales and Northend, "The Outdoor Living Room," 22.

24. Stickley, *Craftsman Homes*, 97.

25. Fales and Northend, "The Outdoor Living Room," 22–23.

26. Ruby Ross Goodnow and Rayne Adams, "The Pleasure of Porches," *The Honest House* (New York: Century, 1914), 127.

27. Letter from Margaret Fuller to James Gotendorf, 1845, in *Love-Letters of Margaret Fuller, 1845–1846* (London: T. Fisher Unwin, 1903), 228; accessed from North American Women's Letters and Diaries database published online by Alexander Street Press at http://www.alexanderstreet.com.

28. "Summer," *Life* 6, no. 138 (August 20, 1885): 103.

29. Alison Bent, "The Outdoor Living Room," *Good Housekeeping* (June 1907): 586; available online at http://books.google.com.

30. "Disturbing a Sleeper," illustration by A. B. Frost in Thomas W. Knox, "Summer Clubs of Great South Bay," *Harper's New Monthly Magazine* 61, no. 362 (July 1880): 211.

31. *Keith's Magazine on Home Building*, 11 (Minneapolis: Keith Co., 1904), 305; available online at http://books.google.com.

32. *Building with Assurance* (Morgan Woodwork Organization, 1921), 138.

33. Goodnow and Adams, "The Pleasure of Porches," 128.

34. Wheeler, *Rural Homes*, 205, 207.

35. Richard Saunders, "Introduction to the Dover Edition," *Heywood Brothers and Wakefield Company Classic Wicker Furniture, The Complete 1898–1899 Illustrated Catalogue* (New York: Dover, 1982), intro.

36. Goodnow and Adams, "The Pleasure of Porches," 127.

37. "$22.50 for a Porch Swing Such as This," *Evening Chronicle*, Spokane, Wash., April 14, 1905, 4; available online at http://books.google.com.

38. Rhea C. Scott, *Home Labor Saving Devices*, 2nd ed. (Philadelphia: Lippincott, 1917), 65; available online at http://books.google.com.

39. Tim Dirks, "Review of *It's a Gift*" (1934), Filmsite; accessed at http://www.filmsite.org/itsag2.html. A video clip of this porch scene from *It's a Gift* may be accessible through online video sites.

CHAPTER 3. CLASSICAL ORDER

1. Asher Benjamin, *Practice of Architecture, Containing the Five Orders of Architecture, and an Additional Column and Entablature, with All Their Elements and Details Explained and Illustrated. For the Use of Carpenters and Practical Men* (Boston: Asher Benjamin, 1833), 24; available online at http://google.books.com.

2. Vitruvius, bk. 4, "Proportions of Doric

Temples," *Ten Books of Architecture*, trans. Morris Hicky Morgan (Cambridge: Harvard University Press, 1914) 109–13; available online at http://gutenberg.org. F. C. Browne, F. A. Bourne, and H. V. von Holst, "The Classic Greek and Roman Orders," *Cyclopedia of Architecture, Carpentry and Building* (Chicago: American Technical Society, 1916), 8:274–75.

3. Jean-Claude Marsan, *Montreal in Evolution* (Montreal: McGill-Queen's Press, 1990), 193–94. Leslie Maitland, *Neoclassical Architecture in Canada* (Ottawa: Parks Canada, Ministry of Supply and Services Canada, 1984), 62.

4. James Stevens Curl, *A Dictionary of Architecture* (Oxford: Oxford University Press, 1999), 336, 587.

5. Ibid., 169–70.

6. Stuart & Revett's *Antiquities of Athens*, St. Louis Public Library, Steedman Exhibit; available online at http://exhibits.slpl.org/steedman/index.asp.

7. "The Study of Orders," in Browne et al., *Cyclopedia of Architecture, Carpentry, and Building*, 8:10, 12.

8. Asher Benjamin, *The American Builder's Companion* (Boston: R. P. & C. Williams, 1826), plate K.

9. Benjamin, *Practice of Architecture*, 34–35.

10. *The Woodlands, 4000 Woodlands Avenue, Philadelphia, Philadelphia, PA*, Historic American Buildings Survey, American Memory from the Library of Congress; accessed at http://hdl.loc.gov/loc.pnp/hhh.pa1367.

11. *Benjamin Conklin House, 302 East Main Street, Cambridge City, Wayne County, IN*, Historic American Buildings Survey, American Memory from the Library of Congress; accessed at http://hdl.loc.gov/loc.pnp/hhh.in0086.

12. Curl, *Dictionary of Architecture*, 513.

13. "The Study of Orders," in Browne et al., *Cyclopedia of Architecture, Carpentry, and Building*, 68.

14. Asher Benjamin, *The Builder's Guide* (Boston: Perkins & Marvin, 1839), 24.

15. Ibid., 67–70.

16. Nathalie Clerk, *Palladian Style in Canadian Architecture* (Ottawa: Ministry of the Environment, 1984), 95.

17. Xenophon, *The Memorabilia Recollections of Socrates, Book III*, trans. H. G. Dakyns, (New York: Macmillan, 1897), chap. 8; available online at http://gutenberg.org.

18. Christiane L. Joost-Gaugier, "The Iconography of Sacred Space: A Suggested Reading of the Meaning of the Roman Pantheon," *Artibus et Historiae* 19, no. 38 (1998): 21–42; accessed at http://www.jstor.org/stable/1483585. C.H.O. Scaife, "The Origin of Some Pantheon Columns," *Journal of Roman Studies* 43 (1953): 37; accessed at http://www.jstor.org/stable/297777.

19. "De Architectura," Wikipedia.org.

20. Vitruvius, *Ten Books of Architecture*, 180; available online at http://gutenberg.org.

21. Ibid., 182.

22. Ibid., 186.

23. One of the earliest-known surviving examples of a portico added to a private mansion is the mid-1600s portico at the Vyne in Basingstoke, Hampshire, England; accessed at http://www.nationaltrust.org.uk/main/w-vh/w-visits/w-findaplace/w-thevyne/w-thevyne-history.htm.

24. William H. Pierson Jr., *American Buildings and Their Architects* (Garden City, NY: Doubleday, 1970), 111–12.

25. Ibid., 142–44. "Redwood Library Introduction and History," Redwood Library and Athenaeum; accessed at http://www.redwoodlibrary.org/General_info/introduction_and_history.html.

26. Pierson, *American Buildings and Their Architects*, 145. Marcus Whiffen and Frederick Koeper, *American Architecture 1607–1860* (Cambridge, MA: MIT Press, 1981), 78.

27. Whiffen and Koeper, *American Architecture*, 81. "Church Info—Historical Overview: St. Michael's Episcopal Church—Charleston, SC," accessed at http://www.stmichaelschurch.net/02c_history.php.

28. Pierson, *American Buildings and Their*

Architects, 111–17. "Mount Airy, Virginia," Signers of the Declaration of Independence, National Park Service; accessed at http://www.nps.gov/history/history/online_books/declaration/site51.htm.

29. *The Woodlands, 4000 Woodlands Avenue, Philadelphia, Philadelphia, PA*, Historic American Buildings Survey, American Memory from the Library of Congress; accessed at http://hdl.loc.gov/loc.pnp/hhh.pa1367.

30. Pierson, *American Buildings and Their Architects*, 215–21.

31. "Virginia State Capitol, City of Richmond, Virginia," Application for Inclusion of a Property in the U.S. World Heritage Tentative List (Richmond: Virginia State Historic Preservation Office, 2007), 27; accessed at http://home.nps.gov/oia/topics/worldheritage/Applications/Virginia%20Capitol.pdf.

32. Whiffen and Koeper, *American Architecture*, 103–9.

33. Buford Pickens, "Wyatt's Pantheon, the State House in Boston and a New View of Bulfinch," *Journal of the Society of Architectural Historians* 29, no. 2 (May 1970): 124–31; accessed at http://www.jstor.org/stable/988646. *Maine State House, State & Capitol Streets, Augusta, Kennebec, ME*, Historic American Buildings Survey, American Memory from the Library of Congress; accessed at http://hdl.loc.gov/loc.pnp/hhh.me0047.

34. *First Parish Church, Town Green, Thayer Drive, Lancaster, Worcester, MA*, Historic American Buildings Survey, American Memory from the Library of Congress; accessed at http://hdl.loc.gov/loc.pnp/hhh.ma0952.

35. Bryant Franklin Tolles, Carolyn K. Tolles, and Paul F. Norton, *Architecture in Salem: An Illustrated Guide* (Hanover, NH: University Press of New England, 2004), 38.

36. "Nickels-Sortwell House," Historic New England; accessed at http://www.historicnewengland.org/visit/homes/nickels.htm.

37. Pierson, *American Buildings and Their Architects*, 402–3.

38. Gene Waddell, "The First Monticello," *Journal of the Society of Architectural Historians* 46, no. 1 (March 1987): 10; accessed at http://www.jstor.org/stable/990142.

39. "Tudor Place"; accessed at http://www.tudorplace.org.

40. Earl Rostenthal, "The Antecedents of Bramante's Tempietto," *Journal of the Society of Architectural Historians* 23, no. 2 (May 1964): 55–74; accessed at http://www.jstor.org/stable/988161. Mark Wilson Jones, "The Tempietto and the Roots of Coincidence," *Architectural History* 33 (1990): 1–28; accessed at http://www.jstor.org/stable/1568546.

41. Whiffen and Koeper, *American Architecture*, 108. *University of Virginia, Pavilions & Hotels, University Avenue & Rugby Road, Charlottesville, VA*, Historic American Buildings Survey, American Memory from the Library of Congress; accessed at http://memory.loc.gov/pnp/habshaer/va/va0000/va0051/sheet/00001r.tif.

42. Brian McNeill, "UVa Preservation Project Creates Colorful Debate," *Daily Progress* (Charlottesville, VA), July 6, 2009.

43. Osmund R. Overby and Henry C. Edwards, "St. Paul's Episcopal Church," (National Park Service, 1959), included as data pages with *St. Paul's Episcopal Church, State & Court Streets, Windsor, Windsor, VT*, Historic American Buildings Survey, American Memory from the Library of Congress; accessed at http://hdl.loc.gov/loc.pnp/hhh.vt0082.

44. Capt. Basil Hall, *Travels in North America* (Edinburgh, 1828), 1:130.

45. Carl David Arfwedson, *The United States and Canada in 1823, 1833 and 1834* (1834; reprint, New York: Johnson Reprint Corp., 1969), 127.

46. Marsan, *Montreal in Evolution*, 197.

47. *Swanwyck, 65 Landers Lane, New Castle Vicinity, New Castle County, DE*, Historic American Buildings Survey, American Memory from the Library of Congress; accessed at May 29, 2010 at http://hdl.loc.gov/loc.pnp/hhh.de0052.

48. Haliburton House Museum, Nova Scotia

Museum; accessed at http://museum.gov.ns
.ca/hh/index.htm.

49. Diane Maddex, ed., *Master Builders: A Guide
to Famous American Architects* (Washington,
DC: Preservation Press, 1985), 182–88.

50. Pierson, *American Buildings and Their Architects*, 373, 477. "Arlington House Architecture
& Construction," U. S. National Park Service;
accessed at http://www.nps.gov/archive/
arho/tour/history/architecture.html. "NPS
Historical Handbook: Custis-Lee Mansion";
accessed at http://www.nps.gov/history/
history/online_books/hh/6/hh6b1.htm.

51. *Monumental Church, Richmond, Virginia*, Historic American Buildings Survey, American
Memory from the Library of Congress; accessed at http://hdl.loc.gov/loc.pnp/hhh
.va1448.

52. Whiffen and Koeper, *American Architecture*,
151.

53. *U.S. Naval Asylum, Biddle Hall, Gray's Ferry
Avenue, Philadelphia, Philadelphia County, PA*,
Historic American Buildings Survey, American Memory from the Library of Congress;
accessed at http://hdl.loc.gov/loc.pnp/hhh
.pa0668.

54. William Strickland, communication to the
commissioners of the navy hospital fund, December 1, 1829, American State Papers 025,
Naval Affairs vol. 3, 21st Congress, 1st sess.,
publication no. 404, p. 482.

55. *U.S. Naval Asylum, Biddle Hall, Gray's Ferry
Avenue, Philadelphia, Philadelphia County, PA*,
Historic American Buildings Survey, American Memory from the Library of Congress;
accessed at http://hdl.loc.gov/loc.pnp/hhh
.pa0668. "Welcome to Naval Square," Toll
Brothers, Inc.; accessed at http://www
.navalsquare.com.

56. "St. Andrew's Protestant Episcopal Church,"
data page 2, Historic American Buildings Survey, American Memory from the Library of
Congress; accessed at http://hdl.loc.gov/loc
.pnp/hhh.pa0793. Whiffen and Koeper, *American Architecture*, 159. Jeffery A. Cohen, "John
Haviland," in *Master Builders*, 36.

57. *Andalusia, State Road Vicinity (Bensalem
Township), Andalusia, Bucks County, PA*,
Jack Boucher, photographer, 1976, Historic American Buildings Survey, American
Memory from the Library of Congress; accessed at http://hdl.loc.gov/loc.pnp/hhh
.pa0213.

58. *David Ross McCord's house "Temple Grove,"
Cote des Neiges, Montreal, QC, 1872*, McCord
Museum of Canadian History, Montreal;
accessed at http://www.mccord-museum.qc
.ca/en.

59. Daniel Robbins, *The Vermont State House*
(Montpelier: Vermont Council on the Arts,
1980), 20–23.

60. John Claudius Loudon, "The Rise, Progress
and State of North American Architecture,"
*Architecture Magazine and Journal of Improve-
ment in Architecture, Building, and Furnishing,
and in the Various Arts and Trades Connected
Therewith* (London) 4 (1837): 18; available online at http://books.google.com.

61. Charles Dickens, *American Notes and Pictures
from Italy* (London, 1846; reprint, London:
Oxford University Press, 1970), 71.

62. "Texas Governor's Mansion," Official Site of
the Friends of the Governor's Mansion; accessed at http://www.txfgm.org/historical_
info.php.

63. *Belmont, Belmont Boulevard & Wedgewood,
Nashville, Davidson, TN*, Historic American
Buildings Survey, American Memory from
the Library of Congress; accessed at http://
hdl.loc.gov/loc.pnp/hhh.tn0013. *U.S. Custom
House, Twentieth & Post Office Streets, Galveston, Galveston, TX*, Historic American Buildings Survey, American Memory from the
Library of Congress; accessed at http://hdl
.loc.gov/loc.pnp/hhh.tx0092.

64. David R. Starbuck, *Massacre at Fort William
Henry* (Hanover, NH: University Press of New
England, 2002), 16.

65. Wheeler, *Homes for the People*, opposite 246.

66. *Nick Prevost House, 105 North Prevost Street,
Anderson, Anderson County, SC*, Historic
American Buildings Survey, American

Memory from the Library of Congress; accessed at http://hdl.loc.gov/loc.pnp/hhh.sc0054.

67. *Benjamin Harrison House, 1230 North Delaware Street, Indianapolis, Marion, IN*, Historic American Buildings Survey, American Memory from the Library of Congress; accessed at http://hdl.loc.gov/loc.pnp/hhh.in0055.

68. *Rockcliffe Mansion, 1000 Bird Street, Hannibal, Marion County, MO*, Historic American Buildings Survey, American Memory from the Library of Congress; accessed at http://hdl.loc.gov/loc.pnp/hhh.mo1118.

69. Historical marker sign on building. Curl, *A Dictionary of Architecture*, 473.

70. *Pennsylvania Station, 370 Seventh Avenue, West Thirty-First, Thirty-First-Thirty-Third Streets, New York, New York, NY*, Historic American Buildings Survey, American Memory from the Library of Congress; accessed at http://hdl.loc.gov/loc.pnp/hhh.ny0411.

71. "Lincoln Memorial," Lincoln Memorial Documentation Project, 1993, sheet 1, Historic American Buildings Survey, American Memory from the Library of Congress; accessed at http://memory.loc.gov/pnp/habshaer/dc/dc0400/dc0472/sheet/0001r.tif.

72. Patricia Murphy, "Cass Gilbert," in Dianne Maddex, ed., *Master Builders: A Guide to Famous American Architects* (Washington, DC: Preservation Press, 1985), 110–13.

73. "The Court Building," Supreme Court of the United States; accessed at http://www.supremecourtus.gov/about/courtbuilding.pdf.

74. "Jefferson Memorial," Sheet 1, Jefferson Memorial Documentation Project, 1994, Historic American Buildings Survey, American Memory from the Library of Congress accessed at http://lcweb2.loc.gov/pnp/habshaer/dc/dc0400/dc0473/sheet/0001r.tif.

75. William MacDonald, "Some Implications of Later Roman Construction," *Journal of the Society of Architectural Historians* 17, no. 4 (Winter 1958): 2–8; accessed at http://www.jstor.org/stable/987944.

76. Edson Armi, "Orders and Continuous Orders in Romanesque Architecture," *Journal of the Society of Architectural Historians* 34, no. 3 (October 1975): 173–88; accessed at http://www.jstor.org/stable/989027.

77. "Presbytere (The)," National Historic Landmark Program; accessed at http://tps.cr.nps.gov/nhl/detail.cfm?resourceId=929&resourceType=building. "Cabildo (The)," National Historic Landmark Program; accessed at http://tps.cr.nps.gov/nhl/detail.cfm?resourceId=254&resourceType=building. "History," Mission San Miguel; accessed at http://www.missionsanmiguel.org/about.

78. "Mayor Menino Reopens Historic Courtyard at the BPL, November 15, 2000," Boston Public Library; accessed at http://www.bpl.org/news/courtyardopening.htm.

79. Mount Airy, State Route 646 vicinity, Warsaw vicinity, Richmond, VA Historic American Buildings Survey, American Memory from the Library of Congress, Washington, DC; accessed at http://hdl.loc.gov/loc.pnp/hhh.va0892.

80. Asher Benjamin, *The Architect or Practical House Carpenter* (Boston: Mussey, 1845), 50; available online at http://books.google.com.

81. Downing, *Cottage Residences*, 142.

82. Calvert Vaux, *Villas and Cottages: A Series of Designs Prepared for Execution in the United States* (New York: Harper, 1857), 98–99.

83. *Bethany College, "Old Main" Building, Route 67, Bethany, Brooke, WV*, Historic American Buildings Survey, American Memory from the Library of Congress; accessed at http://hdl.loc.gov/loc.pnp/hhh.wv0057.

84. *Stanford University Quadrangle, Stanford University Campus, Stanford, Santa Clara, CA*, Historic American Buildings Survey, American Memory from the Library of Congress; accessed at http://loc.gov/pictures/item/ca1002.

85. "Noble Benefaction," *Saint Johnsbury Republican*, December 17, 1891.

86. *Trinity Episcopal Church, Copley Square, Boston, Suffolk County, MA*, Historic American

Buildings Survey, American Memory from the Library of Congress; accessed at http://hdl .loc.gov/loc.pnp/hhh.ma1359.

87. Peter Austin, "Rafael Guastavino's Construction Business in the United States: Beginnings and Development," *APT Bulletin* 30, no. 4 (1999): 15–19.

88. *Union Station, 50 Massachusetts Avenue Northeast, Washington, District of Columbia, DC*, Historic American Buildings Survey, American Memory from the Library of Congress; accessed at http://loc.gov/pictures/item/ dc0254. *Los Angeles City Hall, 200 North Spring Street, Los Angeles, Los Angeles, CA*, Historic American Buildings Survey, American Memory from the Library of Congress; accessed at http://loc.gov/pictures/item/ ca1261.

CHAPTER 4. VARIOUS FORMS

1. Henry Glassie, *Folk Housing in Middle Virginia* (Knoxville: University of Tennessee Press, 1975), 137.

2. Robert Blair St. George, "'Set Thine House in Order': The Domestication of the Yeomanry in Seventeenth-Century New England," in Dell Upton and John Michael Vlach, eds., *Common Places: Readings in American Vernacular Architecture* (Athens: University of Georgia Press, 1986), 340.

3. *Daniel Shute House, Main & South Pleasant Streets, Hingham, Plymouth County, MA*, Historic American Buildings Survey, American Memory from the Library of Congress; accessed at http://hdl.loc.gov/loc.pnp/hhh .ma0870.

4. Peter Benes, "The Templeton 'Run' and the Pomfret 'Cluster': Patterns of Diffusion in Rural New England Meetinghouse Architecture, 1647–1822," *Old-Time New England* 68 (Winter–Spring 1978): 1.

5. *Old Ship Church, 88 Main Street, Hingham, Plymouth, MA*, Historic American Buildings Survey, American Memory from the Library of Congress; accessed at http://hdl.loc.gov/ loc.pnp/hhh.ma0440.

6. James D. Kornwolf, *Architecture and Town Planning in Colonial North America*, (Baltimore: Johns Hopkins University Press, 2002), 3:1379. "Provincial Historic Sites: Commissariat House," Newfoundland and Labrador, Canada; accessed at http://www.seethesites .ca/the-sites/commissariat-house.aspx.

7. Charles E. Peterson, annotator, *The Rules of Work of the Carpenters' Company of the City and County of Philadelphia 1786* (Mendham, NJ: Astragal Press, 1992), 35.

8. *General Samuel Strong House, North Side of West Main Street, Vergennes, Addison County, VT*, Historic American Buildings Survey, American Memory from the Library of Congress; accessed at http://hdl.loc.gov/loc.pnp/ hhh.vt0023.

9. Two clues help to support the age of this structure. The circa 1890 photograph of the Robinson family sitting on this porch shows the bases of the front newel posts to be very weathered and decayed, as might be expected after more than seven decades of exposure. The boards around the bases of the newel posts have since been replaced, but when repairs were made to the porch during the 1990s, hand-hewn timbers in the roof structure also provided evidence of the circa 1814 date of construction.

10. Catherine E. Beecher, *A Treatise on Domestic Economy* (New York: Harper & Brothers, 1845), 263; available online at http:// gutenberg.org.

11. H. Hudson Holly, "The Entrance," *Modern Dwellings in Town and Country Adapted to American Wants and Climate* (New York: Harper & Brothers, 1878), frontispiece.

12. *Henry W. Longfellow Place, 105 Brattle Street, Cambridge, Middlesex County, MA*, and "Supplemental Material," Historic American Buildings Survey, American Memory from the Library of Congress; accessed at http://hdl .loc.gov/loc.pnp/hhh.ma0260.

13. *General George Hutchinson House, 4311 West Seneca Turnpike, Onondaga Hill, Onondaga County, NY*, Gilbert Ask, photographer,

Historic American Buildings Survey, American Memory from the Library of Congress; accessed at http://hdl.loc.gov/loc.pnp/hhh .ny0994.

14. *Crawford-Cassin House, 3017 O Street Northwest, Washington, DC*, J. Alexander, photographer, 1969, Historic American Buildings Survey, American Memory from the Library of Congress; accessed at http://hdl.loc.gov/ loc.pnp/hhh.dc0077.

15. "Letters from the South," *American Agriculturalist* (May 1847): 152; available online at http://books.google.com.

16. *Valery Nichols House, 723 Toulouse Street, New Orleans, Orleans Parish, LA*, Historic American Buildings Survey, American Memory from the Library of Congress; accessed at http://hdl.loc.gov/loc.pnp/hhh.la0021.

17. Solon Robinson, "A Cheap Farm-House," *American Agriculturalist* (July 1847): 217; available online at http://books.google.com.

18. "Review of the June Number of the *Agriculturalist*," *American Agriculturalist* (November 1847): 350; available online at http://books .google.com.

19. Holly, *Modern Dwellings*, 112–13.

20. Frederic Gomes Cassidy and Joan Houston Hall, *Dictionary of American Regional English* (Cambridge, MA: Belknap Press of Harvard University Press, 1985), 113.

21. Capt. Basil Hall, *Travels in North America in the Years 1827 and 1828* (Edinburgh, 1830), 3:139–40; available online at http://books .google.com.

22. *Charles Edmonston House, 21 East Battery Street, Charleston, Charleston County, SC*, C. O. Greene, photographer, 1940, Historic American Buildings Survey, American Memory from the Library of Congress; accessed at http://hdl.loc.gov/loc.pnp/hhh.sc0045.

23. Fredrika Bremer, *The Homes of the New World; Impressions of America* (New York: Harper & Brothers, 1853), 279; available online at http://digital.library.wisc.edu.

24. Fred Kniffen, "Folk Housing: Key to Diffusion," *Annals of the Association of American Geographers* 55, no. 4 (December 1965): 559; accessed at http://www.jstor.org/ stable/2569440.

25. *Montgomery Place, Annandale Road, Barrytown Vicinity, Dutchess County, NY*, Historic American Buildings Survey, American Memory from the Library of Congress; accessed at http://hdl.loc.gov/loc.pnp/hhh.ny0148.

26. Samuel Sloan, *Architectural Review and American Builder's Journal* 1 (January 1869): 430; available online at http://books.google.com.

27. Carroll L. V. Meeks, "Romanesque before Richardson in the United States," *Art Bulletin* 35, no. 1 (March 1953): 17; accessed at http:// www.jstor.org/stable/3047457.

28. *Godey's Lady's Book and Magazine* (1860): 89.

29. Irene L. Rogers, "Island Homes," *Island Magazine* 1 (Fall/Winter, 1976): 9; available online at http://www.islandarchives.ca/node/76.

30. *F. D. Carpenter House, Lorain Road, North Olmsted, Cuyahoga County, OH*, Historic American Buildings Survey, American Memory from the Library of Congress; accessed at http://hdl.loc.gov/loc.pnp/hhh.oh0193. *Abraham Matson House, Matson Vicinity, St. Charles County, MO*, Historic American Buildings Survey, American Memory from the Library of Congress; accessed at http://hdl .loc.gov/loc.pnp/hhh.mo0871.

31. Gervase Wheeler, *Homes for the People in Suburb and Country; the Villa, the Mansion, and the Cottage, Adapted to American Climate and Wants* (New York: American News Co., 1867), 327.

32. James H. Hammond, *The Farmer's and Mechanic's Practical Architect: and Guide in Rural Economy* (Boston: John P. Jewett, 1858), 29–31, 55–58; available online at http://books .google.com.

33. Tara Harrison, *John Roberts' Houses: A Walking Tour in Burlington, Vermont* (Burlington, VT: Preservation Burlington, 2003).

34. An outstanding study of loggia porch houses in Quebec, written and privately published by Danielle Pigeon and Robert Lemire in 2010 as *Les maisons à loggia des Cantons-de-l'Est*,

has documented fifty examples in the Eastern Townships of Quebec and in adjacent regions of Vermont and New Hampshire. Landscape scholar Christopher Lenney also has identified nineteen examples of buildings with recessed balcony porches in the Connecticut River valley, with five of these having served as hotels or inns. See Christopher J. Lenney, *Sightseeking: Clues to the Landscape History of New England* (Hanover, NH: University Press of New England, 2005), 245.

35. Information on the history of the Simeon Ide House in Windsor, Vermont, was provided by email by a former owner of the house, Bill Ballantyne, on January 12, 2009.

36. *Rowell's Inn, State Route 11, Simonsville, Windsor, VT*, Historic American Buildings Survey, American Memory from the Library of Congress; accessed at http://hdl.loc.gov/loc.pnp/hhh.vt0074. Also, historical information from a marker sign at the site in Grafton, Vermont.

37. More research may help to identify any original "hearth" sources, but the geographical distribution of this innovative porch design suggests a correlation with well-traveled stagecoach routes through a predominantly English-speaking region that maintained cultural and familial connections across state and national boundaries. To understand how such a distinctive vernacular building tradition could have spread across this specific area, it is important to consider its geography and cultural history. Geographical and cultural edges that surrounded the region of gable loggias included the transit-limiting mountainous terrain of the Green Mountains on the west and the White Mountains on the east, a predominantly French-speaking population to the north, and a more highly developed and urbanized region to the south. The construction of railroads, increased distribution of books and periodicals, expanding industrialization, population mobility, and effects of the American Civil War would all soon discourage the development of such

distinctive regional vernacular building traditions in North America, however.

38. Information on this example, drawn from her study of loggia porches in Quebec, was provided by Danielle Pigeon by e-mail correspondence in December 2008.

39. Tom Shaw, "Thomas Galbraith Herbert House," National Register of Historic Places Registration Form, National Park Service, South Carolina Department of Archives and History, 1996; accessed at http://www.nationalregister.sc.gov/lexington/S10817732025/S10817732025.pdf.

40. William Strickland, communication to the commissioners of the navy hospital fund, December 1, 1829, American State Papers 025, Naval Affairs vol. 3, 21st Congress, 1st sess., publication no. 404, p. 482.

41. *Waring House, Slave Quarters, 351 Government Street (now South Claiborne Street), Mobile, Mobile County, AL*, E. W. Russell, photographer, 1935, Historic American Building Survey, American Memory from the Library of Congress; accessed at http://hdl.loc.gov/loc.pnp/hhh.a10437. *Front Street (Commercial Buildings), Natchitoches, Natchitoches Parish, LA*, Historic American Buildings Survey, American Memory from the Library of Congress; accessed at http://hdl.loc.gov/loc.pnp/hhh.la0454.

42. Kingston William Heath, *The Patina of Place: The Cultural Weathering of a New England Industrial Landscape* (Knoxville: University of Tennessee Press, 2001), 146, 147. *Monadnock Mill Tenement, 1–18 Crescent Street, Claremont, Sullivan County, NH*, Historic American Buildings Survey, American Memory from the Library of Congress; accessed at http://hdl.loc.gov/loc.pnp/hhh.nh0178.

43. A. J. Downing, *Cottage Residences: or, A Series of Designs for Rural Cottages and Cottage Villas, and Their Gardens and Grounds. Adapted to North America* (New York: Wiley and Putman, 1842), opposite 117.

44. Ibid., 120.

45. Date based on examination of physical

evidence uncovered during building rehabilitation, reported by preservationist Blaine
Cliver, June 2009.

46. Calvert Vaux, *Villas and Cottages: A Series of
Designs Prepared for Execution in the United
States* (New York: Harper, 1857), 138.

47. *Beekman House, East California Street, Jacksonville, Jackson, OR*, Historic American
Buildings Survey, American Memory from the
Library of Congress; accessed at http://hdl
.loc.gov/loc.pnp/hhh.or0119.

48. Kniffen, "Folk Housing," 191-92. John Michael
Vlach, *By the Work of their Hands: Studies in
Afro-American Folklife* (Charlottesville: Uni-
versity of Virginia Press, 1991), 195-197.

49. W. E. Burghardt Du Bois, ed., *The American
Negro Family*, Atlanta University Publications,
no. 13 (Atlanta: Atlanta University Press,
1908), 51–52; available online at http://books
.google.com.

50. U.S. Department of Labor, Bureau of Labor
Statistics, *Monthly Labor Review* 10, no. 1
(January 1920): 217; available online at
http://books.google.com.

51. *Norwood-Williams House, Carmen Church Vicinity, Lowndes County, MS*, Historic American
Buildings Survey, American Memory from the
Library of Congress; accessed at http://hdl
.loc.gov/loc.pnp/hhh.ms0046.

52. *Drane's Rental House B, 109 Hudson Lane,
Americus, Sumter County, GA*, Historic American Building Survey, American Memory from
the Library of Congress; accessed at http://
hdl.loc.gov/loc.pnp/hhh.ga0630.

53. John W. Morris, "Seminole Oil Field Camps,"
Economic Geography 19, no. 2 (April 1943):
133.

54. *Biggs House, 912 Fifth Avenue, Columbus,
Muscogee County, GA*, Historic American
Building Survey, American Memory from the
Library of Congress; accessed at http://hdl
.loc.gov/loc.pnp/hhh.ga0715.

55. "Benjamin Henry Latrobe," White House Profiles, White House Historical Association;
accessed at http://www.whitehousehistory
.org/06/subs/06_d01.html. "Timelines—

Architecture," White House Historical Association; accessed at http://www
.whitehousehistory.org/05/subs/images_
print/05_f.pdf.

56. Vaux, *Villas and Cottages*, 74.

57. *Lyndhurst, Main House, 635 South Broadway,
Tarrytown, Westchester, NY*, Historic American
Buildings Survey, American Memory from the
Library of Congress; accessed at http://hdl
.loc.gov/loc.pnp/hhh.ny0869.

58. *Lawnfield, 8095 Mentor Avenue (U.S. Route
20), Mentor, Lake, OH*, Historic American
Buildings Survey, American Memory from the
Library of Congress; accessed at http://hdl
.loc.gov/loc.pnp/hhh.oh0408.

59. Dana Gatlin, "With Loving Wishes for a
Happy Birthday," *Century Magazine* 88 (1914):
535; available online at http://books.google
.com.

60. *John Farson House, 217 South Home Avenue,
Oak Park, Cook, IL*, Historic American Buildings Survey, American Memory from the Library of Congress; accessed at http://hdl.loc
.gov/loc.pnp/hhh.il0897.

61. Doug Moffat, "The Histories of the Henry
Ford Estate," *Michigan Today* 30, no. 3 (Fall
1998); accessed at http://www.ns.umich
.edu/Mt/98/Fa198/mt14af98.html. "Fair
Lane (Henry and Clara Bryant Ford House),"
Michigan Historical Center, Department of
History, Arts and Libraries, Michigan State
Housing Development Authority; accessed at
http://www.michigan.gov/mshda.

62. *Tivoli Theater, 709–713 Broad Street, Chattanooga, Hamilton County, TN*, Jack E. Boucher,
photographer, 1983; Historic American Buildings Survey, American Memory from the Library of Congress; accessed at http://hdl.loc
.gov/loc.pnp/hhh.tn0076. "Tivoli History,"
Chattanooga Symphony and Opera; accessed
at http://www.chattanoogasymphony.org/
index.cfm?pageId=tivoliHistory.

63. *Pan Pacific Auditorium, 1600 Beverly Boulevard, Los Angeles, Los Angeles County, CA*,
Marvin Rand, photographer, 1977, Historic American Buildings Survey, American

Memory from the Library of Congress; accessed at http://hdl.loc.gov/loc.pnp/hhh .ca0244. Michael Lev, "Fiery Finale for an Art Deco Palace Hollywood Dreams Were Made On," *New York Times*, June 4, 1989.

64. *Greyhound Bus Station, 1200 Blanding Street, Columbia, Richland, SC*, Historic American Buildings Survey, American Memory from the Library of Congress; accessed at http://loc .gov/pictures/item/sc0758.

65. John Hohmann, Don W. Ryden, Margaret "Peg" Davis, Donald Irwin, and Deborah Parmiter, "An Historical Architectural Survey and National Register of Historic Places Eligibility Recommendations for Structures Present along One (1) Mile of Fifth Street (SR 95), Hawthorne, Mineral County, Nevada," prepared for the Nevada Department of Transportation by Louis Berger & Associates and Ryden Associates, March 4, 1997, p. 27; accessed at http://www.nevadadot.com/divisions/ pdfs/013/Mineral_hawthorne_fifth_st.pdf.

CHAPTER 5. VICTORIAN PORCH STYLES

1. Dates provided by Blaine Cliver in interview with author, June 4, 2010.

2. *Lyndhurst, Main House, 635 South Broadway, Tarrytown, Westchester, NY*, Historic American Buildings Survey, American Memory from the Library of Congress; accessed at http://hdl .loc.gov/loc.pnp/hhh.ny0869.

3. *Kingscote, Bellevue Avenue & Bowery Street, Newport, Newport, RI*, Historic American Buildings Survey, American Memory from the Library of Congress; accessed at http://hdl .loc.gov/loc.pnp/hhh.ri0060.

4. A. J. Downing, *Cottage Residences: or, A Series of Designs for Rural Cottages and Cottage Villas, and Their Gardens and Grounds. Adapted to North America* (New York: Wiley and Putman, 1842), 24–25.

5. A. J. Downing, "Hints on the Construction of Farm-Houses," *American Agriculturalist* (August 1846): 248–49; available online at http:// books.google.com.

6. A. J. Downing, *Rural Essays* (New York: Leavitt & Allen, 1856), 246; available online at http://quod.lib.umich.edu/m/moa.

7. John Jacob Thomas, "Gingerbread-work," *Illustrated Annual Register of Rural Affairs* (Albany, NY: Luther Tucker & Son, 1863), 3:253; available online at http://books.google.com.

8. A. J. Downing, *A Treatise on the Theory and Practice of Landscape Gardening, Adapted to North America* (New York: Wiley & Putnam, 1841), 326.

9. Downing, *Cottage Residences*, 45.

10. A. J. Downing, *The Architecture of Country Houses; Including Designs for Cottages, Farm-Houses, and Villas, with Remarks on Interiors, Furniture, and the Best Modes of Warming and Ventilating* (New York: D. Appleton, 1850; reprint, New York: Dover, 1969), 119–20.

11. "Bowen, Henry C., House," National Park Service, National Historic Landmarks; accessed at http://tps.cr.nps.gov/nhl/detail.cfm ?resourceId=1735&resourceType=building. Anne A. Grady, "Henry C. Bowen House (Roseland Cottage) National Historic Landmark Nomination," 1991, United States Department of the Interior, National Park Service; accessed at http://pdfhost.focus.nps .gov/docs/NHLS/Text/77001414.pdf.

12. New York State Agricultural Society, *The Cultivator* (January 1849): 25. Original from Harvard University; available online at http:// books.google.com.

13. Gervase Wheeler, *Rural Homes: or, Sketches of Houses Suited to American Country Life, with Original Plans, Designs, &c.* (New York: C. Scribner, 1851), 110–11.

14. Ibid., 68–69.

15. Gervase Wheeler, *Homes for the People in Suburb and Country; the Villa, the Mansion, and the Cottage, Adapted to American Climate and Wants* (New York: American News Co., 1867), 289.

16. Ibid., 259.

17. *U.S. Military Academy, Officer's Quarters, West Point, Orange County, NY*, Historic American Buildings Survey, American Memory from the

Library of Congress; accessed at http://hdl
.loc.gov/loc.pnp/hhh.ny1417.

18. *Collins-Davis House, Main Street, Washington, Mason County, KY*, Historic American Buildings Survey, American Memory from the Library of Congress; accessed at http://hdl.loc.gov/loc.pnp/hhh.ky0047.

19. Robert Lugar, *Architectural Sketches for Cottages, Rural Dwellings and Villas in the Grecian, Gothic and Fancy Styles with Plans Suitable to Persons of Genteel Life and Moderate Fortune* (London, 1805), 12, 20.

20. Downing, *Cottage Residences*, 176, 180.

21. Wheeler, *Rural Homes*, 219.

22. Ibid., 29.

23. Wheeler, *Homes for the People*, 291, 335.

24. Ibid., 295–96.

25. Ibid., 346–47.

26. Downing, *Cottage Residences*, 92.

27. Wheeler, *Rural Homes*, 71.

28. Ibid., 159.

29. Lewis F. Allen, *Rural Architecture: Being a Complete Description of Farm Houses, Cottages, and Out Buildings* (New York: C. M. Saxton, 1852), 117; available online at http://books.google.com.

30. Calvert Vaux, *Villas and Cottages: A Series of Designs Prepared for Execution in the United States* (New York: Harper, 1857), 111, 163.

31. George E. Woodward and Edward G. Thompson, *Woodward's National Architect* (New York: Geo. E. Woodward, 1869), plate 88.

32. Ibid., "Design No. 1. Carpenters' Specifications." All of the following specs are also from this source.

33. Carl G. Beebe, Jessy Flanigen, Robert T. Russell, and W. Leroy White, "Data Concerning Points of Interest in Part of the Village of Center Sandwich," *Nineteenth Annual Excursion of the Sandwich Historical Society* (Sandwich, NH: Sandwich Historical Society, 1938), 31.

34. *Captain Edward Penniman House, Fort Hill Road, Eastham, Barnstable County, MA*, Historic American Buildings Survey, American Memory from the Library of Congress; accessed at http://hdl.loc.gov/loc.pnp/hhh

.ma0017. *Benjamin Pomeroy House, 658 Pequot Road, Southport, Fairfield County, CT*, Historic American Buildings Survey, American Memory from the Library of Congress; accessed at http://hdl.loc.gov/loc.pnp/hhh.ct0028.

35. George E. Woodward, *Woodward's Architecture and Rural Art* (New York: George Woodward, 1868), 2:56.

36. "Chambly Canal National Historic Site of Canada, Witnesses of History," Parks Canada, 2009; accessed at http://www.pc.gc.ca/lhn-nhs/qc/chambly/natcul/natcu12/natcu12d.aspx.

37. "The Superintendent's House Gets a Facelift," Parks Canada interpretive sign at the Chambly Canal site.

38. *Boston City Hall, 41–45 School Street, Boston, Suffolk County, MA*, quotation from data page 8, Historic American Buildings Survey, American Memory from the Library of Congress; accessed at http://hdl.loc.gov/loc.pnp/hhh.ma0445.

39. *Dwight D. Eisenhower Executive Office Building, Washington, DC*, and "Building Overview," U.S. General Services Administration; accessed at http://www.gsa.gov/portal/ext/html/site/hb/category/25431/actionParameter/exploreByBuilding/buildingId/461.

40. *State, War & Navy Building, Southeast Corner of Pennsylvania Avenue & Seventeenth Street Northwest, Washington, DC*, Historic American Buildings Survey, American Memory from the Library of Congress; accessed at http://hdl.loc.gov/loc.pnp/hhh.dc0271.

41. *A Souvenir: The Thousand Islands of the St. Lawrence River* (Watertown, N.Y, Jno A. Haddock, 1895), 664, reproduced by CIHM Microfiche Series, Library of the Public Archives of Canada; accessed at http://www.ourroots.ca.

42. "History," Grand Isle Lake House; accessed at http://www.grandislelakehouse.com/history. Edward C. Moody, *Handbook History of the Town of York from Early Times to the Present* (Augusta, ME: Kennebec Journal Co., 1915), 176; available online at http://archive.org.

43. Orson Squire Fowler, *A Home for All: or, A New Cheap, Convenient, and Superior Mode of Building* (New York: Fowlers and Wells, 1850), 72.

44. Orson Squire Fowler, *A Home for All: or, The Gravel Wall and Octagon Mode of Building; New, Cheap, Convenient, Superior and Adapted to Rich and Poor* (New York: Fowlers and Wells, 1854), 110.

45. Rebecca Lawin McCarley, "Orson S. Fowler and a Home for All: The Octagon House in the Midwest," *Perspectives in Vernacular Architecture* 12 (2005): 61. Robert Kline and Ellen Preuzer, "Inventory of Older Octagon, Hexagon and Round Houses," accessed at http://www.octagon.bobanna.com/. *Alonzo Benedict House, Prairie du Chien, Crawford, WI*, Historic American Buildings Survey, American Memory from the Library of Congress; accessed at http://hdl.loc.gov/loc.pnp/hhh.wi0002.

46. *Armour-Stiner House, 45 West Clinton Avenue, Irvington, Westchester County, NY*, Historic American Buildings Survey, American Memory from the Library of Congress; accessed at http://hdl.loc.gov/loc.pnp/hhh.ny1158.

47. *John J. Glessner House, 1800 South Prairie Avenue, Chicago, Cook, IL*, Historic American Buildings Survey, American Memory from the Library of Congress; accessed at http://hdl.loc.gov/loc.pnp/hhh.il0118. "House," Glessner House Museum; accessed at http://www.glessnerhouse.org/House.htm.

48. *Pequot Library, 720 Pequot Road, Southport, Fairfield County, CT*, Historic American Buildings Survey, American Memory from the Library of Congress; accessed at http://hdl.loc.gov/loc.pnp/hhh.ct0017.

49. Vincent J. Scully Jr., *The Shingle Style and the Stick Style*, rev. ed. (New Haven: Yale University Press, 1971), xlvii, 2, 4. Virginia McAlester and Lee McAlester, *A Field Guide to American Houses* (New York: Knopf, 1988), 256.

50. The history of decorative chamfering of exposed timbers on colonial American timber-frame buildings has been documented in Abbott Lowell Cummings, *The Framed Houses of Massachusetts Bay, 1625–1725* (Cambridge, MA: Belknap Press, 1979).

51. See Charles Eastlake, *Hints on Household Taste in Furniture, Upholstery, and Other Details* (London: Longmans, Green, and Co., 1869); available online at http://archive.org.

52. *Frances M. MacKay House, 10 Follen Street, Cambridge, Middlesex, MA*, Historic American Buildings Survey, American Memory from the Library of Congress; accessed at http://hdl.loc.gov/loc.pnp/hhh.ma0242. *Isaac P. White House, 66 Ayrault Street, Newport, Newport County, RI*, Historic American Buildings Survey, American Memory from the Library of Congress; accessed at http://hdl.loc.gov/loc.pnp/hhh.ri0090. *Emlen Physick House, 1048 Washington Street, Cape May, Cape May, NJ*, Historic American Buildings Survey, American Memory from the Library of Congress; accessed at http://hdl.loc.gov/loc.pnp/hhh.nj0034.

53. H. Hudson Holly, *Modern Dwellings in Town and Country Adapted to American Wants and Climate* (New York: Harper & Brothers, 1878), 17–18.

54. Ibid., 19.

55. Ibid., 19–20.

56. Ibid., 86.

57. "The Builder," *Canadian Architect and Builder* 12, no. 4 (1899): 83; accessed at http://digital.library.mcgill.ca.

58. McAlester and McAlester, *A Field Guide to American Houses*, 264.

59. *John L. Wisdom House, 535 East Main Street, Jackson, Madison County, TN*, Historic American Buildings Survey, American Memory from the Library of Congress; accessed at http://hdl.loc.gov/loc.pnp/hhh.tn0101.

60. "Historical Time Line of the Association," New Hampshire Veterans Association History; accessed at http://www.weirsbeach.com/Largejpgs/nhvahistory.html.

61. Nancy Hunt et al., "Historic and Archaeological Resources," Bakersfield Town Plan 2009, Town of Bakersfield, Vermont, 13; accessed at

http://nrpcvt.com/TownPlans/
BakersfieldTownPlan.pdf.

62. *O'Dea House, 5804 Ruatan Street, Berwyn
Heights, Prince George's County, MD*, Jack
Boucher, photographer, 1989, Historic American Buildings Survey, American Memory
from the Library of Congress; accessed at
http://hdl.loc.gov/loc.pnp/hhh.md1167.

63. *Jeremiah Nunan House, 635 Oregon Street,
Jacksonville, Jackson County, OR*, Historic
American Buildings Survey, American Memory from the Library of Congress; accessed at
http://hdl.loc.gov/loc.pnp/hhh.or0072.

64. Vincent Scully, *The Architecture of the American Summer: The Flowering of the Shingle Style*
(New York: Rizzoli, 1989), 8–9.

65. *William G. Low House, 3 Low Lane, Bristol,
Bristol County, RI*, Historic American Buildings Survey, American Memory from the Library of Congress; accessed at http://hdl.loc
.gov/loc.pnp/hhh.ri0006.

66. *Annie Longfellow Thorpe House, 115 Brattle
Street, Cambridge, Middlesex, MA*, Historic
American Buildings Survey, American Mem-
ory from the Library of Congress; accessed
at http://hdl.loc.gov/loc.pnp/hhh.ma0257.
Mary Melvin Petronella, ed., *Victorian Boston
Today: Twelve Walking Tours* (Boston: North-
eastern University Press, 2004), 223.

67. *Hill-Stead, Pope-Riddle House Complex, 35
Mountain Road, Farmington, Hartford County,
CT*, Historic American Buildings Survey,
American Memory from the Library of Congress; accessed at http://hdl.loc.gov/loc.pnp/
hhh.ct0700. "Hill-Stead," National Historic
Landmarks Program; accessed at http://tps.cr
.nps.gov/nhl/detail.cfm?resourceId=2121
&resourceType=building.

68. *Building with Assurance* (Morgan Woodwork
Organization, 1921), 341, 342.

**CHAPTER 6. POST-VICTORIAN
STYLES**

1. "History," Munger Place Historic District;
accessed at http://www.mungerplace.com/
history.htm.

2. *John Farson House, 217 South Home Avenue,
Oak Park, Cook, IL*, Historic American Buildings Survey, American Memory from the Library of Congress; accessed at http://hdl.loc
.gov/loc.pnp/hhh.il0897.

3. *J. B. Butler House, 327 South Twelfth Street,
Fort Dodge, Webster County, IA*, Historic American Buildings Survey, American Memory
from the Library of Congress; accessed at
http://hdl.loc.gov/loc.pnp/hhh.ia0176.

4. Katherine Cole Stevenson and H. Ward Jandl,
*Houses by Mail: A Guide to Houses from Sears,
Roebuck* (New York: Preservation Press and
John Wiley, 1986), 264, 265, 282, 284.

5. Gustav Stickley, *Craftsman Homes* (1909; reprint, Guilford, CT: Lyons Press, 2002), 9.

6. W. H. Butterfield and H. W. Tuttle, *A Book of
House Plans* (New York: McBride, Nast & Co.,
1912), 77; available online at http://books
.google.com.

7. Stickley, *Craftsman Homes*, 97.

8. Ibid.

9. C. E. Schermerhorn, "Planning the Bungalow," *Bungalows, Camps and Mountain Homes*
(New York: William T. Comstock Co., 1915;
reprint, Washington, DC: American Institute
of Architects Press, 1990), 18.

10. This and the following five examples are from
Keith's Magazine on Home Building, (Minneapolis: Keith Co., 1904), 235, 303, 237, 247,
301, 305; available online at http://books
.google.com.

11. *The Home Decorator* (Cleveland: Sherwin-
Williams Co.) 4, no. 4 (1913): 10; available
online at http://books.google.com.

12. William A. Radford, ed., *Portfolio of Plans*
(Chicago: Radford Architectural Co., 1909).

13. Frank Lloyd Wright, "A Fireproof House for
$5000," *Ladies' Home Journal* (April 1907);
reproduced at Antique Home Style; accessed
at http://www.antiquehomestyle.com/plans/
lhj/1907/flw0407-fireproof.htm.

14. *Gordon-Van Tine Homes* (1923), reprinted as
177 House Designs of the Twenties (Mineola,
NY: Dover Publications, 1992), 126 for porch
designs.

15. Vincent Scully Jr., *Modern Architecture* (New York: George Brazillier, 1966), 25–27, 30, fig. 41, fig. 42, fig. 69, fig. 74, fig. 76, fig. 77, fig. 82.

16. David Leatherbarrow, *Topographical Stories* (Philadelphia: University of Pennsylvania Press, 2004), 97. *Frederick C. Robie House, 5757 Woodlawn Avenue, Chicago, Cook County, IL*, Cervin Robinson, photographer, 1963, Historic American Buildings Survey, American Memory from the Library of Congress; accessed at http://hdl.loc.gov/loc.pnp/hhh .i10039; "National Register of Historic Places Inventory—Nomination Form: Mrs. Thomas H. Gale House"; accessed at http://gis.hpa .state.il.us/hargis/PDFs/200528.pdf. *Fallingwater, State Route 381 (Stewart Township), Ohiopyle Vicinity, Fayette County, PA*, Jack E. Boucher, photographer, 1985, Historic American Buildings Survey, American Memory from the Library of Congress; accessed at http://hdl.loc.gov/loc.pnp/hhh.pa1690.

17. *Horatio West Court Apartments, 140 Hollister Street, Santa Monica, Los Angeles, CA*, Historic American Buildings Survey, American Memory from the Library of Congress; accessed at http://hdl.loc.gov/loc.pnp/hhh.ca0298.

18. *Gropius House, 68 Baker Bridge Road, Lincoln, Middlesex County, MA*, Historic American Buildings Survey, American Memory from the Library of Congress; accessed at http://hdl .loc.gov/loc.pnp/hhh.ma1367. "Photographic Tour of Gropius House," Historic New England; accessed at http://www .historicnewengland.org.

19. *Mr. & Mrs. Charles Collier House, 6080 Leesburg Pike, Falls Church Vicinity, Fairfax County, VA*, Jet Lowe, photographer, 1983, Historic American Buildings Survey, American Memory from the Library of Congress; accessed at http://hdl.loc.gov/loc.pnp/hhh.va1240.

20. Mies van der Rohe's involvement with the design of the porch screens on the Farnsworth House was confirmed through a series of e-mail messages in June 2008 from Whitney French, Algis Novickas, and Vincent Michael, who have been involved with the efforts of Friends of the Farnsworth House, Landmarks Illinois and the National Trust for Historic Preservation to preserve this historic landmark.

21. Borrego Modern; accessed at http:// borregomodern.com/blog.

EPILOGUE

1. Michelle Willard, "Council to Vote on Porch Sofas," *Murfreesboro Post* (Murfreesboro, TN), November 28, 2007. "Sofa Ordinance," City of Boulder, Colorado; accessed at http:// www.bouldercolorado.gov/index.php?option =com_content&task=view&id=853&itemid =319.

2. "Good Neighbor Ordinances," City of Lawrence, Kansas; accessed at http://www.ci .lawrence.ks.us/legal/good_neighbor.

3. Jane Holz Kay, "Design Notebook: The Return of a Native; The Front Porch," *New York Times*, June 8, 1989.

4. Margaret Hartley, "Greenpoint: Out to Dry," DailyGazette.com, Schenectady, NY, June 15, 2009. Julie Young, "Clotheslines Blow through Culture Again," *Richmond Times-Dispatch* (Richmond, VA), June 26, 2009.

5. This study of the impact of roofing colors on porch temperatures was conducted by the author in July 2008 on a house in Burlington, Vermont. The screened porch used for this study has a shed roof that slopes toward the east at a 3-in-12 pitch. Surface temperature sampling was done using a handheld Extech RH401 infrared thermometer.

Glossary of Porch Terms

apron.   Screening between ground level and porch floor, often of lattice or decorative scroll-sawn boards, providing ventilation. Also sometimes called a skirt.

arcade.   A porch or open walkway lined with a series of arched supports.

architrave.   The lower section of an entablature.

arcuated.   Describing a structure built with support of arches or vaults, rather than horizontal lintels and vertical posts or columns.

balcony.   From the Italian word *balcone*. An elevated platform that projects from the wall of a building.

baluster.   One of a series of decorative vertical elements, typically with circular cross-sections that fill the space beneath the top rail of a balustrade.

balustrade.   A horizontal railing, typically constructed of a top rail and a series of vertical balusters that either extend to the porch deck or to a lower rail.

banister.   The top rail of a balustrade.

battered.   A type of porch support post, pier, or parapet with sides angling in toward the top, commonly associated with Craftsman-style and bungalow building forms of the early twentieth century.

bole.   A section of a rough tree trunk, sometimes used as a post for rustic porches.

bracket.   A structural or decorative element that braces or embellishes a connection between a vertical and a horizontal surface, such as between a porch post and roof beam or between a wall and an overhanging roof. In its simplest form, a porch bracket is straight and angled, but decorative brackets of curved shapes are characteristic of the Italianate style of architecture, and brackets with cutout geometric patterns are typical of the Queen Anne style.

capital.   A decorative element at the top of a column that characterizes its architectural order or treatment.

chamfer.   An angled beveled edge along the length of a post, bracket, or beam or other element.

colonnade.   A type of classical porch with a long row of columns supporting an entablature. Generally the term is used when the row has eight or more columns, and the term *portico* is applied when there are six or fewer columns.

colonnette.   A slender column, typically associated with Gothic, Gothic Revival, Romanesque, and Romanesque Revival styles.

column.   A cylindrical or tapered round vertical support of an entablature in classical architecture or supporting an arch in Gothic, Gothic Revival, Romanesque, and Romanesque Revival styles.

cornice.   The upper section of an entablature; also the horizontal molding at the top of a wall.

corredor.   Spanish term for a porch that connects rooms. See also *portal*.

crenellated. Describing a series of openings along the top of a parapet or wall that simulate the gaps used to fire projectiles from a castle, typically associated with the Gothic and Gothic Revival styles.

crepido.   A platform or base (typically three steps high in classical architecture) on which a colonnade stands. See also stylobate.

cresting.   Ornamentation, typically of metal or wood, that extends along an edge or ridge of a roof or parapet.

dentil, denticulated.   Small blocks aligned in a series (like teeth) below the cornice of an entablature.

entablature.   The collection of elements above the columns in classical architecture, comprised of the architrave, frieze, and cornice.

fascia.   A horizontal band that may be defined or divided by horizontal moldings.

finial.   A decorative cap at the top of a vertical element.

frieze.   The middle section of an entablature.

fretwork.   Decorative ornamentation featuring designs of openings created with intersecting lines. Sometimes is sawn from a panel with a fret-saw. May serve as screening on balustrades.

gable.   The triangular area of a wall beneath a double-pitched roof. Also, a common type of double-pitched roof with two planes of opposite slopes that intersect at a ridge. See also pediment and tympanum.

gallery, *galerie*.   A shallow porch used as a promenade. Also, a single or multistory porch or balcony on buildings associated with a French-speaking heritage.

half-wall.   A low wall or parapet that surrounds a porch deck, also known as a knee-wall.

I-post.   A veranda post with an I-shaped cross section. See also open post.

joist.   A supporting framing piece for floors.

knee-wall.   A low wall or parapet that surrounds a porch deck, also known as a half-wall.

lattice.   A crossed framework of thin strips of wood, metal, or other material installed with open spacing to provide ventilation or partial screening, as for the apron between a porch floor and the ground or as for a trellis. Often framed with narrow boards. When oriented at right angles, perpendicular strips usually face the outside. Also installed diagonally.

loggia.   From the Italian term with the same spelling; a porch, gallery, arcade, or colonnade that provides seating with a view. Commonly used to refer to a porch that is recessed into the body of the building and flanked by side walls.

modillion.   A console bracket or decorative block, typically mounted in regular series on soffits of cornices in the Corinthian or Composite classical orders.

newel.   A short post, often decorated, that terminates a balustrade or railing.

open post.   A veranda post with an opening between two thin outside supports, often filled with lattice or scrollwork. See also I-post.

Palladian.   The classical architectural style based on the works and publications of the Italian Renaissance architect Andrea Palladio (1508–1580).

parapet.   A low wall, typically without openings, at the edge of a porch or balcony floor or at the edge of a roof. One at the edge of a deck is also sometimes called a half-wall or knee-wall. It serves a function similar to that of a balustrade or railing.

pedestal.   The structure beneath the base of a column, post, or pier that may terminate or interrupt a balustrade, often ornamented with panels and moldings.

pediment.   A low-pitched triangular element, like a gable, that is often used in classical architecture to accent entrances and above portico entablatures.

perron.   An archaic word for a flight of ascending steps, typically of stone, leading to a raised building entrance. Also used in Quebec French to describe a stoop or small porch.

piazza.   An archaic word for a porch or veranda that is used as a living space instead of just as a covered entry, occasionally still heard in New England and the Carolinas, but rarely elsewhere. Derived from the Italian word for a plaza, around which arcades were common building features.

pier. A solid supporting wall between openings or arched spans or a freestanding support that is more massive than a column.

pila. A slender pier that is freestanding and not associated with the classical orders. Also called a pillar.

pillar. The common name for slender pier that is freestanding, but a term not associated with the vocabulary traditionally used to describe columns of classical orders. Also called a pila.

plate. A horizontal framing member supported by posts or a wall that supports timbers or rafters above.

pommel. A ball-shaped finial used to cap a pyramidal roof.

portal. Spanish term for a porch that extends along a side of a building to connect rooms. See also *corredor*.

porte-cochere, porte cochère. Literally a carriage entrance in French, but commonly used to describe a covered space adjacent to a building entrance through which carriages or other vehicles may drive to load or discharge passengers.

portico. Most commonly, a roofed entry porch supported by columns on at least one side. Types are designated by the number of columns: four, tetrastyle; six, hexastyle; eight, octastyle; and by whether they create a space that projects out from a wall, prostyle; that is flush with a wall, engaged; or that is recessed into a wall, in antis. See also colonnade.

purlin. A supporting framing piece for roofing that runs horizontally, parallel to ridge and plate.

rafter. A supporting framing piece for roofing that is typically pitched from ridge to eaves.

railing. A horizontal barrier that provides protection or convenience along an edge of a porch, balcony, or stairway. See also balustrade.

screens. Fine wire cloth stretched over frames to provide relief from annoying insects.

scupper. A drain opening at the base of a parapet or knee-wall.

sill. A horizontal supporting beam at the base of a perimeter wall or at the outside edge of a floor or deck, typically supported by a foundation wall or piers.

skirt, skirting. Screening between ground level and porch floor, often of scroll-sawn boards or lattice, providing ventilation. Also called an apron.

skirt-roof. The projecting roof of a veranda that extends around a house.

soffit. The underneath part of a cornice, beam, balcony, arch or vault.

spindlework. Ornamental turned wood decoration.

stickwork. Ornamental square-edged wood decoration.

stoop. Derived from the Dutch word *stoep*, for step, a set of steps leading to a building entrance, sometimes with side railings or parapets, and a platform that may be covered or not. Colloquially also used to describe a small entrance porch with side benches.

stop. Triangular termination detail of a chamfer that may be a flat, curved or embellished.

stylobate. The top level of a platform or base (typically three steps high in classical architecture) on which a colonnade stands. See also crepido.

trabeated. Describing a structure built with horizontal lintels or beams supported by vertical posts or columns, rather than arcuated with support of arches or vaults.

trellis, treillage. Open framework of thin wooden or metal lattice, often of oriental character, for supporting vines and flowing plants, and for providing privacy and shade on porches.

tympanum. The surface area within a pediment between its cornices.

valance. An ornamental screen beneath veranda eaves; often made of lattice, stickwork, or spindlework. Also sometimes called an apron.

veranda, verandah.   An open, projecting part of a house or other building that provides protection from the weather with a simple roof and enough space for walking or sitting.

volutes.   The features that look somewhat like spiral rolled cushions or scrolls on the capitals of Ionic and some Corinthian columns.

Index

Note: Page numbers in *italics* refer to the illustrations.